Advice for Callow Jurists and Gullible Mendicants on Befriending Emirs

World Thought in Translation

A joint project of Yale University Press and the MacMillan Center for International and Area Studies at Yale University, World Thought in Translation makes important works of classical and contemporary political, philosophical, legal, and social thought from outside the Western tradition available to English-speaking scholars, students, and general readers. The translations are annotated and accompanied by critical introductions that orient readers to the background in which these texts were written, their initial reception, and their enduring influence within and beyond their own cultures. World Thought in Translation contributes to the study of religious and secular intellectual traditions across cultures and civilizations.

Advice for Callow Jurists and Gullible Mendicants on Befriending Emirs

ʻAbd al-Wahhāb ibn Aḥmad ibn ʻAlī al-Shaʻrānī

Translated by Adam Sabra

Yale UNIVERSITY PRESS
New Haven and London

This publication was made possible in part by a grant from the Carnegie Corporation of New York. The statements made and views expressed are solely the responsibility of the author.

Set in Adobe Caslon Pro and Whitney type by Newgen North America.
Printed in the United States of America.

Library of Congress Control Number: 2016938753
ISBN 978-0-300-19865-2 (hardcover : alk. paper)

A catalogue record for this book is available from the British Library.

This paper meets the requirements of ANSI/NISO Z39.48–1992 (Permanence of Paper).

10 9 8 7 6 5 4 3 2 1

To the memory of my first and best teacher,
Abdelhamid Ibrahim Sabra (1924–2013)

Contents

Acknowledgments

The text translated here was published as a critical edition in Arabic by the Institut français d'archéologie orientale in Cairo in 2013. I am grateful to IFAO for its interest in this project, without which this translation might not have been possible.

Andrew March encouraged me to submit a proposal to Yale University Press to publish an English translation as part of a series of works on Islamic political theory. Jaya Chatterjee oversaw the editorial process from beginning to end. I am grateful for the Press's interest in exposing English-language readers to a work on Sufi political theory from the sixteenth century. I am also grateful to Mary Pasti and Jessie Dolch for their work in preparing the manuscript for publication.

My work on al-Shaʿrānī began some years ago when I was a National Endowment for the Humanities fellow at the American Research Center in Cairo and continued when I was a member and NEH fellow at the School of Historical Studies at the Institute for Advanced Study in Princeton. During that time, I was a faculty member at the University of Georgia, before moving to my current post at the University of California, Santa Barbara. I thank the staff and my colleagues at those institutions for their support over the years. In particular, I am grateful for the support and friendship of Sylvie Denoix, Amina Elbendary, Richard McGregor, Nicolas Michel, and Mustafa Mughazy.

Note on the Translation

The critical edition on which this translation is based is ʿAbd al-Wahhāb al-Shaʿrānī, *Kitāb Irshād al-mughaffilīn min al-fuqahāʾ wa-al-fuqarāʾ ilā shurūṭ ṣuḥbat al-umarāʾ wa-mukhtaṣar Irshād al-mughaffilīn min al-fuqahāʾ wa-al-fuqarāʾ ilā shurūṭ ṣuḥbat al-umarāʾ*, ed. Adam Sabra (Cairo: Institut français d'archéologie orientale, 2013). The numbers in brackets in the translated text refer to the page numbers in the critical edition.

The page numbers in the *Abbreviation*—*The Abbreviation of Advice for Callow Jurists and Gullible Mendicants on Befriending Emirs* (*Mukhtaṣar Irshād al-mughaffalīn min al-fuqahāʾ wal-fuqarāʾ ilā shurūṭ ṣuḥbat al-umarāʾ*)—also refer to the critical edition. Due to the considerable overlap between the two works, only excerpts of the *Abbreviation* are translated here.

Advice for Callow Jurists
and Gullible Mendicants
on Befriending Emirs

Translator's Introduction

The Middle East in the Sixteenth Century

The sixteenth century was a turning point in the history of the Middle East, when a series of medieval states were swept away and replaced by two major powers: the Safavid dynasty in Iran and the Ottoman Empire, which conquered Syria, Egypt, and the Hejaz in 1516–17. To these, one might add the Mughal dynasty, which came to dominate much of the Indian Subcontinent. These new dynasties proved to be much more stable and long-lived than most of their predecessors. They combined dynastic rule, military innovation, and increasingly complex bureaucracies to build states that we can call early modern. Although nomadic peoples continued to play an important role in Middle Eastern history, the cycle of nomadic conquest and state formation that had dominated much of the region since the eleventh century played a lesser role in its politics.

The largest and most successful of these early modern powers was the Ottoman Empire. The Ottomans began as a small emirate in western Anatolia in approximately 1300 CE. Initially, they expanded into southeastern Europe, mostly at the expense of the Byzantine Empire. Although the Ottoman dynasty was almost extinguished by Timur (Tamerlane) in 1402 at the Battle of Ankara, it quickly rebounded, and the conquest of Constantinople by Mehmed II in 1453 made the Ottomans a world power that could vie for supremacy in the Middle East and in Europe. The Ottomans' principal competitor at this time was the Mamluk Empire, which had been founded in Egypt, Syria, and the Hejaz after 1250. The Mamluks legitimized their rule by presenting themselves as defenders of Islam against the Mongols, and later Timur. Using slave soldiers from Central Asia or the Caucasus who were imported and converted to Islam at a young age, the Mamluk sultans used the presence of a powerless Abbasid caliph in Cairo to provide a veneer of legality to their rule. They also presented themselves as the protectors of the holy cities of Mecca and Medina, and therefore of the Hajj, which was the basis of their own claim to supremacy in the Muslim world.

It was perhaps inevitable that these two states would come into conflict. They fought a major war in 1485–91, during the reigns of Sultan Bayezid II and Sultan Qāyitbāy. The war was fought in eastern Anatolia and the eastern Mediterranean, and it ended in a draw. Over the next two decades, however, the balance of power in the region shifted dramatically against the Mamluks. The first blow came with the arrival in the Indian Ocean of a Portuguese fleet led by Vasco de Gama in 1498. In a series of expeditions, the Portuguese used their naval superiority to undermine the Mamluk monopoly over the spice trade to the Mediterranean. As a result, the Mamluk sultans lost a key source of revenue. Sultan al-Ashraf Qānṣūḥ al-Ghūrī (reigned, 1501–16) instituted a series of new and unpopular taxes, something that the Ottomans would later use to delegitimize his reign. Increasingly, the Mamluks were obliged to depend on Ottoman naval expertise, and Anatolian merchants became an important part of the Cairene commercial scene.

In 1501, a new power arose in Iran. Shah Ismail (reigned, 1501–24) led a force of Turkoman nomads to found a new empire based on messianic Shīʿism. Although the Safavid lineage was originally a Sunnī Sufi lineage based in Ardabil, in the late fifteenth century under Ismail's father, Shaykh Ḥaydar, the Safavids recast themselves as Shīʿīs and descendants of the Prophet Muḥammad and the Twelve Shīʿī Imāms. Their most devoted followers were Turkoman nomads called Qizilbash ("Redheads") because of their red headgear on which there were twelve gores, symbolizing the Twelve Shīʿī Imāms. Although the Safavids later turned to a more conventional form of Imāmī Shīʿism, during this period the Qizilbash worshiped Shah Ismail as the manifestation of God, a claim that he asserted in his poetry. The Safavid movement quickly established control over the historical territories of Iran and Iraq. From an Ottoman point of view, this development was particularly worrying since many of the Turkomans of eastern Anatolia held beliefs similar to those of the Qizilbash and might be recruited to the Safavid cause.

After the death of Bayezid II in 1512, the civil war between his sons was won by Selim I (reigned, 1512–20). In 1511, there had been a large Shīʿī uprising in eastern Anatolia, and Selim was eager to put an end to this threat. In 1514, he invaded Safavid territory and inflicted a major defeat on the Safavids at the Battle of Çaldiran. The Safavid capital of Tabriz fell, but Selim withdrew for fear of a counterattack. Shah Ismail was quickly able to recover control over most of his realm. Sultan Qānṣūh al-Ghūrī refused Sultan Selim's demand to join in the Ottoman campaign against the Safavids, something that Selim later used as a pretext to invade the territory of the Mamluk Empire, despite its being a fellow Sunnī Muslim state.

In the summer of 1516, Selim turned his attention to the conquest of the Mamluk Empire. Whether he initially intended a full conquest or simply an annexation of Mamluk territories adjacent to those of the Ottomans is unknown, but the matter was decided when the aged Qānṣūh al-Ghūrī fell dead on the battlefield, perhaps of a stroke. As it was, the Ottomans held an advantage in their use of field artillery and had also managed to persuade one of the Mamluk commanders, Khā'irbak, to defect to their side at a key moment. Selim quickly seized Aleppo and Damascus, while Qānṣūh al-Ghūrī's successor, Ṭūmān Bāy, prepared an ineffective defense of Cairo. On January 24, 1517, the Mamluk capital fell and Selim became the master of Egypt.

The conquest of the Mamluk Empire had several consequences for the Ottomans. Selim vastly expanded the Ottomans' territories and acquired new sources of taxation. Culturally, the newly conquered lands were Arabic-speaking, overwhelmingly Sunnī Muslim, and well-established centers of Arab-Islamic learning. Cairo became the second capital of the Ottoman Empire and was at least as significant a center of learning as Istanbul. The Mamluk Empire was also the most developed bureaucratic state in the Middle East, and its absorption contributed to the increasingly bureaucratic culture of the Ottoman Empire. Economically, the Ottomans now controlled the Middle Eastern routes to the Indian Ocean and the spice trade, although the Portuguese would continue to present problems for some time. Egypt in particular was a great economic asset, with its relatively large and dense population in the Nile valley. Egypt was an important source of grain and tribute for Istanbul for the next 150 years. The Ottomans also controlled the Red Sea, and the Ottoman sultan became the "Protector of the Two Holy Shrines"—Mecca and Medina.

The Life of 'Abd al-Wahhāb al-Sha'rānī

'Abd al-Wahhāb ibn Aḥmad ibn 'Alī al-Sha'rānī was born most likely in 1493 in the Nile Delta village of Qalqashanda.[1] This was his mother's village, but he soon moved to his father's village of Sāqiyat Abī Sha'ra in the province of al-Munūfiya. His father's family claimed to be descended from Muḥammad ibn al-Ḥanafīya (636–700), the son of the Prophet Muḥammad's cousin and son-in-law 'Alī ibn Abī Ṭālib, which meant that they might be seen as

1. For the life of al-Sha'rānī, see Michael Winter, *Society and Religion in Early Ottoman Egypt: Studies in the Writings of 'Abd al-Wahhāb al-Sha'rānī* (New Brunswick: Transaction Books, 1982), and Muḥammad Ṣabrī al-Dālī, *al-Khiṭāb al-siyāsī al-Ṣūfī fī Miṣr: qirā'a fī khiṭāb 'Abd al-Wahhāb al-Sha'rānī lil-sulṭa wa-al-mujtama'* [Sufi Political Discourse in Egypt: A Reading of 'Abd al-Wahhāb al-Sha'rānī's Discourse on Power and Society] (Cairo: Maṭba'at Dār al-Kutub wal-Wathā'iq al-Qawmīya, 2004).

part of the Prophet's extended family. They also claimed descent from the twelfth-century rulers of Tlemcen. A number of family members are said to have been religious scholars and particularly pious, and in general they seem to have belonged to the class of rural religious scholars. Al-Sha'rānī's father, Aḥmad, died in 1505, making him an orphan, as his mother was already deceased. A village financial official who was a friend of the family took the boy to Cairo, presumably so that he could pursue a religious education. As an orphan, he might have been able to benefit from a number of religious endowments that provided a basic education to needy boys. By this time, it was common for members of the social and political elite to establish endowments (*waqf*, pl. *awqāf*) to benefit religious scholars and Sufis. These endowments included mosques, schools of Islamic law (*madrasa*), Sufi institutions (*khānqāh, zāwiya*), and Qurān schools. The construction of these institutions and the endowments that funded them and provided a living for their functionaries created powerful ties of patronage between the military elite and the religious scholars and Sufis.

In Cairo, al-Sha'rānī, as both boy and young man, came into contact with Sufis. This is unsurprising since Sufism was a popular religious movement whose adherents and admirers came from all classes of society. In his writings, al-Sha'rānī describes how peasants who came to Cairo would stay in Sufi zāwiyas, which were presided over by charismatic shaykhs.[2] In addition to their spiritual functions, zāwiyas were also centers for the distribution of charity, where an orphan with a talent for learning and a pious de-

2. Al-Sha'rānī describes the administration of the zāwiya in his *Taṭhīr ahl al-zawāyā min khabā'ith al-ṭawāyā* [Purifying the Inhabitants of Zāwiyas of Their Inner Evils] (Cairo: Dārat al-Karaz, 2012).

meanor could find a patron. Al-Shaʿrānī lived for five years at the mosque of Abū al-Ḥasan al-Ghamrī, where he encountered his first teacher, Nūr al-Dīn al-Shūnī (d. ca. 1537–38). Al-Shūnī was widely respected in Sufi circles as the propagator of the *maḥyā* prayer, which celebrated the Prophet Muḥammad. Presumably it was al-Shūnī who introduced al-Shaʿrānī to the wider world of Cairene Sufism.

Although al-Shaʿrānī is not shy about expressing his own opinions in his writings, he often quotes the opinions of men he regards as authoritative teachers. It is interesting that most of these figures are older contemporaries or prominent Egyptian scholars or Sufis from the Mamluk period, especially the late fifteenth and early sixteenth centuries. He includes relatively few quotations from earlier texts, despite his obvious familiarity with the Islamic religious canon. As a result, the reader gets a clear sense of how Sufis interpreted Islam in the context of late Mamluk and early Ottoman society. Among the authorities he cites are Zakarīyā al-Anṣārī (d. 1519 or 1520), a former chief judge of the Shāfiʿī school (1481–1500) and commentator on a number of Sufi works. Many other authorities, however, emerged from the world of nonlearned Sufism. Among these are ʿAbd al-Qādir al-Dashṭūṭī (d. 1528), a holy fool who was popular with members of the Mamluk and Ottoman elite, and ʿAlī al-Khawwāṣ (d. 1532), an illiterate Sufi who made a living plaiting palm leaves and pursuing other artisanal occupations. Al-Shaʿrānī quotes ʿAlī al-Khawwāṣ so frequently that one wonders which man is the mouthpiece and which the authorial voice. ʿAlī's teacher Ibrāhīm al-Matbūlī (d. 1472) is another authority figure. Like ʿAlī, Ibrāhīm was illiterate. In the Sufism of the time, illiteracy suggested a parallel with the Prophet, whose authority came from his divine inspiration. Sufi shaykhs of this type claimed to be directly inspired by the Prophet, often in dreams. Although al-Shaʿrānī was a highly learned figure, he cites his own dreams at times and clearly accepts the dream world as a source of divine inspiration. The fact that al-Shaʿrānī places so many of his opinions in the mouths of teachers might suggest a lack of confidence in his own authority, were it not for his clear sense of self-importance. It is more likely that he references these authority figures because he wants to be seen as the heir to their spiritual mantle and because he genuinely regards them as mentors to be emulated. Sufi shaykhs not only possess knowledge, they embody it through their conduct. This respect for authority does not prevent al-Shaʿrānī from offering editorial comments from time to time.

The two major Sufi movements in Egypt in the fifteenth and sixteenth centuries were the Shādhilī and Aḥmadī networks. The Shādhilīs were particularly influential among the religious scholars, merchants, and artisans. Unlike many Sufis, they had a positive attitude toward wealth, provided it was acquired by legitimate means. There are even suggestions that they regarded wealth and power as signs of divine favor. The Aḥmadīs, on the other hand, were a predominantly rural network and appealed to a less learned audience. The festival (*mawlid*) of al-Sayyid al-Badawī, the putative founder of the Aḥmadī network, was the largest saint's festival in Egypt, attracting people from throughout the Nile Delta and beyond to his shrine in Ṭanṭā. Al-Shaʿrānī seems to have associated with both Shādhilīs, such as the powerful Wafā and Bakrī lineages of scholars, and Aḥmadīs, such as ʿAlī al-Khawwāṣ and Afḍal al-Dīn al-Aḥmadī. Al-Shaʿrānī often refers to Afḍal al-Dīn as "my brother." In this way, al-Shaʿrānī combines influences from the two most important worlds of Egyptian Sufism and popular spirituality.

It was presumably through his involvement in Sufism that al-Sha'rānī first came into contact with members of the Ottoman and former Mamluk elite. These contacts were crucial for his rise to prominence and, in particular, for the foundation of a zāwiya under his leadership. The zāwiya seems to have been created in 1524 under the patronage of Emir Muḥyī al-Dīn 'Abd al-Qādir al-Uzbakī. Many endowments were being created at this time by former Mamluk officials as a way to preserve property under the new Ottoman regime. Agricultural lands and urban properties of all kinds could be donated to support religious institutions, with some revenues reserved for the founder and his household members and descendants. This was also the time during which the Ottoman governor Aḥmad Pasha led a rebellion against Sultan Sulaymān. Aḥmad Pasha, a member of Sultan Selim's household who had been passed over for the post of grand vizier, led a rebellion against his former master's son and successor. The rebellion divided the Egyptian provincial elite but was eventually put down by Jānim Bey al-Ḥamzāwī. Jānim Bey went on to play an important role in provincial politics and as a friend to al-Sha'rānī until Jānim Bey's execution in 1538. Al-Sha'rānī is at pains to emphasize his loyalty to the Ottoman dynasty throughout the rebellion, although there is no way to independently assess his claims. Among those who supported the rebellion were tribal shaykhs from the Banī 'Umar and Banī Baghdād, lineages that governed Upper Egypt and al-Munūfiya, respectively.

After the suppression of the rebellion, Sultan Sulaymān sent his grand vizier and favorite, İbrahim Pasha, to establish a new regime in Egypt. On behalf of his master, İbrahim Pasha promulgated a Kanunname, or administrative code, in 1525. Since the reign of Mehmed II, Ottoman sultans had issued codes of laws and administrative measures to organize the governance of their territories, especially those that were newly conquered. The new administrative code was intended to guarantee the central government's control over Egypt, while addressing some of the complaints of Egypt's population. Interestingly, the Banī ʿUmar and Banī Baghdād were left in place as rulers of their subprovinces. Al-Shaʿrānī was particularly close to the Banī Baghdād, although his writings betray considerable ambivalence about their fates as individuals. Given that both families hailed from al-Munūfīya, the relationship between them may have preceded al-Shaʿrānī's arrival in Cairo, but that is difficult to tell.

In any case, the establishment of al-Shaʿrānī's zāwiya made him an important patron in Cairene society. He now had a source of independent financial support and was also in a position to support others. Some of these people were his disciples and their families, many of whom resided in the zāwiya. Others were visitors, especially from the countryside, who stayed there while they were in Cairo. Hundreds more visitors crowded the zāwiya during holidays, when special distributions of food took place. Although al-Shaʿrānī is critical of the practice of Sufis distributing food to the poor on behalf of wealthy and powerful individuals, such distributions only confirmed the role of respected Sufi shaykhs as mediators between the ruling elite and ordinary people.[3]

Given this financial structure, any attack on the endowments that funded the zāwiya threatened to undermine the economic basis of al-Shaʿrānī's livelihood and increasing popularity. In 1551

3. For a study of al-Shaʿrānī's zāwiya as a social institution, see Muḥammad Ṣabrī al-Dālī, *al-Zāwiya wa-al-mujtamaʿ al-Miṣrī fī al-qarn al-sādis ʿashar: dirāsa ḥāla* [The Zāwiya and Egyptian Society in the Sixteenth Century] (Tokyo: Mashrūʿ Dirāsāt al-Ḥaḍāra al-Islāmīya, 2000).

or 1552, the governor of Egypt, ʿAlī Pasha, undertook an investigation into the legality of the donations of lands and real estate to the religious foundations and family trusts in Egypt. The principal target would have been endowments established after the conquest of Egypt by Mamluk officials. It is not improbable that the endowments that supported al-Shaʿrānī's zāwiya fell into this category, but he assures his readers that this was not the case. He voluntarily provided the endowment deeds to ʿAlī Pasha, who declined to seize any of the lands in question. Nonetheless, al-Shaʿrānī found himself caught between ʿAlī Pasha, who wanted to retain the loyalty of the local religious elite who benefited from the endowments, and a new official, the Nāẓir al-Nuẓẓār (chief administrator of endowments), who tried to replace all of the existing administrators of Egypt's endowments. Despite this conflict, al-Shaʿrānī had a good relationship with ʿAlī Pasha, at least according to his own account.[4]

Al-Shaʿrānī and Sufi Political Theology

Although al-Shaʿrānī came through these events safely, they must have shaken him deeply. Throughout his writings, he displays a keen sense of the volatility of political life and the instability of political relationships. Politics, and the parallel struggle among religious authorities to obtain political influence, provokes a merciless competition for power whose negative consequences al-Shaʿrānī

4. The inquest is discussed in al-Shaʿrānī's *al-Minan al-wusṭā* [The Middle Gifts] (Beirut: Dār al-Kutub al-ʿIlmīya, 2010), 367. This work is a shorter version of al-Shaʿrānī's autohagiography.

attempts to mitigate by promoting an ethic of reconciliation and a code of conduct in which each party respects the proper role played by the other. Before entering into a discussion of the contents of the *Advice* and a second version of this text known as the *Abbreviation,* however, one must understand al-Shaʿrānī's political theology and, in particular, his appropriation of the political theology of the thirteenth-century mystic Ibn al-ʿArabī (1165–1240).

Although political theory in the Islamic tradition is often treated in legal and philosophical texts, it more commonly falls under theology (*ʿilm al-kalām*). One's choice of theology and leader (*imām*) determined one's sectarian affiliation, especially in the early period when the various sects were in the process of formation. Ibn al-ʿArabī's synthesis of a variety of disciplines, including law, philosophy, and theology, under the rubric of Sufism led him to create a distinctive political theology. Al-Shaʿrānī, like many thinkers of his age, was deeply influenced by Ibn al-ʿArabī's Sufism, especially his *Futūḥāt al-Makkīya* (Meccan Revelations), a book that combines the many strands of Ibn al-ʿArabī's thought. In his *al-Yawāqīt wal-jawāhir fī bayān ʿulūm al-akābir* (Sapphires and Jewels in Explaining the Sciences of Great Men), al-Shaʿrānī brings together quotations from the *Futūḥāt,* arranged as in a theological treatise, alongside quotations from thinkers from the Ashʿarī school of theology, which was dominant among Egyptian Sunnī scholars. In part, his task is to demonstrate the compatibility of Ibn al-ʿArabī's thought with that of Ashʿarism, which for him was orthodox theology.[5]

5. ʿAbd al-Wahhāb al-Shaʿrānī, *al-Yawāqīt wal-jawāhir fī bayān ʿulūm al-akābir* [Sapphires and Jewels in Explaining the Sciences of Great Men] (Cairo: Muṣṭafā al-Bābī al-Ḥalabī wa Awlāduhu, 1959), vol. 2, 127–31.

The key term here is *khilāfa,* which is usually rendered in English as "caliphate," designating either successorship or vice regency. Depending on one's interpretation, the caliph is either the successor to the Prophet Muḥammad or God's vice-regent on earth. In this context, however, it might be best to translate khilāfa as "sovereignty," albeit sovereignty derived from God. For al-Shaʿrānī, there are two kinds of sovereignty, manifest and hidden, which correspond to the political and the spiritual, the body and the spirit, respectively. Each of these two branches of human activity has its own hierarchy. The manifest hierarchy is led by the political leader, who defends the supreme interests of the Muslim community and who maintains public order, without which it is not possible to observe the Holy Law (*sharīʿa*). The hidden hierarchy, on the other hand, is led by the axial saint (*quṭb*), who presides over the saints. The saints are the authoritative interpreters of the spiritual meaning of the Qurān and Sunna and the means by which humanity's prayers ascend to God and God's mercy descends to humanity. Although each of these leaders is sovereign in his own sphere, the axial saint is superior in that he represents the superiority of religion over politics and the spirit over the body. Although the political leader, as long as he provides the necessary enforcement of public order, is not required to be the best of men in a religious sense, the axial saint must be deserving of his place at the head of the spiritual hierarchy. Thus, the political leader may sin, especially as a private individual, but the axial saint is protected from sin by God, a status that parallels the inerrancy of the prophets. Despite the inferior status of the political leader, al-Shaʿrānī is at pains in the *Advice* and *Abbreviation* to emphasize the divine origins of political sovereignty.

Under most circumstances, the two sovereignties are separate and embodied in two individuals; however, there are certain circumstances in which both types of sovereignty are combined in a single individual. The Prophet Muḥammad was one such individual, as was King David, who was both prophet and king, as well as the first two Muslim caliphs, Abū Bakr (reigned, 632–634) and ʿUmar ibn al-Khaṭṭāb (reigned, 634–644). At the opposite end of the spectrum are purely secular forms of government, in which a kind of cosmic order is maintained without recourse to a revealed law. Such secular governments may protect life and property but cannot provide for the salvation of their subjects. Secular government, however, is not merely an ideal type of rule; it is also a product of certain historical periods in which prophetic guidance is absent. In al-Shaʿrānī's view, the Holy Law of Islam has been in decline since Muḥammad's death, and with the approach of the Islamic millennium (AH 1000/ 1591–92 CE), it has largely been replaced with secular law. When the millennium arrives, the Mahdī, or Muslim messiah, will appear to establish the reign of justice over the entire world. In the meantime, however, religion will continue to decline, as will the ability of the saints to intercede with God for the victims of injustice. Although al-Shaʿrānī did not expect to live to see the advent of the Mahdī, he repeatedly cites the second half of the tenth century as an era in which religion would reach its lowest point since the beginning of Islam. This is not to say that the era lacks an axial saint—that would literally be the end of the world—and there are reasons to believe that al-Shaʿrānī believed himself to be that saint. In his autohagiographical treatise *al-Minan al-wusṭā* (The Middle Gifts) he recounts a dream in which he circles the globe every night bringing relief to the distressed.[6]

6. Al-Shaʿrānī, *al-Minan al-wusṭā,* 211–12.

Al-Sha'rānī's interpretation of the significance of the coming millennium is unreservedly pessimistic. Some of his contemporaries approached the millennium with much greater expectations. Recent research has shown that the sacralization of kingship was an increasingly common phenomenon from the fourteenth through the seventeenth centuries. Figures such as Timur, Shah Ismail, and Akbar the Great drew on the model of Sufi sainthood to combine claims to secular and spiritual authority, presenting themselves as messianic rulers.[7] The Ottoman Empire was no exception to this tradition, which is hardly surprising given the enormous influence Timurid culture had on the Ottomans. There was also the need to compete with the claims to universal monarchy made by the Safavids and the Hapsburgs. During the reign of Sulaymān the Magnificent (1520–66), a faction of his court associated with his favorite, İbrahim Pasha, promoted the idea that the sultan was the Mahdī, both caliph and axial saint, or perhaps a precursor to the Mahdī. When İbrahim Pasha fell from grace and was executed, the messianic image of the ruler lost much of its traction. Sulaymān the Mahdī gave way to Kanuni Sulaymān, Sulaymān the Lawgiver.[8]

The increased use of *kanun* (the body of laws and regulations promulgated by the sovereign) points to the ambivalent character of the ruler. On the one hand, the Mahdī was the just ruler par excellence. The idea that the sultan dispensed justice personally

7. See A. Azfar Moin, *The Millennial Sovereign: Sacred Kingship and Sainthood in Islam* (New York: Columbia University Press, 2012).

8. Cornell H. Fleischer, "The Lawgiver as Messiah: The Making of the Imperial Image in the Reign of Süleyman," in Gilles Veinstein, ed., *Soliman le Magnifique et son temps: Actes du Colloque de Paris, Galaries Nationales du Grand Palais, 7–10 mars, 1990* (Paris: La Documentation française, 1992), 159–84.

suited his messianic role perfectly. On the other hand, kanun was usually understood as secular law, and as such could be seen as being in competition with the Holy Law. Later Ottoman chroniclers and reformers interpreted the rise of kanun as an abandonment of sharīʿa and advocated a return to a state based on God's law.[9] Al-Shaʿrānī's position is more nuanced. He repeatedly condemns kanun as secular law that can never replace God's law. That said, however, he argues that in the historical era in which we are living, one cannot expect full adherence to the Holy Law. Under these circumstances, which increasingly resemble the eras in which there was no prophetic guidance, public order must be maintained. Kanun as such is illegitimate, but in the premillennial era of religious decline, the manifest sovereign is obliged to maintain public order with whatever tools are available.

Another aspect of the personal rule of the sultan in Islamic political theory that was popular with the Ottomans was the Circle of Justice. According to this theory, the flowering of a dynasty depended on the just character of its government. Central to this theory of justice was the idea that it was the responsibility of rulers to intervene to protect their subjects from overly zealous or rapacious officials. Thus, it was important that a mechanism be in place by which subjects could appeal to rulers to obtain justice. Rulers who failed to take proper care of their subjects risked undermining their own power and bringing about the decline and fall of the dynasty. Although this theory has origins in the ancient Near East and was a commonplace of many medieval Islamic political theories, it played a particularly important role in the Ottoman

9. Cornell H. Fleischer, *Bureaucrat and Intellectual in the Ottoman Empire: The Historian Mustafa Âli* (Princeton, NJ: Princeton University Press, 1986), 261–72.

Empire.[10] Al-Sha'rānī refers to the ruler as a shepherd and the ruler's subjects as a flock. This paternalistic image of the ruler could reflect the Circle of Justice, but more likely it refers to the commonly cited tradition in which Muḥammad says, "Each of you is a shepherd and each of you will be asked about his flock." Indeed, although al-Sha'rānī is careful to uphold the ultimate authority of the sultan over his officials and his subjects, there is little to suggest that he believes that an ordinary provincial subject can appeal to the sultan for relief from distress or oppression. He has quite a bit to say about the wrongs done by officials to the peasantry but warns that Ottoman officials who reside in Cairo have little idea what transpires in the countryside. He imagines every emir to be a shepherd responsible for his flock of peasants who live in the villages under his control. Rather than the sultan, the Sufi shaykh is the most likely intercessor with the emir on behalf of the oppressed peasantry. Al-Sha'rānī has more confidence that a local religious figure will be willing and able to intercede with provincial officials than he does in appeals to the central government.

The *Advice* and Its *Abbreviation*

Al-Sha'rāni wrote two books dedicated to the relations between Sufi shaykhs and emirs. The first, which was completed in December 1544, is entitled *Advice for Callow Jurists and Gullible Mendicants on Befriending Emirs* (*Irshād al-mughaffalīn min al-fuqahā'*

10. See Linda T. Darling, *A History of Social Justice and Political Power in the Middle East: The Circle of Justice from Mesopotamia to Globalization* (New York: Routledge, 2012).

wal-fuqarā' ilā shurūṭ ṣuḥbat al-umarā'); the second text is entitled *The Abbreviation of Advice for Callow Jurists and Gullible Mendicants on Befriending Emirs* (*Mukhtaṣar Irshād al-mughaffalīn min al-fuqahā' wal-fuqarā' ilā shurūṭ ṣuḥbat al-umarā'*) and was completed in May 1562.[11] The *Abbreviation* is one of the last works al-Sha'rānī completed, as he died on December 5, 1565. The two texts are of equal length, making it clear that they are two versions of the same work. The version translated here is the *Advice* and is accompanied by some excerpts from the *Abbreviation*. There is a considerable amount of overlap in material between the two versions, which makes it unnecessary to translate both in full. The principal distinction between the two is that the *Abbreviation* is more explicit in identifying the emirs who are the subject of the anecdotes al-Sha'rānī uses to illustrate his arguments. Perhaps al-Sha'rānī felt that he could be more explicit since most of the people concerned were dead by 1562, or perhaps in his old age he no longer feared negative repercussions from powerful people. Many of the people named in the *Abbreviation* belonged to the shaykhly family of the Banī Baghdād, the hereditary rulers of al-Munūfiya with whom al-Sha'rānī clearly had a close personal relationship.

Al-Sha'rānī's discussion of the relationship between emirs and mendicants revolves around a series of key concepts. The first of these is friendship. The term he uses is *ṣuḥba*, which can also be translated as companionship or discipleship. Al-Sha'rānī conceives of friendship as a mutual relationship between the shaykh and the

11. 'Abd al-Wahhāb al-Sha'rānī, Kitāb *Irshād al-mughaffilīn min al-fuqahā' wa-al-fuqarā' ilā shurūṭ ṣuḥbat al-umarā' wa-mukhtaṣar Irshād al-mughaffilīn min al-fuqahā' wa-al-fuqarā' ilā shurūṭ ṣuḥbat al-umarā'*, ed. Adam Sabra (Cairo: Institut français d'archéologie orientale, 2013). The term *faqīr*, translated in the text as "mendicant," is often synonymous with Sufi.

emir, which in some ways resembles a contract or covenant. At the beginning of the friendship, each party undertakes certain responsibilities, and the failure of either party to fulfill his responsibilities voids the friendship. For his part, the shaykh undertakes to provide the emir with spiritual advice that will serve him well in his quest for salvation. In this sense, the emir is like any other believer who seeks the assistance of a spiritual advisor. Since politics is a particularly worldly activity, however, the emir is unlikely to fully repent of his sins and start over, in the manner of a Sufi disciple. At best, the emir may be persuaded to eliminate the worst of his sinful excesses. This fact does not invalidate the need for public order, which the emir provides.

The shaykh is also supposed to aid the emir with his prayers on the emir's behalf and by taking him by the hand and ensuring his salvation on the Day of Judgment. Both of these activities can be considered forms of intercession (*shifāʿa*). The power of intercession properly belongs to the Prophet Muḥammad but can be accessed after the Prophet's death through intermediaries, such as living saints. Such perfect men have renounced all worldly ambitions, beyond the minimum necessary for human existence, and therefore occupy a privileged position as spiritual and moral guides. In particular, shaykhs are supposed to practice precautionary piety (*waraʿ*), which means avoiding anything that could be tainted by illegality or immorality. This would include virtually all property an emir owns. In exchange for the shaykh's intercession, al-Shaʿrānī expects the emir to do his best to repent of his sins and respect the status of the shaykh. For his part, the shaykh must reject any attempt by the emir to use his access to worldly wealth and power to buy the shaykh's support. In particular, he should avoid offering the shaykh his hospitality or sending him gifts. In fact, most, if not all, of the zāwiyas in sixteenth-century Cairo were supported by donations of agricultural lands and real estate to form their endowments. Furthermore, it was typical for wealthy and powerful individuals to make donations to shaykhs to distribute in their names during major religious festivals. Shaykhs also served as loci of charity in that they redistributed alms to the needy and to their disciples. Leading religious scholars and Sufis received stipends from the state in the sultan's name.

The question of who is dependent on whom is often addressed by al-Shaʿrānī in gendered language. For him, masculinity lies in being a provider and not depending on someone else for one's living or upkeep. Allowing oneself to become dependent on someone else places one in the station of a woman or child, who are dependent on a husband or father for financial support.[12] Given the financial resources available to Sufi shaykhs during this period, it is not surprising that they emerged as father figures who ruled over their zāwiyas, including the disciples and their families who lived there. Al-Shaʿrānī applies the same hierarchical concept of gender to the relationship between emirs and mendicants. The shaykh must be sure to play the role of a father vis-à-vis the emir and not allow the emir to usurp that role by becoming the shaykh's provider.

The relationship between the two men (al-Shaʿrānī does not consider the possibility that a spiritual or temporal leader could be a woman) is also governed by a code of conduct (*khuluq*) or good manners (*adab*). The latter term originally referred to the re-

12. This argument is developed in greater detail in Adam Sabra, "The Age of the Fathers: Gender and Spiritual Authority in the Writings of ʿAbd al-Wahhāb al-Šaʿrānī," *Annales Islamologiques* 47 (2013): 133–49.

fined manners of a cultivated member of the court and has been compared to the Greek ideal of *paideia*. By al-Shaʿrānī's time, the term "adab" had long since been adopted by Sufis to describe the ideal conduct between masters and disciples, and among disciples themselves. Al-Shaʿrānī wrote an early work in which he uses "adab" to refer to the ideal conduct of the worshiper in the presence of God.[13] Here, he refers to the adab of the emir in his interactions with the shaykh and vice versa. In particular, al-Shaʿrānī emphasizes the importance of each man understanding the very different role the other plays. Neither should seek to undermine the other's status by demanding that the other act in accordance with the standards appropriate to one's own vocation.

Al-Shaʿrānī's texts are addressed to two groups of people: Sufi mendicants (*faqīr*) and political leaders (*amīr*, commonly transliterated as "emir"). At times, al-Shaʿrānī uses the term *faqīr* to refer to a Sufi disciple, while on other occasions it refers to Sufis in general. This is particularly likely when he juxtaposes *faqīr* with *faqīh*, by which he means a Muslim jurist. The latter term refers to an interpreter of Islamic law, and such people are often seen as critics of Sufi mysticism. Al-Shaʿrānī also uses the term *ʿārif*, here translated as "mystic," to refer to Sufis in general. He often refers to important shaykhs by the honorifics Sayyidī and Mawlānā, both of which mean "my lord."

While the term "emir" usually refers to a military commander or political leader, al-Shaʿrānī uses it in a broader sense to refer to

13. ʿAbd al-Wahhāb al-Shaʿrānī, *Risālat al-anwār al-qudsīya fī bayān ādāb al-Ṣūfīya* [The Treatise of Sacred Lights in Explaining the Conduct of the Sufis], in the margins of *Lawāqiḥ al-anwār fī ṭabaqāt al-akhyār (al-Ṭabaqāt al-kubrā)* [Fecund Lights on the Ranks of the Best Men, or The Greater Ranks] (Beirut: Dār al-Jīl, 1988).

various categories of government officials. These include the Ottoman governor of Egypt (pasha), the chief judge of the province (*qāḍī al-ʿaskar*) and other members of the Ottoman judiciary, commanders of regiments and other high-ranking military officers (*ṣanjaq*), subprovincial governors (*kāshif*), tribal chiefs (*shaykh al-ʿarab*), financial officials (*daftar, daftardār, khāzindār*), tax agents (*ʿāmil*), and the market inspector (*muḥtasib*). In short, the emirs are the members of the *ʿaskarī* class, which originally referred to the military but came to include all of Ottoman officialdom, military and civilian.

The acquisition, and often usurpation, of office is a major preoccupation of al-Shaʿrānī. The respect in which spiritual leaders such as Sufi shaykhs were held made them natural conduits for political influence. While some officials were appointed from Istanbul, many positions were doled out by provincial patrons. Sometimes, officials arriving from elsewhere in the empire were unfamiliar with the local political and religious scenes. A famous scholar like al-Shaʿrānī, who was known throughout the Ottoman lands, would have been in a position to influence appointments to office, especially to religious office, but also to political office. Since religious figures could gain unusual access to powerful individuals because of their roles as spiritual advisors, they were often sought out as intermediaries. People seeking redress for what they considered injustice, whether they were peasants or disgraced officials, might ask a Sufi shaykh to intercede on their behalf. In the highly competitive world of politics, a shaykh's friendship could be important both for his access to political leaders and for his prayers in favor of friends. Particularly dangerous is what al-Shaʿrānī calls partisanship (*ʿaṣabīya*) or pagan zeal. The shaykh must not favor his emir unduly. Rather, he must preserve his status as a spiritual guide whose first obligation is to do what is right. That said, the shaykh should give preference to reconciling the two rivals, rather than to choosing winners and losers. Al-Shaʿrānī tries to persuade emirs that they should act ethically toward their rivals—in their own best interest. He notes that those who conspire or take revenge against their rivals soon find themselves on the receiving end of similar treatment. God retaliates against them for their evil deeds by sending them an enemy who inflicts the same harm on them.

Al-Shaʿrānī's concept of justice is based on adherence to Islamic law, but also on reciprocity. Not only does reciprocity govern relations between humans, but also between humans and God. The presence of an unjust ruler, for example, is God's punishment of his subjects for their injustice. Al-Shaʿrānī has relatively little interest in the Quranic injunction to "command right and forbid wrong." According to this injunction, Muslims have a responsibility to intervene when they witness illegal or irreligious acts. This intervention can take the form of physical intervention, verbal intervention, or simple disapproval. Abū Ḥāmid Muḥammad al-Ghazālī (1058–1111) in his *Revival of the Religious Sciences* (*Iḥyāʾ ʿulūm al-dīn*) emphasized the importance of commanding right and forbidding wrong, and this work had considerable influence among Sufis.[14] Al-Shaʿrānī is skeptical of the value of practicing this precept, especially through physical or verbal intervention. In the corrupt age in which we live, he argues, it is unlikely that one

14. On al-Ghazālī's position, see Michael Cook, *Commanding Right and Forbidding Wrong in Islamic Thought* (Cambridge: Cambridge University Press, 2010), chapter 16.

will be able to reverse unjust acts, and challenging the authority of the sultan and his officials is likely to end badly for the mendicant, or even to undermine public order.

Al-Shaʿrānī's writings also provide a window into popular religious practice of the time. Although he was highly educated, he describes many practices that fall outside the framework of learned religious practice, such as the making of amulets, and he clearly supports most of them. Other practices, such as dream interpretation, straddle the line between learned theology and popular practice. A related belief is that living saints can predict the future. Al-Shaʿrānī does not reject this idea, noting that some shaykhs can view the Protected Tablet (*Lawḥ al-maḥfūẓ*), on which God has written all that will be, but he questions whether most shaykhs can know the future with certainty. Below the Protected Tablet are the Tablets of Affirmation and Erasure, which record contingent events that may yet be altered by an individual's choices and actions. The Devil (Iblīs) can also deceive the shaykh whose insight is less than perfect. It is clear from al-Shaʿrānī's writings that while Sufi shaykhs are expected to act as moral and religious exemplars, such righteous conduct is not enough to attract the support of laypeople, such as emirs. The shaykh is also expected to be a miracle worker who can predict the future and perform other minor miracles. This is a treacherous slope, as al-Shaʿrānī is aware, but he is unwilling to refute these expectations entirely. In the end, he seems to lack the confidence that mere righteousness is sufficient to establish moral and religious authority. The common people demand miracles as visible evidence of a living saint's power.

Although al-Shaʿrānī is very careful never to undermine the authority of the Ottoman rulers of Egypt, one wonders whether his pessimism about politics did not limit the readership for these two books. Of the close to three dozen works al-Shaʿrānī is known to have authored, the *Advice* and *Abbreviation* seem to have been among the least read. They survive in relatively few manuscript copies (only two copies of the *Abbreviation* are known), all of which come from the Arabic-speaking world. Two copies originate in Tunisia, while others appear to come from Egypt or Syria. Two copies that are unavailable to researchers at present are held in Damascus and Taʿiz, Yemen. Remarkably, no copy of either work is known to exist in Turkey. Since more than six hundred manuscripts of various works by al-Shaʿrānī are known to survive in Turkish libraries, this absence is surprising and worthy of note. One can only surmise that al-Shaʿrānī's critique of Egypt's Ottoman rulers, however tactfully crafted, and his emphasis on local religious leaders as political intermediaries made these books politically unacceptable in the Ottoman capital.

Advice for Callow Jurists and Gullible Mendicants on Befriending Emirs

[1][1] Composed by our lord and master, the axial saint,[2] who knows our Exalted Lord, the perfect Shaykh whose footing is firm, Sayyidī al-Shaykh ʿAbd al-Wahhāb ibn Aḥmad ibn ʿAlī al-Shaʿrānī, may Exalted God avail us and all the Muslims through him and his learning. Amen.

1. The numbers in brackets refer to the page numbers in the critical edition (introduction, note 11).

2. The head of the spiritual hierarchy of saints. The axial saint thus corresponds to the caliph, who is the head of the hierarchy of worldly rulers. He is the vehicle by which humanity's prayers ascend to God and by which God's mercy descends to humanity. Hence he is humanity's succor (*ghawth*).

In the name of God, the Compassionate, the Merciful, Whose aid we seek,

Praise God, Lord of the worlds. I testify that there is no god but God alone, who has no partner, the Evident, Real King. I testify that our lord and prophet, Muḥammad, is His servant and messenger to all those under obligation.[3] Oh God, bless and save him, all of the prophets and messengers, his family, and all his companions, perpetually, forever, and for all time. Oh God, amen.

To begin: This is a precious book explaining the conditions under which a mendicant may befriend an emir, and vice versa, and explaining the appropriate conduct[4] of each toward the other. I wrote it for our gullible brethren among the jurists, mendicants, and emirs. I know of no one among the ancients or the moderns who has preceded me in writing one like it. I derived all this from the rays of the light of the purifying Holy Law[5] and from the rays of the light of the active scholars,[6] may God be pleased with them all. The purpose in writing it on these sheets is the hope that it will be of use after my death. A person's book is his substitute in advising his brethren during his life and after his death, in aiding the Holy Law, and in obtaining the resulting reward. This is my

3. A person under obligation to obey God's commands is a *mukallaf*. This category includes all human beings, except those who lack the capacity to be held accountable before God, such as minors and the insane.

4. The term *adab,* here translated as "appropriate conduct," is difficult to translate. Al-Shaʿrānī argues that each party in the relationship between an emir and a mendicant should behave in accordance with a specific code of conduct, which he details in this work.

5. Holy Law (*sharīʿa*) is the set of commands and prohibitions imposed by God on humanity. Adherence to these rules is necessary to obtain salvation.

6. An active scholar (*ʿālim ʿāmil*) is one who lives in accordance with his religious learning as opposed to someone who is learned without practicing.

intention in composing it now, and God knows best. Know, my brother, that I have devoted the writing of this book to the gullible among our brethren, not the clever ones, because the clever man never does something without investigating its good outcome in this world and the Hereafter, unlike the naïve, gullible jurists and mendicants, who may rush to do things without investigating their outcome, as one can observe.

[2] I heard Sayyidī ʿAlī al-Khawwāṣ, may God have mercy on him, say: "Whoever composes a book warning against doing something must begin by warning the jurists and mendicants because these two groups are the exemplars for people in every age. If they stray from the path, the people who follow them will stray. If they stay on the straight path, most people will stay on the straight path." I heard him say: "Every jurist and mendicant whom God makes an exemplar for people must abstain from worldly things, be cautious in matters of religion, avoid those things forbidden by God, and refrain from competing for the friendship of worldly people, such as emirs and the wealthy, lest gullible people imitate him in this and he be recorded among the false leaders."

Sufyān al-Thawrī,[7] may God be pleased with him, used to warn his friends against imitating his every deed without knowing his proof. He would say to them: "Do not imitate me when you are not acquainted with the evidence of my rectitude. I am a man who is devoted to his religion."[8]

7. Sufyān al-Thawrī (716–778), originally from Kufa, was a famous early jurist and scholar of prophetic tradition (*ḥadīth*). He was known for his independence from the political authorities and his exemplary piety.

8. Some manuscripts read, "I am a man who has adulterated his religion." This tradition does not appear in any of the standard collections, and it is unclear where al-Shaʿrānī found it.

I heard Mawlānā Shaykh al-Islām Zakarīyā,[9] may God be pleased with him, say: "People differentiate between the words 'jurists' and 'Sufis' as a matter of terminology, but the correct understanding is that every Sufi is a jurist and vice versa. For the true meaning of a Sufi is that he is a jurist who acts sincerely in accordance with his knowledge, nothing more, and no one can ever rise above this limit. As for the miracles and wonders that occur at the hands of the Sufis, they are the result of acting sincerely in accordance with the Book and the Sunna.[10] Every jurist who acts in accordance with his knowledge is a Sufi, a true Sufi." Among the things said by Imām al-Shāfiʿī,[11] may God be pleased with him, is, "If the scholars are not God's saints, then God has no saints."[12]

Know that I did not write this treatise purely for clever jurists and mendicants, for they have no need of it. I wrote it purely for the gullible among them because they are the ones who do not investigate the outcome of matters and compete to befriend emirs and get close to them in order to obtain some of their worldly goods, even if given as alms. It is obvious that this entails humiliation and opens the door to bringing scorn down upon them, despite their being the bearers of the Qurān and of learning, and exemplars for

9. Zakarīyā al-Anṣārī (d. ca. 1520) was a Shāfiʿī jurist and Sufi in Cairo. He held the post of judge at one point, hence the title shaykh al-Islām.

10. "The Book" refers to the Qurān. The Book and the Sunna (example) of the Prophet Muḥammad are the two sources of Islamic law and practice.

11. Imām al-Shāfiʿī (767–820) was perhaps the greatest of the early Muslim jurists. Born in Yemen, he immigrated to Cairo where he died and was buried. He is revered as the founder of the Shāfiʿī school of law, which predominates in Lower Egypt and is also found in many other parts of the Islamic world. Al-Shaʿrānī belonged to this school of law.

12. "Saint" is a translation of the word *walī* (pl. *awliyāʾ*). The word may be translated more literally as "friend" or "ally of God."

the people in matters of religion. Otherwise, the correct understanding is that sincere friendship for God's sake is obligatory for all people toward one another; it is not specific to some and not others. Furthermore, my brother, it will not escape you that it was clever of the author to warn against only those things he is already safe from committing, lest people see him doing them and say, "How can so-and-so warn against something he himself does?" This, although not a valid argument, is better avoided. They have said, "Among the requirements of someone who calls people to God's presence is that he be protected[13] from violations by virtue of his being a follower of his legator, peace be upon him. Just as his legator is immune from mistakes and slips, he too is protected from them. At a minimum, he benefits from seeing someone who is protected." For this reason, I have warned people in this book of mine and other books against only things I have already mastered in the station[14] of warning against, to the best of my ability, in my best interest and that of my brethren. I ask Exalted God in His goodness to grant to all of the brethren that they act in accordance with their knowledge and avoid what I have warned against in this book, that each of them may be learned, active, a jurist, a Sufi, cautious, self-denying, abstaining from the property of their friends, offering them council, [3] not cheating them, fulfilling

13. "Protected" is a translation of the word *maḥfūz*, indicating God's intervention to prevent a saint from committing a sin. It is parallel to the *ʿisma* (immunity from error) of the prophets. Each saint is an heir to a prophet, who is his legator.

14. The stations (*maqāmāt*) are progressive stages on the Sufi path of spiritual development. Each station refers to a specific virtue that must be mastered before one can move on to the next. Unlike mystical states (*aḥwāl*), which are temporary, stations are permanent attainments.

the obligations of religion and honor, just as was done by the active scholars whom we encountered in the early tenth century[15] in Egypt[16] and its villages. None of them would taste his emir's food or drink or accept his gifts. Despite this, he would share in his joys and sorrows, fulfilling the obligation of friendship, which is the opposite of what most people do today. One of them may eat his emir's food and wear his clothes for years. Then, when the emir suffers adversity, he leaves as if he never knew him.

I heard Sayyidī 'Alī al-Khawwāṣ, may God be pleased with him, say: "Whoever does not devote his friendship to Exalted God with the emirs and other people he befriends, God will afflict with humiliation and disgrace. He is responsible for every peer and other person who slanders him in his absence and offends his honor. Let the servant blame no one but himself if he is insincere in befriending someone." Know this, brethren, and start acting in accordance with the contents of this book by mastering abstention from worldly things, keeping one's hands off of other people's property, and not coveting the worldly objects of temptation that other people possess. Otherwise, each of you will suffer humiliation and disgrace and will be unable to turn himself away from the lust for something, just like a fly that smells the odor of honey and milk. God is my sufficiency, and your sufficiency, and the blessings of the Deputy.[17] There is no power or might save in God, the Most High, the Almighty. Know, brethren, that I have said from the be-

15. The tenth Ḥijrī century corresponds to the sixteenth century of the Common Era.

16. "Egypt" is a translation of the word *Miṣr,* which can also be translated as "Cairo."

17. By "the Deputy," al-Sha'rānī means the Prophet Muḥammad.

ginning of the book to the end, "Among the blessings which God has bestowed upon me is such-and-such" in order to inform you that the door to granting noble stations to [God's] servants will remain open until the Day of Resurrection. Having informed you of this, I say, and success comes from God:

Among the blessings which Exalted God has bestowed upon me is sincerity in befriending emirs and abstaining from their food, drink, and clothing, as well as the other useful worldly things, to the best of my ability, and your poor servant's mentioning a good sum of the conduct of this poor servant with them and their conduct with him, in which he and they fulfill the obligation of friendship to the best of his ability, as will be explained, Exalted God willing. This is in addition to my doing my best—praise be to Exalted God—in advising them, and not cheating them or falling under their governance for selfish purposes, such as pretending to be their partisan supporter against their enemies or helping them to obtain appointment to offices they cannot escape, and the like, from the moment they become my friend until they part with me by death or otherwise. Praise God for that. Let us now get to the point of the book. We say, and success comes from God:

Among the blessings which Exalted God has bestowed upon me is my strong dislike of any emir visiting me, even if he is not distressed, and my dislike of making his acquaintance by my manifesting learning or righteousness, lest this draw him into extreme faith in me, and harm me. If I sense that he believes me to possess perfect knowledge and righteousness, I pray to God, may He be honored and glorified, to drive him away from me and cause him to forget my name so that he barely remembers me [4] or thinks of me. I have done something like this with many emirs—*ṣanjaq*s and *daftardārs*[18]—such as Emir Jānim al-Ḥamzāwī, Muṣṭafā the pasha of Zabīd,[19] and Ḥasan the daftardār, among others, when I thought it likely they had decided to visit me, and God turned their hearts away from me.

I heard Sayyidī ʿAlī al-Khawwāṣ, may God have mercy on him, say: "Take care not to allow any emir to visit you. All of your righteous deeds and their reward may not repay him for his single visit to you, just as you cannot repay him for this single visit seventy times over. Entreat God to conceal your righteousness and learning from him, and turn him away from you, even by sending you an enemy who disparages you in his presence and tells him your faults in a legitimate manner. Then you should forgive him for this and ask Exalted God to forgive him to the extent humanly possible for selfishly taking revenge on his brother's honor, thereby protecting yourself, for befriending emirs is full of pitfalls in this world and the Hereafter. Were any of you to contemplate himself with insight, you would discover that all of your deeds are dissimulation and hypocrisy, none of which are worthy of being accepted by the Real.[20] If you learn that an emir has excessive faith in you, swear by God to him that you are not pious, thereby acting in accordance with your best estimate of yourselves." I heard him say: "If an emir comes to you seeking your friendship, say to him: 'We don't need you. We are incapable of fulfilling the duty of being your friend,

18. The title *ṣanjaq* refers to a commander of one of Egypt's military regiments or to a small province. A *daftardār* was the chief financial official of the province.

19. The title *pasha* was bestowed upon the governor of a province, in this case Zabīd, the capital of Ottoman-ruled southern Yemen.

20. "The Real" (*al-Ḥaqq*) is used in Sufi texts to mean God.

or of sharing your misfortunes and the calamities you may suffer in this world and the Hereafter. Had we known ourselves to be capable of this, we would have befriended you.'" This is something that can be said only by someone who has mastered the station of depriving himself of this world and its temptations and who fears anything that distracts him from God, may He be honored and glorified, even for a single moment of his life. I saw one of my brethren who was famous for learning and righteousness frequent one of Egypt's daftars.[21] I said to him, "What is the reason for your frequenting him?" He said, "I have heard that he loves the learned and the righteous among my peers." I said to him, "What makes you think you are a peer of the learned and righteous men such that you should seek his love?" He didn't know what to say. My son 'Abd al-Raḥmān, may God protect him, whispered in his ear, "Tell my father: I merely frequented him because he loves learned and pious men, regardless of whether I am one of their number." He took note and said this to me. I said to him: "This is not your rank. Your rank is of someone who has mastered the station of depriving yourself of worldly things, loves the emir's veneration for his peers, and gives them precedence over himself such that if the ruler deprives him of all of his offices and gives the offices to his peers he is overjoyed and glad."

I heard my brother Afḍal al-Dīn, may Exalted God have mercy on him, say, "Beware lest you allow any emir to visit you without a righteous intention that neither of you suffers any consequences to your faith." He, may God be pleased with him, used to say: "I

21. Al-Sha'rānī uses this term as a shortening of *daftardār,* the title of the chief financial officer of the province of Egypt.

swear to God, I protect the emir who has faith in me from keeping company with someone like me. Perhaps his good nature will steal some of my evil nature."

I heard Mawlānā Shaykh al-Islām Zakarīyā, may God have mercy on him, say: "Every mendicant who considers himself worthy of being frequented by ordinary people, much less emirs and important people, is deceiving himself. There are some emirs who may be more modest than he, [5] and therefore of a higher rank. A ṣanjaq once wrote to me, saying, "If I weren't afraid to pollute your presence, by being present or being impolite to you by sending you greetings with the tongue with which I have sinned against God, I would have done so." Therefore, any mendicant whom you witness saying something like this, my brother, is one of your brethren! Know this, my brethren, and take precautions for your own sake and for the sake of the emirs and others whom you befriend; don't deceive yourselves and your friends. Praise God, Lord of the worlds.

Among the blessings which Exalted God has bestowed upon me is that I will not befriend an emir unless I think it likely that he will obey me voluntarily and willingly such that he would consider disobeying me a sin for which he must repent immediately. There is no higher conduct to which one may ascend. The emir who befriends a mendicant is like a novice who does nothing without his shaykh's command. If the shaykh says to him, "Discharge yourself from the office of emir and give all of your property to the poor," and he hesitates, he ends his friendship with the mendicant and must repent and begin the friendship anew.

I heard Sayyidī 'Alī al-Khawwāṣ, may God have mercy on him, say: "Every emir who is not pleased and whose heart is not overjoyed to abandon all of his offices and all of his property, to divorce his wives, manumit his slaves, and donate his homes and gardens to charity if his shaykh commands it, is not fit to be befriended by a mendicant, for he does not have enough faith in him.[22] If he truly had faith in the shaykh, he would see that all of the worldly goods he abandoned are viler than a lump of dirt in comparison with the stations to which the shaykh wishes to raise him, which contain the glory of the two abodes,[23] such as being in the company of God, may He be honored and glorified, devoting himself to worshiping Him, and not avoiding anything pleasing to Him." Know from what we have related that I will not agree to let an emir whom I have befriended bend me to his own purpose, such as if he wants me to take his side against his enemy or curse him, as those do who befriend emirs for the sake of something other than God. No, before I befriend him, I make it a condition that I will not be governed by him or by his purposes in anything that agrees with his selfish whim. If he asks me to repel his enemy's stratagem, I pray God, may He be honored and glorified, and ask Him for the sake of His prophets and chosen ones, to make that enemy one of His righteous servants who neither fear nor grieve. For if Exalted God answers my prayer for his enemy, he will place him at the forefront of those brought close to Him, and not use him to do anything harmful to any Muslim, much less this emir. This is a good policy that I derived from His saying, may He be exalted, "Repel with that which is fairer and behold, he between whom and thee there is enmity shall be as if he were a loyal friend."[24] I have acted in accordance with this ethic a number of times with

22. Literally, al-Sha'rānī uses the expression, "make an endowment of his homes and property."

23. There are two abodes (*dār*): this world and the Hereafter.

24. Sūrat Fuṣṣilat 41:34.

emirs [6] who befriended me, and have enemies. I never curse an enemy with something harmful to his faith, body, property, or family, because that would amount to abandoning the station of justice. Both emirs are servants of God, may He be honored and glorified, and our brothers in Islam. We are obliged to love them both out of respect for Him whose servants they are. If there must be judgment between them, we ask God, may He be honored and glorified, to judge between them in such a way as to harm neither party. Rather, both should be pleased with God's judgment.

I heard Sayyidī 'Alī al-Khawwāṣ, may God have mercy on him, say: "Beware lest you take up the burden of an emir who seeks an office that is already held by someone who deserves it, for that is abandoning justice for selfish gain, even if he sends you leading scholars or others. Avoid him more and assist him by asking God, may He be honored and glorified, to make it harder for him to obtain this office, out of mercy for him, and for the current office holder. Then, if he disobeys your directive, tries to obtain it for some worldly purpose, then receives it, and the holder of this office defeats him and tries to have him dismissed and punished in return, beware taking up his burden; rather, abandon him to the will of God, may He be honored and glorified. If He punishes him, that will be part of what he deserves, and if He forgives him, He is all-forgiving and merciful." Know this, my brethren, and act upon it, praise God, Lord of the worlds.

Among the blessings which Exalted God has bestowed upon me is that I will not enter into a friendship with an emir who wants me to get God to solve his problems quickly, unless he prefers me to all of my customary peers, the scholars and righteous men in my town or region. This is because the speed or slowness in fulfilling his needs depends on the degree to which the needy person has faith in the mendicant, not on the elevation of the station of the mendicant. Whoever claims to have great faith in a mendicant, who then betrays him and aids his enemy against him and harms him in every way possible, does not make a true claim. If he were truthful, Exalted God would have protected him against the stratagem of his enemies and enviers, and he would not have enabled any of them to do him harm. The emir in the guardianship of the mendicant's training is like a lioness's cub at her bosom; if anyone tries to take him from her bosom, she will tear him apart and mangle him.

There is a story that Abū Yazīd al-Bisṭāmī,[25] may Exalted God be pleased with him, came to a well to drink. Not finding a rope or a bucket, he stood bewildered. Some young girls came without a rope, whispered something to themselves, and the water rose to them until they were able to fill their jars. Abū Yazīd was amazed [7] by this and said to them, "What did you say to the well?" They said, "We said, 'Oh well, rise by the blessing of Abū Yazīd.'" He said to them, "I am Abū Yazīd, but the well water did not rise for me." The youngest of the girls said: "The well obeyed us because we truly believe in your righteousness. It would not be correct for you to believe in your own righteousness." Know that when a mendicant seeks to be preferred to his peers by the needy person, it is not because he is more selfish than the human minimum. No, it is a means to solve his problems quickly. Know this, emirs, and do not ask a mendicant to solve your problems unless you fully and

25. Abū Yazīd al-Bisṭāmī (d. 874, or 877 or 878) was a Sufi who was both famous and controversial for his ecstatic utterances.

appropriately believe in his apparent station, even if he is not actually like that. If you don't have faith in him, you will overburden him and your efforts will be in vain. Praise God, Lord of the worlds.

Among the blessings which Exalted God has bestowed upon me is that I will not befriend an emir without stipulating that he not require me to eat his food or accept any of his gifts as long as I am his friend. If he agrees willingly, I befriend him; otherwise, I avoid him. If, having agreed to this, he then sends me gifts of cash, food, clothes, perfume, animals, etc., I inform him that I have ceased to be his friend. Then I rebuke my appetitive soul, saying to it: "If you truly hated to receive gifts from emirs, you would have deflected him with your heart and caused him to forget to send you any gifts on holidays and other occasions. Ask God for forgiveness for your failure to truly hate receiving his gifts." This is an unusual ethic, rarely acted upon by my brethren. Praise God, Lord of the worlds.

Among the blessings which Exalted God has bestowed upon me is that I really hate for an emir to have faith in me, except for a legitimate purpose. Indeed, I would prefer that he strongly reject me and stay away from me, to the extent humanly possible. Rare is the emir who befriends a mendicant purely for God's sake, or vice versa. Most mendicants may befriend an emir to obtain some of his worldly goods, just as an emir may befriend a mendicant so that he will bear his burden during hard times in exchange for the gifts the emir sends him. They say, "Whoever accepts the watchman's wage is obliged to repel attacks," unlike someone who does not accept the watchman's wage: he may repel the attack if he chooses, or leave it up to Exalted God.

I heard Sayyidī ʿAlī al-Khawwāṣ, may God have mercy on him, say: "One sign that an emir has faith in a mendicant is that he respects him too much to send him any worldly goods. Sending him these sorts of things is a sign that he has contempt for him and considers him one of the imposters and beggars who are of no significance to God." I heard him say: "The more gifts an emir gives to a mendicant, the greater the proof of his lack of faith in him, and of his love [8] of worldly things. Had he known that the mendicant hates worldly things, and that they cause him distress, he would not have sent them to him." I heard him say, "The acceptance by the mendicant of the emir's gift or eating his food is harmful first of all to the emir because the mendicant's prayers on his behalf will not be answered." The food of emirs is usually tainted relative to the station of the mendicant, and what is permitted to the emir may be forbidden or tainted for the mendicant in view of his station, as will be explained in the second part on the topics on precautionary piety.[26]

I heard Sayyidī ʿAlī al-Khawwāṣ, may God have mercy on him, say, "The emir who befriends a mendicant must not prefer any of the shaykhs present in his time to him, and one sign of this is that he does not give the shaykh gifts, feed him his food, or clothe him in his clothes, lest he distract the shaykh's heart and prevent his prayers from being answered. Indeed, if it is the mendicant's practice to accept gifts from emirs and eat their food, and he requests this from the emir, the emir is obliged to refuse him in his own best interest and in the interest of protecting his shaykh's faith." I heard him say: "The speed with which needs are fulfilled depends on the faith of the needy person in the mendicant, and not on the

26. "Precautionary piety" is a translation of the Arabic word *wara*ʿ, meaning the avoidance of anything about which there might be any suspicion. The text contains no specific subject headings to identify the section referred to here.

mendicant himself. If the needy person has little faith in the ability of the axial saint, humanity's succor, to fulfill his needs, the axial saint will not be able to fulfill his needs. If he had great faith in an ordinary person, Exalted God would fulfill his need and make him worthy of that." Exalted God swore an oath on one of the divine scriptures, by His honor and majesty, that whatever locus through which his servant requests help, the Exalted Real will be present in that locus and solve his problems lest the servant be forsaken. The presence of the Exalted Real in every purpose is supported by His saying, may He be exalted, about the mirage, "there indeed he finds God."[27] This is an obscure secret that few people understand. Praise God, Lord of the worlds.

Among the blessings which Exalted God has bestowed upon me is that if I discover that an emir has changed his mind so that he has little faith in me, I guide him to exchange my friendship for that of one of my peers. If I notice that he has little faith in him, I do my best to improve his faith in him, saying: "Choose for yourself. Either have more faith in me than him to solve your problems quickly, or have more faith in him than me to solve your problems. Or you can ask neither of us to solve your problems. Their solution depends on your faith in one righteous man, so place your faith in one of them to solve your problems; otherwise, your efforts will be in vain." It so happened that one of my friends would come to me with little faith, asking me to solve his problems, but I would be unable to solve them, neither with God, [9] nor with men, while someone unknown to me would come to me with great faith, and I would solve his problem with God's permission as quickly as possible. I might give the faithful one, whom the doctors were unable

27. Sūrat al-Nūr 24:39.

to treat, a stick made of dirt and tell him, "Burn it as incense." He would do so and be cured. Once, someone came to me with dropsy so severe that his stomach almost reached his beard. I said to him, "This can be cured only by someone in whom you have such great faith that if all of the inhabitants of Egypt were in one pan of a scale and he in the other pan, he would outweigh them all in your eyes." He said, "That is how I see you." I gave him a stick to burn as incense before going to sleep. He did that and came to me the next morning free of illness. By this I knew how strong his faith was in me, even if I did not actually deserve it. Know this, my brethren. Praise God, Lord of the worlds.

Among the blessings which Exalted God has bestowed upon me is that if I befriend an emir who is learned in the Holy Law and he asks me to accept his gift, I refuse it only with a legal basis, not on the basis of his assumed integrity. For example, I say to him: "I fear that my acceptance of this sort of thing amounts to trading my faith for worldly goods, especially as my shaykhs made me promise not to eat the food of those who believe me to be righteous. I think that you believe me to be righteous, so keep this with you until your faith in me changes and you come to think of me as a liar and an imposter." And I resent him, Exalted God willing, if I have need of someone like him. For the emir is embarrassed to say to me, "I have come to think of you as a liar and an imposter." As long as he continues to believe me to be righteous, I won't accept anything from him lest I violate my promise to my shaykhs. This will be discussed at length in the second part of the book, where it will also be said that were I really righteous, as this emir thinks, I would have traded my righteousness for some worldly good, and if I weren't righteous, I would have consumed something forbidden by deceiving people.

In the testament of my shaykh, may God be pleased with him, it says: "Take care lest you eat the food of one who believes you to be righteous. The correct conduct is that you eat the food of those who love you as a mother loves her child. She gives him the best food to eat and is most solicitous of his welfare, even if he is a great sinner. When he sins, she says, 'That comes from Iblīs,[28] not from him.' She says: 'May God disgrace you, Iblīs; you did something to my son's mind and made him do such-and-such, although it is not his habit to do that. You think little of the sin he committed.'" Similarly, lovers, when they feed you, do this out of love for you, not for the sake of your faith, so that if they saw you commit some sin, you would not be diminished in their estimation. You may eat their food because they do not feed you on account of your righteousness, but you will rarely find this type of person. At the beginning of the discussion, we excluded someone "learned in the Holy Law," but were he ignorant, we would have the right to refuse his gift without explaining to him the legal basis for refusing it. Know this my brethren. Praise God, Lord of the worlds.

Among the blessings which Exalted God has bestowed upon me is that I do not entreat God to aid the emir who has befriended me against his enemy until I meet with him and inquire about the issue. Perhaps my emir is unjust, thereby making me appear to be his partisan supporter against his rival without justification. [10] An example of this would be if my emir seeks an office justifiably held by that enemy, in an unjustifiable attempt to take it away from him. Then if God allows this enemy to defeat him and aids the enemy against him, I must not aid him, for he is a wrongdoer

28. The Qurānic name for Satan.

in the appearance of the victim of wrongdoing. I often tell my emir: "Taste the bitterness of the harm you previously caused your enemy—how long you mistreated him and made his life unpleasant so you could take his office, or try to take it, without justification. Take what you deserve for your actions and don't ask me to help you prevent the punishment your enemy inflicts on you, making me smell of injustice and wrong, or to entreat Exalted God to turn his heart from hatred of you to love, for this is a most difficult task." They say that it is easier for a mendicant to move a mountain than to change the heart of an emir. That is because the mountain has no intellect, nor vision of human affairs, unlike the emir. Praise God, Lord of the worlds.

Among the blessings which Exalted God has bestowed upon me is that I pretend to befriend the enemy of my emir with the intention of promoting his welfare. This is because were I to allow him to see my partisanship for my emir against him, even for a legitimate reason, he would cease to obey me and would tire my heart and my emir's heart. This is something unknown to many emirs. My emir might think that I love his enemy and hate him, when in fact I love him, in order to make him favorably disposed to me so I can persuade him to forgo the harm that most enemies do to one another. For the mendicants are above intervening between their friends for corrupt reasons because of their extreme self-denial with regard to this world and its temptations, unlike those who desire worldly things. Each of them may be led wherever he is taken by the objective of someone who gives him some worldly good, whether he likes it or not. Let the emir who befriends a mendicant beware lest he think that the mendicant who loves his enemy loves him for some selfish purpose; this is a sign of the emir's violating his covenant with him. This is a situation I experienced often with the Banī Baghdād, Banī ʻUmar,[29] and other emirs among the ṣanjaqs, such that one of them thought I intervened with his enemy for my own purpose, making an analogy between me and most mendicants, who are desirous of worldly things. Praise God, Lord of the worlds.

Among the blessings which Exalted God has bestowed upon me is that I never befriend any emir until I make a covenant with him in God's name that I will not taste his food or accept his gifts. If he ever sends me a gift of food or something else, the friendship will be null and void, and no love or brotherhood will remain between us, as we have just said. Al-Fuḍayl ibn ʻIyāḍ,[30] may God be pleased with him, said, "Whenever a mendicant stretches out his hand to take an emir's food or accepts his gifts, God removes from the emir's heart awe for him and respect for him, and he no longer has any motive to follow his advice or accept his intercession on behalf of the victims of wrongdoing." The shaykhs are in agreement that it is the station of the shaykh to feed and clothe the disciple, not vice versa. They say: "The emir is under the guardianship of the mendicant's training as if he were the mendicant's disciple or wife. Whoever allows his disciple or wife to provide for him abandons the station of being a man and a shaykh, and

29. The Banī Baghdād were a lineage of tribal chiefs who governed the subprovince of al-Munūfiya during the late Mamluk and early Ottoman periods. The Banī ʻUmar were a similar lineage who governed much of Upper Egypt during the same period.

30. Al-Fuḍayl ibn ʻIyāḍ (d. 803) was a highway robber who underwent a conversion and became a pious ascetic. He was regarded as a saint within the Sufi tradition.

his disciple ceases to benefit from him because of the humiliation incurred by his charity toward him."

[11] Sayyidī ʿAlī al-Khawwāṣ, may God have mercy on him, used to say to the emir whom he befriended, "If you want me to remain your friend, don't visit me on any of the holidays, and never put my name in your register of alms, presents, and gifts, especially if you want my prayers for your needs to be answered." They say, "The food of emirs is mixed with the blood of the poor." That is because the emirs force the poor to perform their sowing and harvesting and to pay the land tax on the lands they usually cultivate. Consuming this sort of food causes the mendicant's prayers to be refused. I heard him say: "Do not accept a gift from an emir, whether broadcloth, muslin, wool, clarified butter, honey, rice, sugar, chickens, geese, or sheep. Most of that comes from tax agents, whether village heads or subprovincial governors, and it is well-known that the gifts tax agents give to their emirs are bribes, as is affirmed in authentic reports. It is not appropriate for a shaykh to accept any of these bribes that the emir gives him; indeed, he commits a grave sin by accepting them and diverges from the path of the people.[31] Let the mendicant who befriends emirs be on his guard against this sort of thing and return whatever gifts he received from his emir, even if they come unasked."

I heard Sayyidī ʿAlī al-Khawwāṣ, may God have mercy on him, say: "Every mendicant who claims to befriend an emir for the sake of God, may He be honored and glorified, then is given some worldly good by the emir, this is proof of his not being truthful. Were he truthful, he would erase his name from the emir's heart

31. By "the people" (*qawm*), al-Shaʿrānī means the Sufis.

when the emir distributes meat, sweets, or other gifts. It is a condition of a friendship for God's sake, that each love his brother for the sake of God, without the instrument of a gift or charity. On the contrary, the greater the absence of gifts and charity, the greater the mendicant's love for the emir." Praise God, Lord of the worlds.

Among the blessings which Exalted God has bestowed upon me is that I won't befriend an emir whom I believe wishes my help in being appointed to an office unless it will not burden him in this world or the Hereafter. I may say to him: "My brother, not a single hair on my body will help you to obtain this office. Indeed, I am one of your strongest opponents, out of love and concern for you. If you wish, enter on this condition; otherwise, go to someone else." All of this is acting in accordance with [the Prophet's] saying, may God bless and save him, "Giving good advice is a religious act." They said, "To whom, oh Messenger of God?"[32] He said, "To God and His Messenger, the Muslim leader, and the ordinary Muslims." I know and have determined that assisting my emir to assume an office that he cannot escape is a betrayal of myself, of him, and of the Muslims. Even if he is pleased by this in this world, he will be angered by it in the Hereafter. They have said, "If a mendicant is incapable of witnessing conditions in the Hereafter, its accounts, and its measures while in this abode, his friendship does more harm than good."

I heard my brother Afḍal al-Dīn, may God have mercy on him, say: "If you see an emir or someone else who wants to befriend you in order to be appointed market inspector, judge, administrator of a religious endowment, tribal chief, or tax agent, drive him away as

32. The "Messenger of God" refers to the Prophet Muḥammad.

best you can. He wants you [12] to be his partners in worldly disgrace and punishment in the Hereafter, if you succeed in obtaining it. Each of you has enough on his back with his own burdens and with other people's." Praise God, Lord of the worlds.

Among the blessings which Exalted God has bestowed upon me is that I strongly warn my emir against speaking ill of his enemy to any important person, especially a new governor, who enters the country without knowing people's circumstances. The attack on this person's integrity in his presence may become inscribed on his heart, and it may be difficult to remove it later. Furthermore, God, may He be honored and glorified, may send him an enemy who impugns his integrity in the presence of a new governor, which is only just. Anyone whose integrity is impugned in the presence of emirs and others can blame no one but himself.

I heard Sayyidī 'Alī al-Khawwāṣ, may God have mercy on him, say: "A mendicant who befriends an emir must warn him in the strongest possible terms against speaking ill of his enemy. Everything he does to his enemy God pays back in kind, whether it be infrequent or frequent, good or evil." Praise God, Lord of the worlds.

Among the blessings which Exalted God has bestowed upon me is that I won't attend the feast of an emir whom I have befriended, much less eat there. For if I eat his food I will become one of those leaders who lead people astray because they would follow my example; and if I don't eat anything I will ruin the occasion for him and some of the attendees. They will watch to see what I do and may stop eating in imitation of my example. The emir's face will turn pale and they will embarrass him and accuse him of eating forbidden food, saying, "If it was permissible, his shaykh would have eaten it." So my attendance will not be enough to please him. I may cause people to tarnish his reputation, accuse him of eating forbidden food, and think that his feast was all amassed from the property of his subjects,[33] either by the sword of shame, because they are afraid of him, or for lack of good intentions. This is prevalent in emir's feasts and food that they have had prepared in celebration of the circumcision of their sons, their marriages, votive offerings, offering condolences, or for meals on Fridays or at the end of the month. Rarely are they free of the problems we have noted, so it is better to block the door in a legitimate manner by the mendicant not attending his emir's feast. Praise God, Lord of the worlds.

Among the blessings which Exalted God has bestowed upon me is guiding my emir and helping him to ascend the stations until he is able to see the Protected Tablet[34] and know what Exalted God has foreordained and not foreordained for him. That is so he will not suffer a great worry, concern, or fear if a holy fool[35] says to him, "Give me a dinar," for example, and he refuses, unlike most emirs who may give the holy fool something out of fear that he will be ruined or some affliction will befall him if he refuses. This is counted among the transactions not undertaken for God's sake, and one is almost never rewarded for that. Happy is the emir who endures his shaykh's training until he comes to know the obscure

33. The people under the emir's jurisdiction are his *ra'īya,* or "flock." When speaking of the ruler's *ra'īya,* the term is usually translated as "subjects." Presumably, al-Sha'rānī has in mind peasants living in the emir's villages and other people dependent on his protection.

34. The Protected Tablet (*al-Lawḥ al-Maḥfūẓ*) is where God has written all that will occur in Creation, from the beginning to the end.

35. "Holy fool" is a translation of *majdhūb* (pl. *majādhīb*), or saints who are literally "attracted" by God. Such figures often behave strangely or violate Islamic law but are not considered responsible for their actions.

affairs and other things God has foreordained for him, without fearing holy fools if he refuses them the worldly goods they seek.

[13] I heard Sayyidī ʿAlī al-Khawwāṣ, may Exalted God have mercy on him, say, "One who sees all matters as coming from God fears no one's anger." Know this, emirs, and give holy fools and others some of the property of Exalted God[36] that they seek, without fearing them or seeking any reward. Praise God, Lord of the worlds.

Among the blessings which Exalted God has bestowed upon me is that I won't befriend an emir whom I recognize as having often praised me in gatherings if he has interacted with me and knows my station in self-denial and precautionary piety, unless his intentions are good and he protects me whenever he praises me with verses and invocations so that I don't become enamored with myself, even in a momentary thought. If he is not like that, I won't befriend him. Indeed, I dismiss him from my company, heart and soul. On the other hand, if he conceals my states from people, or makes them public with good intentions while protecting me, I don't dismiss him from my company, but I warn him severely against praise, because of the likelihood that in praising me and preferring me to my peers, he is guilty of partisanship and pagan zeal.

I heard Sayyidī ʿAlī al-Khawwāṣ, may God have mercy on him, say, "No mendicant should befriend an emir unless he thinks that the emir will keep his secrets, lest he diminish his faith." I heard him say: "Take care not to befriend those who accept your opinions and publicize your merit, unless you are cautious, for they will

36. By God's property, al-Shaʿrānī presumably means alms. The payment of an alms tax (*zakāh*) is obligatory in Islam.

strike you in the heart and raise your standing in people's hearts for illegitimate purposes. Befriend only those who know your merit and conceal it from your friends and enemies, revealing it only to those who love you and imitate your example. Friends may be moved to envy you, as is prevalent among friends these days, while enemies may prepare snares for you and attempt to destroy you, unlike a true devotee whom you are safe from turning against you, in most cases." I heard him say: "Any mendicant who finds pleasure in hearing himself praised by his emir in gatherings, his friendship is not for God's sake; and any mendicant who finds bitterness and pain in his emir's praise of him in gatherings, this is a sign that his friendship is sincere; this is a scale that can be tipped by a speck of dust. A mendicant should not condone pleasure except the minimum humanly possible, which is like a single hair on the body of a bull." Praise God, Lord of the worlds.

Among the blessings which Exalted God has bestowed upon me is that I advise all of the emirs who befriend me not to oppose me with regard to anything he gives to the mendicants for me to receive or distribute to them because this results in the degradation of the station of the mendicants insofar as the emir most likely will think himself superior to the shaykh and his followers, in addition to the grief and depression I will suffer if I see anything that attracts worldly desires to me or my followers. I say to him, "If you would give something to the mendicants, give it to my deputy,[37] without informing me; your transaction is really with God, not me."

37. "Deputy" is the translation of *naqīb,* the person runs the shaykh's *zāwiya* on a day-to-day basis on his behalf.

I heard Sayyidī Abū al-Su'ūd al-Jāriḥī,[38] may Exalted God have mercy on him, say: "If an emir brings you some worldly goods to distribute to your followers, do not allow him to see that you are pleased by this, or you will humiliate yourself and make him prideful. Furthermore, if [14] it so happens that you accept this on behalf of the mendicants, do not accept it if you know that there is someone needier than you in the same town, or you will be the cause of the emir's reward being diminished. Instead, guide him to the needier person so that you cause his scale to tip in the Hereafter as a result."[39] Know this, oh emirs, and act upon it. Praise God, Lord of the worlds.

Among the blessings which Exalted God has bestowed upon me is that I befriend an emir only once I think that I have so mastered the station of renouncing the world that I am unhappy to receive him, and I so love every enemy who opposes my receiving him that he becomes one of my dearest friends. Similarly, I am pleased and overjoyed whenever God makes my life harder, in imitation of the example of the prophets and saints. If I don't think it most likely that I have perfected the station of renouncing the world before befriending the emir, I will not befriend him, in the best interest of my faith and that of the emir; for one who pursues worldly goods and its temptations will inevitably flatter the emir about his religiosity and be too embarrassed to rebuke him, either because of the worldly goods he received from the emir or because of his hope of receiving them from him in the future. The one who

38. Abū al-Su'ūd al-Jāriḥī (d. ca. 1520s) was a leading Cairene saint in the late Mamluk period and after the Ottoman conquest.

39. In the Hereafter, the deceased's good deeds and evil deeds are weighed against each other on a scale.

renounces the world, on the other hand, will not flatter the emir about his religiosity or be too embarrassed to rebuke him.

I heard Sayyidī 'Alī al-Khawwāṣ, may God have mercy on him, say: "Whoever has not mastered the station of renouncing the world must necessarily love to receive charity and gifts from the emir whom he has befriended, and that diminishes his authority. It is unseemly for a shaykh to be dependent on an emir, for the emir will come to see him like one of the pages who serves at his table or wardrobe. Because of his contempt for them in his heart, he will rarely accept their intercession on behalf of an aggrieved person. There is a common saying, 'Contemptible in your eyes is the one who depends on you.'" I heard him say: "Whoever wants to know his station in honor and dishonor, let him observe himself, for example, when his emir gives him one hundred dinars, and he accepts them or returns them. He will find that the emir honors him when he returns them and despises him when he accepts them. Even if the emir wants to belittle him after he returns them or honor him after he accepts them, he cannot." One pasha in Egypt offered me five hundred dinars, but I returned them to him. In my heart, I sensed that he held me in higher esteem than he held himself because I denied myself something he desires.

I heard Sayyidī 'Alī al-Khawwāṣ, may God have mercy on him, say, "A shaykh who claims to truly follow the path must not allow an emir or official to be more abstemious in worldly goods than he." I said to him, "How can that be?" He said: "He accepts the money, food, clothes, or the like that they offer him. They offer him that only once they have denied it to themselves. Had none of them denied it to himself, no mendicant could extract it from their possession by any ruse in exchange for something that officials, whom they accuse of mistreatment, oppression, and low station, deny to themselves. How can it be appropriate for one who claims to be a saint and a righteous man to receive something from him, and for the officials to be more abstemious than he in worldly goods?" This is the greatest of wonders, so consider this, my brethren. Praise God, Lord of the worlds.

[15] Among the blessings which Exalted God has bestowed upon me is my great love for my emir if he distributes dirhams, dinars, or other things, and he gives me less than one-tenth what he gives to my peers, for I interpret his reduction of my gift as his believing that I harbor great love for him and that I deny myself most worldly goods—unlike what my peers may think. When someone is like this, he deserves his shaykh's great love. This is the opposite of how officials these days are with their shaykhs. A shaykh may believe that an emir's giving him many gifts is due to his great station in his eyes, while the emir thinks that whoever loves him most is more deserving than others of frequent gifts, and he may be ignorant of the situation of mendicants. For a true mendicant never accepts emirs' gifts, much less becomes annoyed if they give him few gifts but give many gifts to his peers. Praise God, Lord of the worlds.

Among the blessings which Exalted God has bestowed upon me is that I do not regard myself as superior to any of the emirs whom I befriend, if I take one of them by the hand during a crisis, with God's permission; rather, without thinking twice, I consider them superior to me. For this reason, I would rise for one of them, kiss his foot, ask him to pray for me, and escort him to the door of the house or zāwiya. I see this as part of what I owe him due to his superior station in humility and his abandoning his haughtiness and grandeur on my behalf. Had he not thrown off his haughtiness and grandeur, he would not have come to visit me.

I heard Sayyidī ʿAlī al-Khawwāṣ, may God have mercy on him, say: "Do not consider yourselves superior to any emir who visits you; this is ignorance and arrogance on your part. High rank in God's eyes is due to great humility. As the tradition says, 'Whoever humbles himself before God, God raises him up.' There is no doubt that the emir is more humble than you because his manifest station is high, unlike one of you, whose station it is to sit on the ground, below which there is nowhere to descend." I heard him, may God have mercy on him, say: "It is correct conduct on our part with our emirs that we honor them out of respect for God who bestowed on them the robe of command and gave them governance over their subjects. It is only those who honor them for their worldly goods that are blameworthy." I heard him say: "If one of you meets an emir, ask him to pray for you that you repent and are forgiven. Hope that his prayer for you will be answered, as you hope that the prayers of the righteous will be answered." Then he said, "This is our conduct with our emirs in this abode, and Exalted God will teach us, God willing, the correct conduct with them when we are transferred to the abode of the Hereafter. He said, may He be exalted, 'And surely the world to come is greater in ranks, greater in preferment.'"[40] I heard him say, "Any mendicant these days who looks at himself with insight will find the emir who visits him more humble before God; he must honor him because of his more lofty station." An important emir befriended me. I said to him, "Do you need anything?" He said, [16] "Yes, something indispensable." I said to him, "What is it?" He said: "Beseech God on my behalf that he grant me one of the characteristics of a dog. I have examined my character and found it to be

40. Sūrat al-Isrāʾ 17:21.

worse than a dog's character." Another emir befriended me, then broke off the friendship, writing to say to me: "Forgive me for not coming to see you, or sending you greetings. I am embarrassed to befoul your presence or send you greetings with the voice I have used to sin against God." They brought to my attention something of which I was unaware. Look, brother, at this great humility by these two important emirs, and follow their example. Praise God, Lord of the worlds.

Among the blessings which Exalted God has bestowed upon me is that I rarely neglect to guide my emir to pardon and leniency with the friends of the emir who preceded him in his office. I say to him, "If you are unsteady in your office, this will suffice for you; if you are firmly ensconced in it, this is part of being thankful for consolidating your position and for your increased honor." The tradition says, "God makes his servant more forgiving that he may be more honored." Which means that he who is not forgiving and lenient, He increases in humiliation and degradation. Rare is the mendicant who guides his emir to this, either because he is unaware of it or because he is too lenient to rebuke him. Praise God, Lord of the worlds.

Among the blessings which Exalted God has bestowed upon me is that I do not allow my emir to see my anger if he rejects my intercession, or speak rudely to him, unlike the way he behaves toward me, for I know that emirs are most often veiled from what the mendicant requests of them. He said, may He be exalted, to Moses and Aaron with respect to Pharaoh, "yet speak gently to him,"[41] that is, if he speaks rudely to you. Rare is the mendicant who perseveres in this. He becomes angry with the emir and ruins

41. Sūrat Ṭāhā 20:44.

his ability to intercede with him. Both he and the emir end up in the losing pan of the scale. Know this, my brethren, and act upon it. Praise God, Lord of the worlds.

Among the blessings which Exalted God has bestowed upon me is that I do not ask an emir who befriends me to respect my honor and power and to accept my intercession unless I have already mastered the station of self-denial with respect to worldly goods. Otherwise, I ask too much of him. If he sees that I love worldly goods, perhaps he will say, "This shaykh and I are no different in our love for worldly goods; so why should I revere him and why should he ask me to imitate his example?" Abu 'Abdallāh al-Aṣma'ī[42] entered and was rude to the caliph. The caliph said to him, "Abū 'Abdallāh, do you know why you have the courage to speak to me rudely, and why we patiently put up with this from you?" Al-Aṣma'ī was silent. The caliph said, "The reason for that is your renunciation of the world and your lack of desire for our money." The intelligent man will draw the appropriate conclusion. Praise God, Lord of the worlds.

[17] Among the blessings which Exalted God has bestowed upon me is that I will not befriend an emir unless I think that his love for me will increase the more I rebuke him, the more severe I am with him, and the more I point out his faults. If he is not like that, I send him away with a kind phrase, for there is no value in a mendicant befriending an emir except to admonish him and so that he may profit in this world and in the Hereafter. In the ab-

42. Abu 'Abdallāh al-Aṣma'ī (ca. 740–828) was an Iraqi grammarian and tutor to the sons of the caliph Hārūn al-Rashīd. He was known for his piety and abstemious lifestyle.

sence of admonition, there enters deceit, and one loses this world and the Hereafter.

I heard Mawlānā Shaykh al-Islām Zakarīyā, may God be pleased with him, say: "Once, I overdid it in admonishing Sultan Qāyitbāy,[43] may God have mercy on him. He scowled at what I said. I took his hand, and said, 'I swear to God, I overdid it in admonishing you because of my love for you, and for fear that this body of yours might become one of the coals of Hell.' The sultan said, 'This is what I thought you intended, may God repay you with goodness on my behalf.'" My brother, befriend those whose love for you increases when you admonish them; otherwise, leave them alone. Praise God, Lord of the worlds.

Among the blessings which Exalted God has bestowed upon me is that I make it a condition of every emir who befriends me that he not visit me without a legitimate necessity, to save him and me the trouble and to save him the stain of visiting one such as me, especially if he is a daftar. If the tax agents see one of their own frequenting a mendicant, they will ask the mendicant to ask the daftar to obtain for him some of the sultan's money or forgive him some of it if he finds himself in need. The mendicant will have no choice but to intercede, and the daftar will have no choice but to accept the mendicant's intercession in this sort of thing. He is authorized to prepare the money owed the sultan and to speed up its collection so that he can spend it on armies for jihad and other things. The mendicant and the emir will find themselves in conflict; sometimes the mendicant will become angry with the

43. Sultan Qāyitbāy ruled the Mamluk Empire from 1468 to 1498. He was known to admire Sufis.

emir, and sometimes the emir will become angry with the mendicant. Among the daftars of Egypt who fulfilled their covenant not to visit me were Muḥammad, Abū Zayd, Ibrāhīm, and Ḥasan. When one of them passed by the zāwiya, he would not approach and would say, "We are fulfilling our covenant." May Exalted God repay them with goodness on my behalf. Praise God, Lord of the worlds.

Among the blessings which Exalted God has bestowed upon me is that I am not overjoyed when an emir who frequents me is appointed to office unless it is free from people's troubles, and is unoccupied, not in someone's possession. What value can there be in being overjoyed by an emir being appointed to an office when another emir is disappointed, both emirs being the mendicant's brothers in Islam? Furthermore, if the emir who has befriended the mendicant is righteous in his faith, he is besmirched by this appointment. If he is not righteous, his faith is further besmirched, so why would the mendicant be overjoyed? This is something that one rarely can avoid with the exception of those mendicants who have mastered the station of renouncing the world. Otherwise, one will be overjoyed by one's emir's appointment to office, whether one likes it or not.

I heard Sayyidī 'Alī al-Khawwāṣ, may God have mercy on him, say, "An intelligent man should not congratulate anyone for being appointed to office in this age, not even a teaching post or the administration of a mosque, because this entails considerable annoyance at the hands of students and beneficiaries, and their demanding in the homes of the rulers that he be the subject of an inquest, etc., should they turn against him." He said, "Anyone who doubts this, let him find out for himself." Praise God, Lord of the worlds.

Among the blessings which Exalted God has bestowed upon me is that I will not agree to curse my emir's enemy, as has already been indicated in this treatise, in imitation of the Messenger of God, may God bless and save him. Every time he was asked to curse someone after Exalted God, may He be honored and glorified, revealed "We have not sent thee, [18] save as a mercy unto all beings,"[44] he warned him[45] against cursing him and prayed that he would become righteous. One emir asked me for the sake of God, may He be honored and glorified, to curse his enemy, but I did not agree to that. That night, I prayed to God on behalf of his enemy that Exalted God would make him one of his saints who neither fear nor grieve. My tongue was pleased by that while prostrating myself until I had repeated it for about twenty minutes and found evidence that the prayer was answered. This is something that can be done only by someone who has mastered the station of renouncing the world, who goes where it pleases God, not where it pleases man, and acts in accordance with His saying, may He be exalted, "Repel thou the evil with that which is fairer."[46] If one's enemy becomes one of God's saints, may He be honored and glorified, Exalted God will protect him from being employed to harm anyone unjustly, as has previously been explained. Praise God, Lord of the worlds.

Among the blessings which Exalted God has bestowed upon me is that I will befriend an emir only once I prepare myself mentally to act on his behalf in a legitimate manner. I grieve when he grieves, am joyful when he is joyful, fall sick when he is sick, and

44. Sūrat al-Anbiyā' 21:107.
45. The text has "warned you."
46. Sūrat al-Mu'minīn 23:96.

when he is in distress I won't approach my wives, relax in a garden, laugh, or wear a perfumed robe, except in a legitimate manner, until that distress passes. I consider that part of what he is entitled to for befriending me. This is an unusual quality in this age; rare is the mendicant who acts in accordance with it. No, one of them may consume an emir's food, wear his clothes, and accept his gifts, and then not share his worries and troubles. Instead, he has intercourse with his wife, laughs, plays, and relaxes in gardens and by rivers. Meanwhile, his emir languishes in prison or under house arrest,[47] but the mendicant can barely remember a single one of his kind deeds. This kind of friendship is a curse upon him, in this world and in the Hereafter. Praise God, Lord of the worlds.

Among the blessings which Exalted God has bestowed upon me is that I will agree to befriend an emir only if I am extremely shy and bashful before God and that emir, fearing that I will be guilty of deceiving him by claiming to be righteous and a saint. One requirement of a righteous man and saint who befriends an emir is that he not think any evil thoughts that would embarrass him before God and that emir; and what mendicant can claim to be free of something like that? No mendicant is worthy of befriending an emir until his balance sheet is purified of sins. That is so he may claim to pray that the emir achieves his legitimate goals, and the Real answers his prayers most of the time. If one's [19] balance sheet contains a single sin, one's prayers cease to be answered. If he swears by the Real, the Glorious, the Lofty, that his prayers are answered, the voice of the presence of the Real, the Glorious, the Lofty, says: "Why don't you understand what you are

47. House arrest (*tarsīm*) was a common punishment to force payment of a debt.

told? The Exalted Real forbade you, but you paid no attention. He commanded you, but you did not obey when He called to you. As a commensurate punishment, He did not answer your prayer."

I heard Sayyidī ʿAlī al-Khawwāṣ, may God have mercy on him, say: "It is extremely ignorant of a mendicant to befriend an emir who is stained by his sins when he too has not repented of his sins, for his prayers on behalf of that emir and on his own behalf will not be answered. Let the mendicant and the emir purify themselves of all their sins and only then enter into a friendship. Otherwise, the friendship is useless, especially if the mendicant consumes the emir's food, for his prayers are unlikely to be answered because of the prevalence of taint in emirs' food. The food that is laid out at their table, whether chicken, geese, sheep, clarified butter, or bee's honey, may all be collected involuntarily from destitute peasants, as people who mix with emirs these days know. No intelligent person befriends an emir unless all of the conditions have been met." Praise God, Lord of the worlds.

Among the blessings which Exalted God has bestowed upon me is that I will befriend only an emir who respects me too much to send me any gifts or alms. They say, "One way in which an emir honors a mendicant is to think him too good to eat his food or accept his gifts for fear that the mendicant would be contaminated by something like this and cease to be of benefit to the emir." We have already said that one sign of an emir's veneration of a mendicant is that he not send him any presents, whether food, clothing, a mount, or a eunuch, without his permission for the duration of their friendship.

I heard Sayyidī ʿAlī al-Khawwāṣ, may God have mercy on him, say: "How can an emir claim to venerate a mendicant whom he often visits bearing alms and gifts, as he does with beggars? If he really venerated him, he would think that the mendicant had no need of him, either because he is content with what he has and exercises self-restraint, or because he has renounced the world." The Messenger of God, may God bless and save him, said, "Contentment is an inexhaustible treasure." In another tradition, it says: "You must deny yourself worldly goods and be content with a modest living. A little suffices, and a lot won't make you satisfied." Whoever contemplates the contentment of the mendicants will find that they are more satisfied than emirs. For the mendicant has ceased to seek more worldly goods while most emirs seek more until they die.

I heard Sayyidī ʻAlī al-Khawwāṣ, may God have mercy on him, say: "The superiority of the mendicants over ordinary people lies only in their voluntary renunciation of worldly goods. Had they renounced them out of necessity, they would have no advantage over worldly people." When the inhabitants of Egypt spread a rumor that one of the pashas had great faith in me, and I believed this rumor because of his behavior, he later offered me four hundred dinars at the hand of his personal treasurer. I stopped believing people about his faith in me and changed my opinion of him. I said: "If he truly believed, he would not have sent me any money gathered from unacceptable sources. No, he would consider my station to be above this sort of thing"—as has previously been indicated in this book. Know this, praise God, Lord of the worlds.

[20] Among the blessings which Exalted God has bestowed upon me is that I will befriend only those emirs who have faith in my total honesty in renouncing the world. If I come to the conclusion that the emir thinks that if he offers me his money I will only reject it to preserve my reputation among people, not because of my hidden aversion to it, I won't befriend him. I will befriend only

those who believe that I am extremely troubled by those who offer me worldly goods; then they will fear for my opinion and not send me anything. Ḥasan the daftardār of Egypt sent me one hundred dinars. I said to him, "Give it to someone needier than I." He was annoyed by this and pretended to have great faith in me. I believed him. Then, once he had left the zāwiya, he sent it again with his slave, telling him: "Give it to him when the two of you are alone. Perhaps he refused this money to protect his reputation among the group who were in his company." From this I realized how little faith he had in me. I returned it to the slave and said, "How can I accept from you what I would not accept from your master?"

I heard Sayyidī 'Alī al-Khawwāṣ, may Exalted God have mercy on him, say: "A mendicant must not befriend an emir until the emir believes that worldly goods are like carrion or excrement for the shaykh; touching them would befoul his hand and pollute his heart. Then the emir will not dare to send him any such carrion out of respect and veneration." Praise God, Lord of the worlds.

Among the blessings which Exalted God has bestowed upon me is that I will not agree to befriend an emir and allow him to visit me unless I come to the conclusion that he will not distract me from God, may He be honored and glorified. If I come to the conclusion that the emir will distract me from a single *tasbīḥa, tahlīla,* or *takbīra,*[48] I will not befriend him. If I have already entered into a friendship with him, I forbid him to visit me, especially when I am at my invocations,[49] when my brethren gather in

48. Here, al-Sha'rānī refers to three pious phrases, *tasbīḥa* (*subḥān Allāh,* praise God), *tahlīla* (*lā ilāha illā Allāh,* there is no god but God), and *takbīra* (*Allāhu akbar,* God is great).

49. "Invocations" is a translation of *awrād* (sing., *wird*), which refers to the ritual repetition of one of the names of God or a pious phrase.

the morning or at night, for example. If I give him my attention and interrupt my private conversation with God, I will be guilty of being rude to God, and if I don't turn my attention to him, and pay him no heed, he will be annoyed, if only to the minimum degree humanly possible.

It was the practice of Sayyidī Yūsuf al-ʿAjamī,[50] may God have mercy on him, to accept alms from God's presence at the hand of emirs and other people. Whenever an emir came to his zāwiya to visit him, he would say to the doorkeeper, "Don't open the door unless he has something permissible to give to the mendicants." When asked about that, he said: "The most precious possession of a mendicant is his time, and the most precious possession of worldly people is their worldly goods. If they give us their most precious possession, we will give them our most precious possession in the best interest of the mendicants. Otherwise, we have no need for their visits."

I heard Sayyidī ʿAlī al-Khawwāṣ, may God have mercy on him, say: "The company of emirs is more harmful to a mendicant in his faith than a ferocious beast because it distracts him from most pious acts. None of them is worthy for the mendicant to propagate any knowledge or secrets in his heart, just as a true mendicant does not desire any of the emir's worldly goods because he has renounced worldly goods for fear of God, may He be honored and glorified." This is a quality [21] that has become rare these days. Rare is the mendicant who befriends an emir without being distracted from God. It is best not to befriend emirs at all, unless

50. Yūsuf al-ʿAjamī (d. 1367) was a Sufi shaykh of the Suhrawardī network who relocated from Persia to Egypt.

with a legitimate aim and without deceiving oneself. Praise God, Lord of the worlds.

Among the blessings which Exalted God has bestowed upon me is that I will not befriend an emir who accepts offices whose obligations he cannot fulfill because one of the duties of friendship is that one share one's friend's hardships in this world and the Hereafter so that one may bear people's charges for him. This is rarer than red sulfur these days.[51] A mendicant, if he looks with insight, will find himself incapable of bearing his own burdens, much less other people's burdens. It is wrong for a shaykh who claims to be righteous not to bear any of his emir's responsibilities. No, al-Shiblī,[52] may God have mercy on him, used to say, "Whoever has not prepared himself mentally to go to Hell on his friend's behalf—if he deserves to go to Hell—and free him from going there is not entitled to befriend him."

I heard Sayyidī 'Alī al-Khawwāṣ, may God have mercy on him, say: "A mendicant must not befriend an emir until he has prepared himself mentally to bear all of the suspended misfortunes and trials that would befall him were he not to take up their burden for him. As for those who are confirmed, he cannot bear their burden. Rather, he must ask Exalted God to prepare him well for them."

I heard Sayyidī 'Alī al-Khawwāṣ, may God have mercy on him, say, "Let the mendicant beware if he bears his emir's suspended misfortunes and trials lest he think that he thereby is superior to

51. In alchemy, red sulfur was derived from the philosopher's stone and was believed to allow the transmutation of one metal into another. Sufis compared the search for red sulfur to the quest for spiritual enlightenment.

52. Abū Bakr al-Shiblī (ca. 861–945) was an influential Sufi shaykh in Baghdād.

him, indeed lest he not think that this is one of the duties of friendship." I heard him say, "It is impermissible for an emir to think that he is superior to a mendicant because he sends him wheat, rice, lentils, and other things at his zāwiya. For the mendicant, when he befriended him, entered into a contract to bear his hardships, even if only in spirit, so how can an emir be obliged to think himself superior because of some worldly goods that in God's eyes weigh less than a mosquito's wing?" Praise God, Lord of the worlds.

Among the blessings which Exalted God has bestowed upon me is that I am overjoyed whenever an emir criticizes me, even unfairly, ceases to visit me, and starts to meet with someone else, in whom he has the greatest faith, because that is in the best interest of my faith and that of my emir. They say, "Whoever is overjoyed when his emir visits him might as well ask for misfortunes and trials to descend upon him, as this is prevalent among the emirs who frequent mendicants." One of them, as long as he is powerful and influential and safe from his enemy's snares, etc., will visit a mendicant only on rare occasions because he has no need of the mendicant, unlike if he is in the opposite situation. Any mendicant who seeks to have his emir visit him frequently might as well seek to have misfortunes and trials descend upon him. This is something of which mendicants are rarely aware. Know this, brethren, and be joyful when emirs do not visit you. Ask God to grant you happiness in both abodes and keep them far away from you. Praise God, Lord of the worlds.

Among the blessings which Exalted God has bestowed upon me is that I will not undertake to bear my emir's burden when his millstone turns to the left and his situation turns against him, unless he has first repented of all his sins and his punishment has reached its end, unlike the situation of most people today. Perhaps

[22] one of them will undertake to bear his emir's burden after he has mistreated people and whole villages, killed people, drunk wine, committed fornication, unjustly seized people's property, and committed uncounted crimes, while he has yet to repent of these sins and his punishment for them has yet to reach an end. This is ignorance on the part of the mendicant and unjust partisanship on behalf of his emir. Let the mendicant who wishes to bear his emir's crimes command him to repent sincerely, return what he has taken unjustly to its proper owners, and endure his punishment until it is almost complete. Then, after that, the mendicant can undertake to bear his burden.

I heard Sayyidī 'Alī al-Khawwāṣ, may God have mercy on him, say: "Do not undertake to bear an emir's burden until he repents of all his missteps, totally humbles himself before his Lord, and his heart is totally broken. Otherwise, undertaking to bear his burden when he is the opposite of what we have mentioned is nothing but drudgery and toil, unlike with someone who is penitent, humble, and heartbroken." Praise God, Lord of the worlds.

Among the blessings which Exalted God has bestowed upon me is that I will not befriend an emir until I reach the conclusion that the Exalted Real will not disgrace me in front of him, indeed, that He will conceal my faults from him until we part at death, or for some other reason. This is because every mendicant whom emirs have faith in must have an enemy or envier who speaks against his honor and accuses him of deceit and fraud in order to drive that emir away from him. For hearts are inclined to desire that the emirs have faith in them exclusively, and only rarely is a mendicant allowed to enjoy the uninterrupted faith of an emir. The prophets and all of their followers sought protection from their enemies' gloating, whether with the human part in the case of non-prophets, or, in the case of the prophets, legislating to their communities or showing that they are too weak to bear disgrace in the eyes of those who have faith in them. How can the pleasure of an emir's faith in a mendicant and his considering him to be the axial saint and a righteous person compare with the bitterness of his believing him to be sinful and an imposter, and his being shamed in front of people until it is as if he is accused of lewdness? That rising is naught but a fall, the soul of the emir having gazed upon the mendicant while he was committing a lewd act, for he will never again accept anyone's good opinion of him. An intelligent man protects himself and never allows his emir to see him misrepresent himself. No, he says to him, I will befriend you only if you will not leave me even if you see me sin. Instead you will stay with me, correct my deviation, and pray that I repent and reform. They say, "A mystic must not flee one who is deviant or straight; a straight man is a dear friend, and if he flees from a deviant, who will correct his deviation?" I have heard that David, may God bless and save him, when his soul was repulsed by the sinners among the Children of Israel out of zeal for the honor of the Real, God revealed to him: "David, the straight man does not need you, and your soul has driven the deviant man from your friendship without correcting his deviancy. Why [23] did I send you?" After that, David never abandoned anyone, whether deviant or straight. Know that just as a mendicant must not abandon an emir if he deviates from the straight path, so too an emir [must not abandon a mendicant who deviates from the straight path]. Praise God, Lord of the worlds.

Among the blessings which Exalted God has bestowed upon me is that I defend my emir's rival's reputation when he is absent, give him his due, and respect his station in perfection to the best of my ability. I do not allow my emir to speak ill of him at any time. No, I rebuke him severely and order him to say only good things about him. I say to him: "All the evil things you say about your rival are your own qualities. The believers are mirrors to one another. When one looks into a mirror, one sees one's own image, not the image of the mirror."

I heard Sayyidī ʿAlī al-Khawwāṣ, may God have mercy on him, say, "Let the shaykh who befriends emirs be extremely careful not to be silent if he hears any slander against his emir's rival out of partisanship for his emir, for this is sinful and it is not worthy of a shaykh to be sinful." He said, "Only someone who has totally renounced the world, and for whom his emir and his rival are equally deserving of respect, is capable of acting this way with his emir, and there are few mendicants of whom this is true." I heard him say: "It may be that the rival of the emir whom the mendicant has befriended violates the honor of the mendicant and his emir by some slanderous statement. Then they slander him until they take what is due them and go too far, and they come to owe him a debt, although they were entitled to slander him. This is a false opinion since their rival has become the aggrieved party and is no longer the wrongdoer. His prayers against you will not be refused because the prayer of a victim of wrongdoing is never veiled from God, even if he be an infidel, as the tradition says." I heard him say: "Let the shaykh who befriends emirs be extremely careful not to show a desire to help his emir against his enemy, even by writing a charm for his emir to wear or a paper that he buries in the threshold of his rival's house to bring about the destruction of the house. This is magic, and the tradition says, 'He who uses magic is an infidel.'" Only someone who befriends emirs for some purpose other than pleasing God would do this. Praise God, Lord of the worlds.

Among the blessings which Exalted God has bestowed upon me is that I will not agree to befriend an emir as long as I still love gold more than dust and love eating tainted food because I know that I must eventually break with him and be disgraced. If I show that I have worldly desires, he will say, if only to himself, "We both love worldly things, so what makes this shaykh better than me?" On the other hand, if I renounce the world and don't differentiate between dust and gold, we will continue to be friends and I will be protected against disgrace until I part from him at death or for some other reason, Exalted God willing.

[24] I heard Sayyidī ʿAlī al-Khawwāṣ, may God have mercy on him, say: "A mendicant must not agree to befriend an emir unless this emir respects him more than he respects the most powerful emirs. It may be that one of them will die still enamored of the world, while the mendicant rose above this the minute he entered on the path. It is well-known that high rank in God's eyes results only from renouncing the world and its temptations." I heard him say: "Whoever has less respect for a mendicant than he has for the sultan does not know the mendicant's significance. For the mendicant who renounces the world is manlier and has more lofty ambition than the kings of the world, any of whom may die still enamored of it."

Al-Junayd[53] used to say to those who came to him seeking the path, "Have you served kings?" If he said, "No," he would say: "Go

53. Al-Junayd (830–910) was the founder of the Baghdad school of Sufism and is often regarded as the greatest of the early Sufi masters.

serve them, then come back. The least demanding conduct with us is beyond the conduct you are obliged to follow with kings." I heard him say: "One who knows the greatness of the path and the glory of its people sees that his station is above that of kings. He protects it for God's sake, not for his own sake, and befriends only those who will raise his station above that of kings. The only person worthy of censure is he who is offended by one who, unmindful of what we have mentioned, despises him and severely rebukes him out of zeal for the knowledge he bears, not for his own sake." Know this, brethren. Praise God, Lord of the worlds.

Among the blessings which Exalted God has bestowed upon me is that I will befriend an emir only if I know that I am capable of breaking with him, fighting with him, and being his open enemy, should he overstep God's boundaries, such as if he mistreats a peasant or servant without justification, and if I intercede with him, my intercession will be refused because he is filthy inside, or so he can preserve his honor. This is a rare quality; few are those who act on it. No, most mendicants befriend an emir for worldly reasons, and when they see him beat a peasant, imprison him, and seize his property unjustly, they lack the courage to say to him, "This is forbidden to you," because their intention is wrong right from the start. Had they befriended him for sake of the Hereafter, and to offer advice, he would fear them more than he does the sultan. This happened to me with a certain emir, who swore to me by God and divorce that he feared me more than he did the sultan, and I believed him. Know this, brethren, and act on it. Praise God, Lord of the worlds.

Among the blessings which Exalted God has bestowed upon me is that if I befriend an emir I never present myself to him as a righteous man or one gifted with revelation, because I consider myself incapable of following the example of the righteous. I fear that eventually I will be exposed. I heard Sayyidī ʿAlī al-Khawwāṣ, may God have mercy on him, say: "Do not seek to cause others to have faith in you, or pretend to a higher station than your peers. If you are given that, you won't enjoy it for long. Furthermore, God is more powerful and more punitive. You should stick to the station of concealment as best you can until God reveals you and supports you with His aid in every situation. God suffices as an ally; God suffices as a helper." I heard him say: "The mendicant who befriends emirs needs an authentic revelation of future events, such as someone's appointment to office, his dismissal, or his death. The emir may ask the shaykh about this. If he finds that he knows nothing about it, he will despise him [25] personally. Had he informed the emir when he first befriended him that he is not a righteous man or one gifted with revelation, he would not have suffered his contempt when he deviated from the example of the righteous or failed to reveal to him the truth about future events about which he inquired." I heard him say: "A mendicant must not expect his friendship with an emir to last unless he is gifted with authentic revelation, is capable of taking the emir by the hand during hardships, and God has given him power over the emir, should he disobey him, to affect his body or have him dismissed from office. If the emir sees that he has this power, he will automatically respect him, especially if he has power over his—the emir's—enemies as well in having them appointed to office, dismissed, or causing them to fall ill. He will respect him, honor him, and remain his friend until death. Whoever expects an emir to honor him without being gifted with revelation or taking him by the hand in times of hardship is asking for the impossible. As long as the mendicant lacks power over the emir and his enemies are sharper than a sword, God permitting, he is of little use. A saintly miracle is to a saint as an evidentiary miracle is to a prophet;[54] whoever lacks a saintly miracle is thought of by people as one of them. They do not regard him as superior to them in any way."

I heard Mawlānā Shaykh al-Islām Zakarīyā, may God have mercy on him, say: "Do not present yourself to the emir whom you befriend as a pious man, one gifted with revelation, even if you have confidence in this, for divine election may fail you and disgrace you in the eyes of people and of the emir. If you have presented yourself as such to your emir, ask Exalted God to protect you in his eyes. Do not relax until you believe that Exalted God has given a decisive answer to your request." I heard him say, "When the second half of the tenth century begins, God will remove power over men from most saints because of the many trials that will befall the people of that age, so that God's providence may be fulfilled." Praise God, Lord of the worlds.

Among the blessings which Exalted God has bestowed upon me is that I will not agree to befriend an emir unless I believe that there is nothing on my conscience, much less in my outward behavior, that God abhors. This is to prevent the sin of deceiving the emir. Whenever I know that I have a bad conscience between me and God, which would repulse the emir if he knew of it, I refuse to become his friend as a precaution against my committing a sin and swindling him. This is conduct rarely observed by the mendicants who befriend emirs. For this reason, smart mendicants rarely

54. "Miracle" is used for the two terms *karāma* and *muʿjiza*. A *muʿjiza* is limited to a prophet and serves as evidence that the prophet possesses authentic revelations from God. A *karāma* is a miracle performed by a saint and is proof of his sanctity.

befriend emirs. You almost never find one who is a friend to emirs. It is the ones with deficient intellects who befriend them.

I heard Sayyidī ʿAlī al-Khawwāṣ, may God have mercy on him, say: "Whoever wishes to befriend an emir must not commit sins between himself and God. That way, he will conform to the faith the emir has in him and be able to bear his burden in times of hardship. Whoever has a sin on his conscience is unsuitable to intercede with God on his own behalf, much less on behalf of someone else." I heard him say: "Whoever befriends an emir intending to intercede with him on behalf of victims of wrongdoing must be more careful than others not to commit sins. The station of intercession is too lofty for one who masters it to commit [26] any of the vices, for it is first and foremost the station of the prophets, may they be blessed and saved. As for some prophets excusing themselves when asked to open the gate of intercession on the Day of Resurrection, this is not due to any real sin. It is an introduction and demonstration of the superior station of Muḥammad, may God bless and save him, on that awesome day when they know that he, may God bless and save him, will be the first to open the gate of intercession. We have said repeatedly that the sins of the prophets in the Qurān and elsewhere are formal, not real. God caused their form to occur through them so they could teach their religious communities how to repent and renounce their real sins when they commit them, and for no other reason. Otherwise, the prophets, may God bless and save them, never leave the station of visionary certitude, much less the station of good conduct. Someone like this cannot commit a real sin. Indeed, the sin itself flees from the prophet just as darkness flees from light, for the sin knows that it has no place where it may attach itself to the person of the prophet." Praise God, Lord of the worlds.

Among the blessings which Exalted God has bestowed upon me is that I will befriend only those emirs who have full faith in me, except when it is in his best interest or mine, so that he has too much respect for my station to send me a gift at any time, as has been indicated previously. They say: "One sign of the perfection of one's respect for a shaykh is that one consider oneself and one's dependents as the shaykh's dependents and reproach any of one's dependents who sends him any of the money he received from his provider. Only those emirs whose faith is not perfect and think that they share property with the shaykh may send him things. Any emir who claims to have complete faith in a mendicant, then sends him a gift of food, clothes, mount, servant, etc., indicates how little faith he has. This is unlike most mendicants who befriend emirs. Unless the shaykh requests something; then there is no harm, and it is as if he is using the emir to hand over some of his own property." Know this, brethren. Praise God, Lord of the worlds.

Among the blessings which Exalted God has bestowed upon me is that I will agree to befriend only an emir whom I believe has full faith in the perfection of my intellect and my renunciation in this world and the Hereafter, and that I consider accepting [gifts] as soiling myself. If the emir is not like that, I will not befriend him, even if he swears by God and divorce that he loves and esteems me greatly, according to his own view. How can I believe him that he believes me to be righteous when he believes that I love the world and its attractions, much like himself or any ordinary person? One of the preconditions to being righteous is to renounce the world and its temptations from the first footstep one takes on the path of the people, to be disgusted by it as one would be by carrion, and to avoid it as one would poison or thorns. How can someone like that befriend anyone or love him for the sake of worldly goods? This is extremely unlikely. Thus it is made clear to you that the emir has little faith in the shaykh if he sends him some worldly goods. If he believed [27] that he had weaned himself from them, and had no motive beyond the human minimum to love them, he would not have sent him anything. No, he would see this as pointless, just as an elderly man is not commanded to suckle a child at his breast, since he has no reason to do this. Know this. Praise God, Lord of the worlds.

Among the blessings which Exalted God has bestowed upon me is that I will not agree to befriend an emir until I have certainly accustomed myself to sharing all of his hardships in this world and the Hereafter, as has already been indicated. If I cannot do this willingly, I will not befriend him for fear of failing in my duty to him.

I heard Sayyidī ʿAlī al-Khawwāṣ, may God have mercy on him, say, "Whoever does not know that he is capable of sharing all his emir's concerns and worries, and of being determined to share all of the hardships and fears that he will suffer in the Hereafter until he succeeds in crossing the bridge,[55] is not permitted to befriend him." I heard him say, "Whoever does not know that he is capable of observing his emir in all of the sins that he would commit were it not for the shaykh's observation, to observe him in all of his judgments between his subjects so that he does not deviate from what is right, and to be present when his spirit exits his body so that it emerges in the Islamic faith, when Munkar and Nakīr[56]

55. The bridge (*ṣirāṭ*) over Hell is crossed by the righteous before they enter Paradise.

56. Munkar and Nakīr are the angels who interrogate the deceased in the grave about his or her faith.

interrogate him so that he answers correctly, at the scales so that they tip in his favor and at the bridge so that he does not fall into Hell, does not have the right to befriend him." I heard him say, "Whoever is not determined to share all of his emir's punishments in his lifetime and after his death because he is incapable of bearing them all on his behalf has no right to befriend him." These days, this is something that has become rarer than red sulfur; it is spoken of but never seen. An intelligent man will not befriend an emir whom he can send away by some ruse. Praise God, Lord of the worlds.

Among the blessings which Exalted God has bestowed upon me is that I will not agree to befriend an emir as long as I am bent on eating his food, wearing his clothes, riding his mounts, etc., because I know if I do this I will cease to be useful to him and do harm to myself and to him, and this would prevent my prayers for him from being answered in times of hardship. Let the emir beware of inviting the mendicant to eat his food, for he will be the first one to suffer.

[28] I heard Sayyidī 'Alī al-Khawwāṣ, may Exalted God have mercy on him, say: "Most emirs who befriend mendicants are ignorant of the states of mendicants. They sometimes invite the mendicant to eat their food or wear their clothes, out of real love for him, but forgetting that this will harm him and them. The mendicant must teach the emir things like this and say to him, 'If you feed us your food, don't blame us later if we fail to bear your burden and our prayers on your behalf are not answered. Choose: either deprive us of your food, or don't ask us to assist you with the hardships that befall you.'" Especially since the food of most emirs is not free of taint due to its filthy ingredients, as has previously been indicated.

I heard Sayyidī 'Alī al-Khawwāṣ, may God have mercy on him, say: "Only great saints are capable of rebuking an emir whose food they have eaten. Most people are likely to be prevented from rebuking him by natural diffidence toward the emir whose food they have eaten. Only a few solitary mendicants feel obliged to rebuke the emir whose licit food they have eaten. It is better not to agree to befriend emirs whose food the mendicant is not determined to avoid eating. Let that be the end of the matter."

Among the blessings which Exalted God has bestowed upon me is that I will not promise the emir who befriends me that he will obtain any of the offices that he seeks in the future, even if the object of my gaze is the Protected Tablet. It may be that the tablet is one set up by Iblīs for those who are not infallible to lure them away from their religion and shame them in front of people, where he writes false things to make a laughingstock of the mendicant who gazes upon it, and make a fool of him, if he reports these things to people. Al-Ghazālī[57] and others have mentioned that Exalted God allowed Iblīs to achieve the station of deception and temptation so that if he sees that the heart of the mendicant receives from the cloud that is located above the Throne, he sets up a cloud for him, or from the Throne, he sets up a throne, or the Pedestal, he sets up a pedestal, or the Lotus Tree, he sets up a lotus tree, etc.[58] If Exalted God supports the servant, he gives him the

57. Abū Ḥāmid Muḥammad al-Ghazālī (ca. 1058–1111) was one of the most influential Muslim thinkers of the Middle Ages. His *Revival of the Religious Sciences,* a comprehensive work on religious reform, was deeply influential in Sufi circles.

58. The Throne refers to the outermost sphere that contains the entire cosmos. Within it is the Pedestal, the sphere that contains the houses of the Zodiac. The Lotus Tree represents the end of the Seventh Heaven.

power to distinguish between what is true and what is imaginary; otherwise, he unwittingly falls into error. Let the mendicant take care not to say to his emir, "You will certainly be appointed to a certain office" or "Your enemy will certainly be dismissed or destroyed at a certain time." This is ignorance, deceit, and a sign that he follows what pleases the emir for worldly reasons, or that he is a brother to devils.

I heard Sayyidī ʿAlī al-Khawwāṣ, may God have mercy on him, say, quoting ʿAbd al-Qādir al-Jīlī:[59] "A mendicant must not inform people of what he sees in the Protected Tablet, much less the Tablets of Affirmation and Erasure.[60] The tablet that he sees might be one set up [29] for him by Iblīs. Instead, he must conceal that and delay until it appears in the world to everyone, for fear that the event will not occur, people will make fun of him and he will lower the people's opinion of the people of the path.[61] This is the custom of the perfect saints; the intelligent man will follow their example in this. Praise God, Lord of the worlds.

Among the blessings which Exalted God has bestowed upon me is that I will not agree to befriend an emir if I believe that he is befriending me only so that I will bear his burden in times of hardship, unless he is one of those who attends the divine processions,[62] in which case there is no blame in my befriending him, Exalted God willing. This is because God may become angry with one who doesn't attend them, dismiss him from his offices, and cut

59. ʿAbd al-Qādir al-Jīlī (1077–1166) was an influential preacher in Baghdad. The Qādirī Sufi network claims him as its founder.

60. The Tablets of Erasure and Affirmation are of a lower order than the Protected Tablet and contain contingent events that may or may not transpire.

61. The "people of the path" are those who follow the Sufi path.

62. Religious rituals such as prayer and fasting.

off divine aid to him, just as happens to those soldiers who reject the processions of kings on earth. To God belongs the highest example. In the tradition, someone says, "Messenger of God, I ask you: May I accompany you in Paradise?" He said, "Occupy yourself with frequent prostration." Every mendicant who befriends an emir who does not attend the divine processions expects too much of himself in bearing that emir's burden, especially if that emir disobeys his Lord while the mendicant bears his burden, by drinking wine, committing fornication or sodomy, or mistreating people, such as unjustly imprisoning a peasant, etc.

I heard Sayyidī ʿAlī al-Khawwāṣ, may God have mercy on him, say: "It is foolish of the mendicant to befriend an emir who commits sins and is not guided to repent of them, for the mendicant cannot abandon him in times of hardship, while the emir deserves his help only once he has repented of all his sins. Only then may the mendicant hope for God to accept his intercession, unlike the persistent sinner and the one who refuses to attend the divine processions. How long will the mendicant who befriends such a person toil, and how futile will his endeavor be!" Praise God, Lord of the worlds.

Among the blessings which Exalted God has bestowed upon me is that I sometimes pray to Exalted God, may He be honored and glorified, that the emir whom I have befriended be dismissed if he deviates from the straight path that is appropriate to one such as he, won't heed my rebuke, and has no patience for my correction of his deviation, or I pray that God forgives him or causes his death. All of this is out of love for him and concern that he will commit sins that will anger his Lord, may He be honored and glorified. Were I to wish that he continue in his deviance, and not pray as has been mentioned, I would be cheating him, cheating myself, and abandoning my duty to him.

I heard Sayyidī ʿAlī al-Khawwāṣ, may God have mercy on him, say: "The mendicant who befriends an unjust emir who does not heed his rebuke must not pray to God, may He be honored and glorified, that he be dismissed, for example, until he has consulted the *aṣḥāb al-nawba*[63] who appointed him to this office, out of courtesy to them. For all tyrannical offices and illegitimate tolls and the like are under their control because they belong to the holy fools, unlike the sober saints who follow the Holy Law, none of whom can assist the emir to obtain oppressive offices with a single hair on [30] his body. One of our brethren was lenient about what we said and prayed to God for the dismissal of an emir appointed with God's permission by the aṣḥāb al-nawba. They caused him to be chronically ill, blinded his sight, and deafened his ears. He stayed that way until he died. The intelligent man is he who heeds advice and does not start down a road whose end he does not know. Let that be the end of the matter."

I heard my brother Afḍal al-Dīn, may God have mercy on him, say: "Don't resemble the masters of states[64] and assist anyone in being appointed to an office from which there is no relief. You will be sinners and partners in the sin that attaches to him. One of the masters of states, on the other hand, can appoint to office oppressive toll collectors and others, with God's permission, while protecting

63. Hidden saints who control who is appointed to and dismissed from office. They are holy fools not bound by Islamic law.

64. The "masters of states" (*arbāb al-aḥwāl*) are a type of saint. Like the aṣḥāb al-nawba, they do not seem bound to stay within the limits of respectable behavior or company.

himself from the consequences. Then he intercedes with God on behalf of that wrongdoer so that Exalted God forgives him and he reconciles with him all of the people who suffered. He does this on his behalf, God willing. One of them may sit in a tavern among women of ill repute and wine drinkers and intercede on behalf of every fornicator, male and female, and every wine drinker and seller, and God accepts his intercession with signs known to him. These are called the 'men of mercy,' were it not for whom Exalted God would cause the sinners to be swallowed up by the earth and transformed into beasts."

I heard Sayyidī 'Alī al-Khawwāṣ, may God have mercy on him, say, "Any mendicant whom Exalted God does not give the power to dismiss tyrannical emirs, to make them lame, blind, etc., has no right to befriend any of them, because this is equivalent to being present where sins are being committed without rebuking those committing them." I heard him say: "Don't befriend an emir who mistreats his subjects unless Exalted God gives you the power to depose or otherwise punish him and prevent him from harm, especially if he has been mistreating your friends. The mendicant is commanded to be patient only with those who mistreat him personally. When someone mistreats his brethren, on the other hand, he is obliged to hold that wrongdoer back from them, for they befriended him specifically so that he would protect them from the harm that befalls them in this world and the Hereafter, so that he may deserve their believing him to be righteous." Sayyidī Ibrāhīm al-Ja'barī,[65] who is buried in his zāwiya outside Bāb al-Naṣr,[66] used to say: "Any mendicant who does not kill as many wrongdoers

65. Ibrāhīm al-Ja'barī (d. 1288) was a Sufi preacher.
66. One of the principal gates to Cairo.

as there are hairs on his head, Exalted God willing, has not done his duty in Holy War. That is because the world never lacks those who mistreat people day and night in every region of the earth. Whenever he learns of a wrongdoer, he asks the Real, may He be honored and exalted, for permission to punish him in a legal manner, and punishes him with death or in some other way." Praise God, Lord of the worlds.

Among the blessings which Exalted God has bestowed upon me is that I will not agree to befriend an emir as long as he forces people to buy his goods at a loss, unless I know that he will accept my intercession not to force anyone to buy anything. Under those circumstances, I will befriend him to benefit people and to protect him from sin. This is something that most mendicants who accept charity and patronage from tyrannical emirs are lax about. They befriend them, then defend them and interpret their behavior in ways no sound mind could accept. People start to mock them, as I have witnessed with those who befriended subprovincial governors and tribal chiefs who mistreat men and whole villages. Among the things 'Umar ibn 'Abd al-'Azīz[67] said was: [31] "Do not befriend any tyrannical emir with the intention of rebuking him as long as you love this world. Tyrannical emirs cannot be counted on to accept being rebuked. It is better for you to avoid befriending them. Let that be the end of the matter."

I heard Sayyidī 'Alī al-Khawwāṣ, may God have mercy on him, say: "Do not befriend a wrongdoer and try to prevent the prayers against him of those he has mistreated from being accepted. This

67. 'Umar ibn 'Abd al-'Azīz (682–720) was caliph from 717 until his death. Unlike the other Umayyad caliphs, who are widely scorned for their unjust rule, Sunnī Muslims consider him to be an exemplar of justice and righteousness.

is not possible for you, because the prayers of the victim of wrongdoing are answered, even if he is an infidel, as it says." Nonetheless, it has become rare for a mendicant to protect a wrongdoer in matters yet to be settled because they depend on the mendicant's food and clothes being licit, and that there be no sin upon him. This is rarer than red sulfur these days. Praise God, Lord of the worlds.

Among the blessings which Exalted God has bestowed upon me is that I will not agree to befriend any emir unless I know that I am capable of stopping myself from eating his food or accepting his gifts, especially if I fear that he will rashly mistreat people through the agency of some imported official he has appointed. For the situation may change and the officials whom he appointed and imported may be dismissed or die. An inquest may be held against him and he might seek to have a statement written in which people testify to his being morally righteous and not unjust. They might present this statement to me to sign, and I would be uncertain whether or not to sign. How could I refuse to sign and testify that he is a good man, having eaten his food and accepted his gifts? This is the hardest thing in the world. Had I not eaten his food and accepted any of his gifts, I would not be in this quandary. This emir has been recorded in the official records and perhaps a chief judge or governor gives the mendicant cash or assigns him a stipend; which he accepts. Then, after a few days, they send him a statement to sign when the subjects have lodged a complaint against him. If he signs it, the common people will rise against him like it is Judgment Day, and his reputation will be in tatters as far as the eye can see. If he refuses to sign, the officials will say to him, "How is it that you consumed our property when you knew it was tainted and you are too cautious to give us a testimonial?" They will mock him in gatherings, unlike he whom Exalted God protects entirely from emirs' property; Exalted God protects him from their snare. Even if they appear to be annoyed with him, they secretly admire him because he fears for his faith. Know this, brethren, praise God, Lord of the worlds.

Among the blessings which Exalted God has bestowed upon me is that I will not befriend an emir unless I think I will be able to prevent myself from abasing myself to him to obtain some worldly goods as long as I am his friend, unlike what happens to some who befriend emirs, hoping that one of them will help him in obtaining some worldly objective, such as the administration of a mosque; a post as a teacher, preacher, or prayer leader; or protecting his ship or beasts from [32] being requisitioned by officials, etc. If I do not know that I am able to protect against abasing myself to him to obtain any of the things I have mentioned, I will not befriend him. This is possible only for someone who has mastered renouncing the world and its attractions, so that he is unhappy when he obtains them and happy when they disappear, and loves every enemy who prevents him from obtaining them more than he loves his friend who helps him to obtain them. This is rarer than red sulfur among most people in this age. Freedom from enslavement to the world and its attachments is possible only for individual perfect men, so that al-Junayd, may God have mercy on him, said, "If one could pray without reciting from the Qurān, it would be valid to recite this verse, which was said by one of them: 'I hope for the impossible from this age / that my eyes behold the face of a free man.'" That is, free from enslavement to others. Once, he was asked about renouncing the world such that there is nothing left to him but the edge of a kernel. He said, "The indentured slave remains a bondsman as long as he owes a single dirham."

They say that Sayyidī Yāqūt al-ʿArshī,[68] may God have mercy on him, said: "I saw a boy who sought the clothes another boy had with him. He said, 'If you act like a dog, I will give them to you.' He replied, 'Yes,' so he gave the clothes to him, placed a rope around his neck, and dragged him around like a puppy. I learned a lesson from this and said, 'Had the boy renounced the clothes, the clothes' owner would not have been able to make a dog out of him.'" He said: "Once I was hungry so I asked someone for a loaf of bread. He said, 'I brought it specifically for this dog, so be patient until I offer it to him.' The dog paid no attention to it. I said to myself, 'Woe is he who is less able to abstain from food and withstand hunger than a dog!'" Let the intelligent man learn a lesson. Praise God, Lord of the worlds.

Among the blessings which Exalted God has bestowed upon me is that I will not befriend an emir unless I know by revelation and certainty, not opinion and guesswork, that I am truly seeking his friendship for God's sake. For it is the nature of the appetitive soul to deceive its master, and the soul may make it appear to him that he is honest in seeking to befriend the emir, and that he befriends him only for God's sake, when the truth is the opposite. Let he who rebukes his soul examine his conscience carefully before entering into a friendship with an emir. For the soul has wiles that may be hidden from many active scholars, not to mention other people.

I heard Sayyidī ʿAlī al-Khawwāṣ, may God have mercy on him, say: "A mendicant must not accept his soul's claim to honesty with regard to any of its states. No, he must be firm in impugning all

68. An early fourteenth-century shaykh in the Shādhilī Sufi network in Alexandria, Egypt.

of its claims, especially its befriending of emirs. For it is its nature to take pleasure in the company of great men, including kings and lesser men. It may claim to be honest in loving the just emir for his justice, when the truth is that it loves him because its merits are mentioned in gatherings until most of the emirs are drawn to him. Let the servant test his soul's honesty: what if that just emir had no faith in him, indeed criticized him, and drove people away from him? If he still would love him, he loves him for God's sake or for his justice, not because the emir praises him. If he is annoyed by this by one hair more than the human minimum, he is a liar in claiming to love the emir for God's sake or for his justice. If the motive to love him were solely justice, he would not be annoyed, since he would not cease to be just. This is a balance that can be tipped by a single grain."

[33] I heard Sayyidī ʿAlī al-Khawwāṣ, may God have mercy on him, say: "One sign of the mendicant's sincerity in befriending the just emir for God's sake is that he love him totally, even if he is one of his strongest critics who hates him. The emir's hatred for him and his criticism fade in comparison with the benefits men obtain due to the emir's justice. Similarly, it is a sign of sincerity if the emir is oppressive but loves the mendicant, has great faith in him, and honors him greatly, that the mendicant hate him, criticize him, and that the emir's love for him fade in comparison with his oppression of men, such that barely a single hair on his body loves him." This too is a balance that can be tipped by a single grain. Only someone who follows what pleases Exalted God, not his own selfish objectives, is capable of being measured by it. We have already said in this book that whenever a mendicant is annoyed when his emir ceases to visit him, criticizes him, and meets with

his peers, this is a sign that he has befriended the emir for something other than God's sake. Praise God, Lord of the worlds.

Among the blessings which Exalted God has bestowed upon me is that I will not agree to befriend an emir, or any subprovincial governor or tribal chief if he asks, until I receive his promise that should he mistreat any of his subjects, whether a peasant or someone else, I cease to be his friend. If he accepts this condition, I befriend him; otherwise, I dismiss him with a kind phrase.

I heard Mawlānā Shaykh al-Islām Zakarīyā, may God have mercy on him, say: "The mendicant must not befriend an emir until he receives his promise that if he mistreats any man, even by forcing him to labor for a single hour to plow, harvest, build, or transport anything, he will pray to God, may He be honored and glorified, that he be dismissed from office and that God take from him what he owes this aggrieved person, even through a long period of imprisonment or a severe beating. If the emir agrees to this, he agrees to befriend him; otherwise, let him forsake him and repel him with a kind phrase."

I heard my brother Afḍal al-Dīn, may God have mercy on him, say: "If you want to know if the emir is sincere in befriending you, and if he will obey you, praise his enemy in his presence and pray that he continues to be honored, supported, and in a good situation. If he is pleased by this, he is sincere in his friendship with you; otherwise, his situation is obvious." Praise God, Lord of the worlds.

Among the blessings which Exalted God has bestowed upon me is that I will not intercede with my emir on behalf of a person who has been imprisoned or beaten until it is clear to me whether he is a victim or a wrongdoer, and the punishment is almost over. Few mendicants understand things like this. They intercede with the pasha or someone else solely on the basis of the statement of the prisoner or victim that, for example, "I am the aggrieved party." Then they are rude to the emir, which is reckless. The emir may have a reliable statement that the prisoner or person being beaten has done wrong, and the person being beaten and the mendicant will be put to shame. For this reason, I used to write to officials with regard to the prisoners they hold, saying, "If so-and-so is aggrieved or a wrongdoer and the punishment is finished, let me intercede on his behalf; otherwise, we are with you against him until he repents or is deterred." That way, I am not put to shame by what they do to this prisoner, since [34] we agree on what is right. Know that a mendicant must not intercede merely because a prisoner claims to have been mistreated and his family says that he has been mistreated, because if it turns out that his intercession is mistaken, he will lose his good name with officials and they will think he is a fool. Almost none of them will rely on his intercession or accept it from now on. A group of students came to me to ask that I intercede for a surgeon with the Emir Māmāy, saying, "The emir's retinue seized him unjustly when they raided some dissolute people." I hesitated, and they swore to me by God that they were telling the truth. I wrote him a letter which said: "Person A, Person B, and Person C testified in my presence that he is being treated unjustly and swore to God that this is the case. If they are telling the truth, let us intercede for him. If they are not telling the truth, we are with you against him until the legal punishment is finished." When the letter was read to him, he said, "This shows that so-and-so's heart is illuminated." Then he had him released from prison. He said to him, "Didn't you confess to the pasha that you are the leader of the gang?" He said, "Yes." He said to him, "Wasn't the property of the inhabitants of such-and-such villages found on your person?" He said, "Yes." The emir said to them, "Where is your testimony before so-and-so that he is being mistreated?" They were ashamed and disgraced.

I heard Sayyidī 'Alī al-Khawwāṣ, may God have mercy on him, say: "Don't intercede for anyone with the emirs unless you have insight into his situation lest they stop trusting your opinion and mind. Few emirs imprison someone without someone's testimony against him, even if it is actually false testimony. The apparent sense of the Holy Law will be on his side, and you will have nothing on your side to oppose it." For this reason, I would not intercede with an emir for a prisoner until I had prayed to God, may He be honored and glorified, that I be willing to intercede for him if he has been mistreated, or unwilling to intercede if he is a wrongdoer. I have continued to do this up to today, unlike some who love the world and accept a wage in exchange for intercession, heedless that this is forbidden. It so happened that one scholar went to see Sulaymān Pasha[69] to intercede for a Christian tax agent, saying, "The Messenger of God, may he be blessed and saved, prohibited mistreating the protected people,[70] saying, 'Whoever oppresses a protected person, I will be his opponent on the Day of Resurrection.'" The pasha said, "Bring this Christian from the prison." When he had been brought, the pasha said to him, "How much of the sultan's money is in your possession?" He said, "Seven purses." The pasha said to him, "Knowingly?" He said, "Knowingly." He said, "Tell this to my lord the shaykh who makes us out to be un-

69. Governor of Egypt, 1525–35 and 1537–38.

70. The "protected people" (*ahl al-dhimma*) are the non-Muslims who fell under the protection of the Muslim state in exchange for the payment of a poll tax (*jizya* or *jawālī*). Their lives, property, and right to practice their religion were protected.

just to you." The shaykh was embarrassed and did not know what to say. He had a big stomach, and when he left, the pasha said to his companions: "It is said that God despises the fat sage," that is, the fat scholar, "and that is because of his lack of precautionary piety. Were he cautious, he most likely would not have found anything to fatten him and would have become like an insect." The intelligent man will learn a lesson from things like this.

I heard Sayyidī ʿAlī al-Khawwāṣ, may God have mercy on him, say: "If you learn that an aggrieved person is being held unjustly by an emir, intercede for him, even if the punishment that the emir desired is not finished, unlike if he is a wrongdoer, in which case, you must not intercede for him until [35] the legal punishment is finished. For example, if the prefect seizes someone whom he observes seducing one of his own slave girls, and whom he wishes to punish, barely controlling his anger, it is not intelligent for someone to intercede for him after the first blow or two; no, one should wait until he thinks that the punishment is finished. Even if a scholar were to intercede for him before that, the prefect might well not listen to him and disregard his opinion. He who intercedes for an aggrieved person must be extremely crafty and be clear about the aggrieved person's situation before interceding for him." Praise God, Lord of the worlds.

Among the blessings which Exalted God has bestowed upon me is that I will not agree to befriend an emir unless I am confident of my sincerity in knowledge and action. If I am not confident of that I will not agree to befriend him lest I need his alms or gift, even without begging. In receiving them from the emir, I would seek to reduce his reward since he would have assisted me in something that involves him in deceit and insincerity. The clarification of this is that Exalted God only guarantees a seeker of knowledge a living in excess of what is necessary if he is sincere in his knowledge and action. One who is not sincere in needing to beg the emir for a living loses his respect. The emir is unable to accept his intercession for aggrieved persons after that. Know that whoever is not sincere in his knowledge and action may be punished by God with a need to beg people whose hearts harden against him. He will not be able to refrain from begging, nor will they give him what he requests. This is counted among the most severe of punishments, according to al-Junayd, among others.

I heard Sayyidī ʿAlī al-Khawwāṣ, may God have mercy on him, say: "Do not befriend an emir and be lax in eating his food and accepting his gifts unless you are sincere in your knowledge and action and unless the food is licit, so that the emir receives full credit for his charity to you and for helping you to seek knowledge. If you are not sincere, you must not be lax in eating his food or accepting his kindness and charity because this entails his helping you to sin by your bad intentions. Otherwise, the search for knowledge as such is counted as a righteous act and one of the best acts of obedience." He said, "This is something that may be hidden from many students." I heard him say, may God have mercy on him, "Whoever has not mastered the station of abstaining from the property of the emirs he befriends may be mocked by the emir if he sees him eating tainted foods, especially during the month of Ramaḍān." It so happened that one of those who claims to be learned and righteous wanted to break his fast during Ramaḍān at the home of our friend Emir Muḥammad al-Dawādār. The emir said to him, "None of our food is worthy for the likes of you to eat." He said to him, "The sea is not made muddy by buckets or altered by carrion." The emir said to his pages: "Get this fellow out of my sight; he is a devil in human form. If the souls of people like us are unwilling to break the fast with this sort of food during the Great Month, how can the soul of one such as this be willing to eat it, when he claims to be learned, righteous, and the axial saint?" Take note, people of vision, and do not befriend [36] an emir, unless you know that you can protect yourself from consuming his property, so that you become a paragon of caution and avoid tainted things for him and others. Otherwise, if you consume tainted things, whom will your emir, and others, imitate if he seeks to practice precautionary piety? I heard him say: "If the learned man does not act on his knowledge, he is liable to be recorded in the roll of false leaders, especially if he befriends an emir, or if the emir and his retinue imitate his lack of caution. He accentuates the matter by abstaining from befriending him."

I heard my brother Afḍal al-Dīn, may God have mercy on him, say: "Every mendicant who befriends an emir and eats his tainted food, saying to him, 'This sort of thing doesn't do me any harm,' is a liar and a fabricator. The prohibited thing in the tainted food alters the heart of the axial saint and succor, not to mention an ordinary person. Indeed, they say, 'Prohibited things are like poison.' Just as consuming poison, even unwittingly, is harmful, so too are prohibited things." Know that there is no objection to the mendicant gifted with revelation for whom the Exalted Real has extracted what is permitted from between the dung of the prohibited and the blood of the tainted foods. Do not rush to denounce a mendicant known for his caution until you know that the food is harmful. Praise God, Lord of the worlds.

Among the blessings which Exalted God has bestowed upon me is that I will not agree to befriend an emir once my soul looks forward to seeking his friendship unless both he and I are purified of all sins and impurities, manifest and hidden. If he and I are not like that, I won't agree to befriend him. At worst, an immoral person befriends another immoral person. Assuming that I want to bear his burden in times of hardship, I am not fit for that, nor is he fit for me to seek his relief, since we are both sinners. This is something of which few people are aware, as has already been indicated in this book. Praise God, Lord of the worlds.

Among the blessings which Exalted God has bestowed upon me is that I will not agree to befriend an emir unless my vision has penetrated into the Hereafter and seen with my heart's eye its hardships, terrors, and judgments. This is so that I may spare the emir everything that I saw that harms his faith and worldly goods. Someone whose vision cannot penetrate to see this sort of thing is liable to order the emir to do something that harms his faith or to help him to obtain an office that he cannot avoid. We have already said that the master of this station has not a single hair that wishes the emir to remain in an office from which he cannot avoid. No, he is the first one to oppose his remaining in it, and the first to pray to God that he be dismissed, out of love for him and concern for his religion, and to fulfill the obligatory duty of friendship.

[37] I heard Sayyidī 'Alī al-Khawwāṣ, may God have mercy on him, say: "If you turn your emir away from your friendship for some reason, do not guide him to befriend one of your brethren, bringing him the grief and worry that you escaped and ceasing to act in accordance with the tradition [that states] 'None of you believes until he wishes for his brother what he wishes for himself.' The intelligent man is as careful for his brother as he is for himself." Praise God, Lord of the worlds.

Among the blessings which Exalted God has bestowed upon me is that I will not believe an emir if he swears to me by God that this food of his is licit, for what he considers licit might not be licit in my eyes, as has already been indicated in the first section of this book. This is a mistake made by callow mendicants and students. They rely on the emir's oath that his food, for example, is licit, and they are unaware that it is likely that by "licit" they mean that which does not result from any new injustices they have imposed on their subjects, as I heard from a certain daftar and subprovincial governor when he offered me some of his food to eat. He said: "This is something not made from new taxes I have imposed on my subjects. Rather, it was my predecessor who originated it." I saw that he is one of those who thinks that the injustices and fines that he did not originate are licit. How can I eat his food after that and rely on his oath when he is ignorant of the rules of the Holy Law? Praise God, Lord of the worlds.

Among the blessings which Exalted God has bestowed upon me is that I am happy when my emir is relieved of his responsibility and people obtain what he owes them, even if he is imprisoned, lashed, and hit with mallets, rushing to purify him of his sins in this world, before the Hereafter, thanks to the strong faith in the Day of Reckoning that Exalted God has bestowed upon me. It has happened to me with some emirs that I may pray to God to kill him if he kills someone unjustly, out of love for him, not hatred. If my emir has already been imprisoned and his family begins to send him a variety of excellent foods in prison, I forbid them from doing this sort of thing and command them to send him dried-out loaves without any accompanying food, one day after another, in hopes of reducing his sentence. Every day that he goes hungry in prison and does not see his family caring for him equals a week or a month of humiliation and punishment, according to his level of manliness. If, however, they make a variety of foods and send them to him, his imprisonment will be long, for then it is as if he is sitting at home. This is something unknown to many people, but act upon it my brethren. Praise God, Lord of the worlds.

Among the blessings which Exalted God has bestowed upon me is that if I bear the burden of my aggrieved emir, aiding him against his oppressive enemy, and his enemy is dismissed and the grief and worry that my emir suffered shift to him, I shift to bearing his burden and abandon my emir entirely. Praise God, I follow what pleases God. Whoever is suffering, I support by helping him with his suffering. This is something that few mendicants do. Indeed, one of them may pray to God to dismiss his emir's enemy, for example; then, when he has been dismissed, he gloats and takes revenge with pagan glee.

I heard Sayyidī ʿAlī al-Khawwāṣ, may God have mercy on him, say: "One sign of a mendicant's sincerity in befriending an emir for Exalted God's sake is that if his emir's enemy is dismissed and he suffers from grief and worry, he shifts to feeling sorry for him, is pained on his behalf, and takes his hand in hard times. He does not avoid [38] this sort of thing to please his emir, for that would be ignorance and selfishness, and the mendicants are above that sort of thing." I heard him say: "The mendicant must prevent his emir from gloating over his enemy if fate turns against him and inform him that anyone who gloats over his enemy may be repaid in kind by Exalted God. It is the emir's obligation to feel very sorry for his enemy lest he be the reason why God censures him. The intelligent man pays attention most of the time to those who are against him, not to those who are on his side." I have dismissed many emirs from my friendship when they became annoyed with me because I showed sorrow for their enemy and undertook to bear his burden, especially the Banī Baghdād. This is something that can be practiced only by someone who befriends his emir for God's sake, not for any selfish end. Praise God, Lord of the worlds.

Among the blessings which Exalted God has bestowed upon me is that I am extremely cautious of emirs who have great faith in me, and that I really dislike this, in accordance with my obligation toward our lord, the sultan, even if he is not aware of it. It is the task of every mystic to protect the authority of our lord, the sultan, lest anyone acquire a comparable following among the emirs. The true mystic is he who is extremely cautious not to do this. This is something that pleases seducers, but it may lead to their being exiled or destroyed in the best interest of the Muslims. The person who brings about their exile may gain a great reward. That is because anyone who enjoys the support and full faith of the sultan's armies is no different from the sultan's enemy who wishes to seize his realm.

I heard my brother Afḍal al-Dīn, may God have mercy on him, say: "One sign of a sincere mendicant is that he is happy with humiliation and defeat. The more that emirs and the powerful degrade him, the happier and cheerier he is, content with God's knowledge, may He be honored and glorified, just as he is happy and cheerful with Exalted God's being pleased with him, unlike the false mendicant." Know this, brethren, and seek that which drives the emirs away from you as best you can, lest you begin to resemble the Supreme Sultan in the loyalty of his subjects. The mystics consider this one of the highest levels of bad conduct. Praise God, Lord of the worlds.

Among the blessings which Exalted God has bestowed upon me is that I abstain from eating permissible, but tainted, foods, which usually prevent one's prayers from being answered, when I fear that my emir will be dismissed or imprisoned, even if I am afraid for a long time, since I hope that my prayers on his behalf will be answered if he suffers an ordeal, thereby fulfilling the duty of friendship. It says: "David, take heed and warn your people against eating tempting foods. The hearts of those who eat tempting foods are veiled from Me." Whoever eats tempting foods at a time when his emir is in distress or when he fears for him, or has intercourse with his wife, violates the obligation he has to him out of friendship, for his prayers will not be answered quickly.

I heard Sayyidī ʿAlī al-Khawwāṣ, may God have mercy on him, say: "A mendicant must not befriend an emir until he has accustomed his appetitive soul to abstain from eating tempting foods when his emir is worried or in distress, even if the period of abstention lasts for a year or more. Whoever has not accustomed his appetitive soul to this must not agree to befriend an emir." I abstained one time on behalf of an emir who befriended me. I did not eat butter, sweets, or any permissible tempting foods for a period of fifty days. Then my appetitive soul tried to persuade me to eat a tempting food and I agreed. Then I saw that my wife, Umm ʿAbd al-Raḥmān, may God have mercy on her, had abstained for a period of five months for the sake of her infant son. I said to myself: "Shame on he who is exceeded in ambition and manliness by women." I returned to abstemiousness until God brought relief to that emir. [39] This is something that people rarely do solely for Exalted God's sake these days. No, one of them may abstain, greedily hoping that the emir will give him charity when he hears that he has abstained on his behalf. Then, if he does get what he hoped for from the emir, he may cite what someone said:

I force my heart to bear night and day
the worries of him whose charity I never receive

Like the fuller whose face is blackened in the sun
working at bleaching other people's clothes

Had this sort of person abstained from temptations for the sake of Exalted God solely in order to fulfill the duty of friendship, he would not have had any regrets or recited these verses. No, he would have sought his reward from Exalted God.

Sayyidī Ibrāhīm al-Matbūlī, may God have mercy on him, used to say, "Any mendicant who takes pleasure in eating, drinking, sex, or any temptation while his emir is sorrowful or worried lacks the qualities of a man; indeed, he belongs to the category of women." He used to say: "One sign of the mendicant's sincerity in befriending the emir is that he feel as if his body is filled with fire from the moment he befriends him until he leaves him by dying, or some other way. That is because the majority of emirs love this world and never cease to feel worry and grieve for a single moment, while it is the task of the mendicant to share his sorrows out of manliness." It has already been said in this book that it is the duty of the mendicant to the emir, if he suffers from worry or grief, that the mendicant not lie down to sleep, approach his wife, eat tempting food, enjoy himself in a garden or by the riverside, wear a perfumed robe, laugh, or neglect the remembrance of God until that worry or grief leaves the emir. Know this, brethren, and act on it. Praise God, Lord of the worlds.

Among the blessings which Exalted God has bestowed upon me is that I will not commit acts that undermine my station in the eyes of the emir whom I befriend, such as inviting him to a feast I wish to hold. He may think initially that I informed him of it only so that he will assist me. It is intelligent and manly not to inform or invite him lest he send me some meat, honey, rice, firewood, or the like. If I accepted it, I would leave the station of precautionary piety; and if I refused it, I would have made myself out to be pious, expelled my emir, and disappointed him. There is no hiding the fault in that.

I heard Sayyidī 'Alī al-Khawwāṣ, may God have mercy on him, say: "A mendicant who wishes to hold a feast must not inform any of his brethren, especially the emirs, in the hope that they will help him lest he impose on them. If he invites them to partake of this sort of food, he shows contempt for them and for their station. This is something done by many people who are imposters. If one of them wants to hold an *'aqīqa,*[71] complete the recitation of the Qurān, or hold a wedding, he acquires the material for his food from a hodgepodge of people, then he invites important people to the feast and converses with them, saying, 'Be kind to me,' which is bad manners." I heard him say: "Whoever has no trade or salary must not hold a feast whose materials he gathers from other people. The souls of important people may shun eating from it, just as they shun [40] cooking the flesh of unclean animals, such as snakes, beetles, weasels, scarabs, worms, etc. Most people make a living from things as unclean as the flesh of these pests." Praise God, Lord of the worlds.

Among the blessings which Exalted God has bestowed upon me is that I frequently protect the emir whom I have befriended with verses and invocations from the Sunna lest his judgments stray from the Holy Law or he mistreat one of his subjects. If he is a tax farmer for villages, I protect their dikes and roads from criminals, lest the dikes burst at the wrong time when the Nile is

71. A naming ceremony held seven days after the birth of a child during which a sheep is slaughtered and the meat is given away as alms.

high, or someone be robbed on the roads. Similarly, [I protect] his pages who collect the land tax and consume the peasant's hospitality lest they transgress God's limits, etc., as we have mentioned in our book called *al-Fulk al-mashḥūn.*[72] Any mendicant who cannot protect his emir, the emir's villages, his pages, and his revenues from the land as we have mentioned has no right to befriend the emir since he is unable to meet his obligations to him. This is something that few mendicants observe, but you should act in accordance with it, my brethren. Praise God, Lord of the worlds.

Among the blessings which Exalted God has bestowed upon me is that I dislike the emir whom I have befriended to appear when I am meeting with a large number of people in a session for invocations, a lesson, or a feast, lest I form a high opinion of myself. Rare is the mendicant who is frequented by important people during his celebrations without his forming a high opinion of himself and being happy when people become acquainted with his noble states. For this reason, the pious predecessors feared sitting in a class or session for invocations if it expanded and many people were present, so that when Ibrāhīm ibn Adham[73] entered the Sacred Mosque and saw that the class of Ṭāwūs al-Yamānī had grown,[74] he shook his head and said in his ear, "If your soul enjoys sitting in this large class, leave." Ṭāwūs rose to leave the

72. The full title of this work is *al-Fulk al-mashḥūn fī bayān anna al-taṣawwuf huwa mā takhallaqa bihi al-'ulamā' al-'āmilūn* (The Ark Filled with Proof That Sufism Is the Conduct Followed by the Active Scholars) is an important work by al-Sha'rānī that is still in manuscript form.

73. A well-known eighth-century ascetic.

74. The Sacred Mosque, located in Mecca, contains the Kaaba. Ṭāwūs al-Yamānī was a scholar who studied with many of the companions of the Prophet.

class without anyone knowing why. Al-Fuḍayl ibn 'Iyāḍ and Sufyān al-Thawrī passed by the class of 'Aṭā' ibn Abī Rabbāḥ[75] in the sanctuary—it having expanded considerably—and they said to him, "Were this the class of 'Umar ibn al-Khaṭṭāb,[76] may God be pleased with him, he would leave it for fear of his soul."

I heard Sayyidī 'Alī al-Khawwāṣ, may God have mercy on him, say, "It is the task of the sincere mendicant to understand that the harm caused by the emir coming into his presence is worse than the appearance of a lion who would devour him, since he must fear that he is liable to develop a high opinion of himself." Furthermore, it is said that Sufyān al-Thawrī used to say, "Someone like us does not have the right to teach classes or dictate tradition to large groups, lest God despise him if he develops a high opinion of himself." When he was dictating traditions and a cloud passed overhead, he would cease dictating and say to his companions: [41] "Wait until this cloud passes. I am afraid it contains stones to pelt us for our lack of sincerity and frequent dissimulation." Know this, brethren, and forbid the emir whom you befriend from meeting you during your litanies and celebrations. Make legitimate excuses to him, lest you engage in hypocrisy. Praise God, Lord of the worlds.

Among the blessings which Exalted God has bestowed upon me is my love for anyone who drives my emir from me and my hatred of anyone who encourages an emir to befriend me, since I

75. 'Aṭā' ibn Abī Rabbāḥ studied with many of the companions of the Prophet.

76. 'Umar ibn al-Khaṭṭāb (579–644) was the second caliph, often seen as the founder of the Islamic Empire, as during his caliphate (634–644), Persia, Syria, and Egypt were conquered.

fear that I will fail in my duty to rebuke my emir. I had doubts for selfish reasons about one of my peers, but when he drove my emir away from his friendship with me, those doubts passed, and I came to love him greatly. I understood that by driving the emir away from me he prevented the harm that resulted from befriending that emir, and I knew that he was one of those who achieved this station. This is unusual behavior that few people can imitate. Most people love anyone who encourages an emir to befriend them and hate whoever drives him away, assuming his intentions to be evil, which is a departure from the character of our people.

I heard Sayyidī ʿAlī al-Khawwāṣ say: "Only someone who has mastered the station of renouncing the world and been weaned from its temptations at the hands of a genuine shaykh is capable of loving those who drive an emir from his friendship or hating all those who encourage an emir to befriend him. Otherwise, one who loves this world necessarily hates anyone who drives a worldly person from him and loves everyone who attracts a worldly person to him." I heard him say: "One sign of the sincerity of one who loves you is that he discourages you from befriending the emir, and the emir from befriending you, because he knows that each of you is incapable of fulfilling the duties of friendship to the other, as can be witnessed by insightful persons. The mendicant may wish to befriend an emir mostly to obtain his charity and patronage or to acquire status, just as the emir may wish to befriend the mendicant mostly so that he will bear his burdens during hard times and help him to get appointed to offices, which cannot be avoided. Undoubtedly, this friendship on both of their parts is for something other than God's sake; for in the friendship between the mendicant and the emir that is purely for God's sake, neither asks the other to assist him for some purpose in this world, or in the Hereafter if it begins in this world." Know this, praise God, Lord of the worlds.

Among the blessings which Exalted God has bestowed upon me is that I will not mention to my emir anything that will burden him in worldly matters, such as if I say to him: "Think of us. We are out of wheat and you know how weak the children's faith is and how worried they are about food." This sort of thing is worse than asking the emir outright. This happens to many callow mendicants and students, and they almost always diminish their station in doing so. The mendicant may mention to his emir his need for wheat, [42] honey, firewood, clothes, etc., without the emir paying the slightest attention, thereby making a complete fool of himself. Let the mendicant who befriends emirs be wary of this sort of thing. If he must accept the emir's charity, let him pray to God, may He be honored and glorified, to move the emir's heart to send him some of the needed items, if he knows that God has allotted this to him and that it is licit. I did something like this with my closest friend among the emirs, and he began to send me what I asked Exalted God to have him send me. I would make a show of returning it, exhibiting self-restraint and protecting the Sufi cloak[77] in a legitimate manner. Acts are judged by their intentions.

I heard my brother Afḍal al-Dīn, may God have mercy on him, say: "One sign of the mendicant's sincerity in befriending the emir for the sake of God is that he is not annoyed if the emir distributes meat, wheat, honey, clothes, etc., and neglects him. No, he is extremely pleased if the emir forgets him or gives what he would have given to him to one of his enemies." This is a scale that can

77. The Sufi cloak (*khirqa*) is the distinctive garb of the Sufis.

be tipped by a speck of dust. Weigh yourselves in it, my brethren, so that you may know whether you are sincere or insincere in befriending the emir. Praise God, Lord of the worlds.

Among the blessings which Exalted God has bestowed upon me is that I am extremely cautious when the emir is of a higher station than I am in the eyes of the rulers so that I need him for some worldly matter, such as help in being appointed to office, being assigned my stipend, protecting my ship from those who would confiscate it for their own use, protecting a village under my administration from a subprovincial governor or a tribal chief who mistreats its inhabitants, etc. It is appropriate for the sincere mendicant that the emir requires him to protect the emir's sources of income, not the reverse. This is a principle that the mendicants rarely follow; most of them need the emir, not the reverse, because they are not weaned of this world. Otherwise, one who has renounced the world is by necessity given power by the Exalted Real over the world's kings, not to mention other people. No one may block his path to his daily bread, or anything else. Exalted God empowers unjust rulers only over worldly people. Any mendicant who claims to have renounced the world and whose path to his daily bread, for example, is blocked, they consider false because had he renounced the world, no one could stand in his way. Exalted God revealed to David, may he be blessed and saved, "Oh David, renounce the world that you may place the kings of the Earth at your disposal, like the sheep under the knife." Praise God, Lord of the worlds.

Among the blessings which Exalted God has bestowed upon me is my refusal to accept anything that would cause most people to besmirch my reputation, such as receiving money from my emir to distribute to unnamed poor and indigent persons. Most people would accuse me of taking some of the money for myself, my children, and those in my care, thinking that I am like them, were one of them to distribute a similar sum of money. If, however, the emir offers me money, I persuade him to distribute it himself, or through one of his servants. I encourage him as best I can to give alms so that he does not change his intention and fail to distribute the money—my having refused to distribute it—and miss out on the good deed and the reward.

Sayyidī ʿAlī al-Khawwāṣ, may God have mercy on him, when someone gave him money to distribute to the poor would return it, saying, "He who accumulates wealth is the best one to distribute it." I asked him about that. He said, "I return it simply because I am afraid that my honor will be sullied in the eyes of the money's owner, especially [43] if he is an emir, and that by accepting it a number of other people will lose benefits that would have been better than my accepting it." I heard him say: "Do not accept money from the emir with whom you intercede in order to distribute it to the poor and indigent. Slanderers may impugn your integrity as a result, the matter may reach the emir and the slander may become fixed in his mind, and he may wish to return you to your station before your integrity was impugned but be unable to do so. It is safer for your faith to return officials' money." Praise God, Lord of the worlds.

Among the blessings which Exalted God has bestowed upon me is that I will not befriend an emir who seeks my friendship until I accustom myself to frequently tolerating hearing my enemies' words from that emir. Competition among peers for the friendship of emirs is prevalent among all those who have not mastered the station of renouncing the world. Enemies may prepare traps and conspiracies against the mendicant in whom the emir has faith, destroying the emir's faith in him, so that each ceases to benefit from the other.

Sayyidī ʿAlī al-Khawwāṣ, may God have mercy on him, used to protect himself and his emir with invocations and verses lest an enemy come between them and destroy their friendship. Indeed, it so happened that one enemy set traps for a mendicant in whom an emir had faith, until it ended with the mendicant being killed. I heard him, may God have mercy on him, say: "If you befriend an emir, get used to hearing your peers insult your honor, such as saying, 'The only reason so-and-so befriended the emir was to acquire the illegitimate goods of this world. We have tried to trick the emirs so that they will have the same faith in us that they do in him, but we can't match his imposture, artifice, deceit, hypocrisy, false modesty, keeping his head bowed, abstinence, and so on.'" I heard him say: "If you befriend an emir, consider the proposition of frequently putting up with your enemies impugning your integrity, accusing you of hypocrisy, and deceiving that emir. If you think that you are capable of enduring that sort of thing, enter into a friendship with the emir. Most often, you have no choice. Similarly, before you enter into a friendship with him, you must be prepared to forgive your enemies for attributing all kinds of failures to you, if you do befriend him. If you are capable of bearing this sort of thing and forgiving them for insulting your honor, thereby honoring God and secondly His Prophet, enter into a friendship. Otherwise, don't. Safety comes before gain." Praise God, Lord of the worlds.

Among the blessings which Exalted God has bestowed upon me is that I won't always ask the emir who befriends me to accept my intercession for one of his subjects who claims to be wronged, as has been said previously. Accepting my intercession for that individual may provoke strife that leads to killing and robbery, as is the case with most criminal peasants. Indeed, I am obliged to withhold judgment about those who claim to be wronged and to make valid excuses for the emir so that I am in agreement with him about his rights, and so he will agree with me as well. For this reason, I used to write to subprovincial governors and other people about the prisoners they held, saying: "If you know that he has been wronged, let me intercede for him. If you know [44] that he is in the wrong, we do not wish to intercede for him." If that prisoner has an enemy who is quarreling with him and asks the emir to take his side against him, I write to him, saying, "You are kindly requested to support whichever of the two parties is wronged," for example, "as you usually do out of kindness and charity," as has previously been mentioned in this book.

I heard my brother Afḍal al-Dīn, may God have mercy on him, say: "Do not be annoyed by someone who refuses to accept your intercession for a person who has been wronged. He may be aware of the ploys of your soul and reject your intercession at that time, although he has decided to accept it in the future, lest you form too high an opinion of yourself, especially if your peers interceded on his behalf before you and he turned them down. Self-complacency would be worse." Let the mendicant be extremely cautious of the emir accepting his intercession. The emirs no longer believe that most mendicants are pious and draw negative conclusions when they try to intercede with them, saying, if only to themselves, "Were it not for the gifts that so-and-so receives from people, he would not intercede with us for any of them." Indeed, I heard one of them say: "So-and-so is only considered a shaykh by peasants and other people because I accept his intercession. Had I refused his intercession, he would not be a shaykh and no one would have faith in him." Let the intelligent man draw the appropriate conclusion. Praise God, Lord of the worlds.

Among the blessings which Exalted God has bestowed upon me is that I will not agree to befriend an emir if he asks me unless I know that I am capable of concealing the secrets that he entrusts to me, especially information about the sultan and his ministers. If I am not confident that I can conceal them from my closest friends, I will not agree to befriend him, out of concern for myself and for him due to the harm caused by the secrets being divulged. I read in *al-Aḥkām al-sulṭānīya*[78] that kings with temporal power have the right to execute anyone who reveals their secrets, corrupts their women, or questions their being qualified for office. Others do not have that right. Imām al-Shāfiʿī, may God be pleased with him, said: "One who does not have confidence in himself must not mix with people who hold secrets. This may lead to his execution, and the blame will fall on himself and whoever divulged his secret." Then he recited,

If an individual reveals his own secret and then blames
another, he is an idiot
If an individual's breast is too small to contain his secret,
the breast of the one to whom he entrusts the secret is
smaller still

They found the following inscribed on the gate to Anushiravan's palace:[79]

78. *Al-Aḥkām al-sulṭānīya* (Rules for Governance) is a highly influential work by Abū al-Ḥasan ʿAlī al-Māwardī (972–1058) on the juridical theory of the caliphate and administration of government in Sunnī Islam.

79. Anushiravan, or Khosrau I, ruled the Sasanid Empire in Iran and Iraq from 531 to 579.

If you befriend kings, don the most splendid clothes of
caution
When you enter, enter blind, and when you exit, exit deaf

Let the mendicant who befriends an emir be extremely careful not to divulge his secret, even if the emir does not so advise him. Indeed, it is sufficient for the emir to glance right and left before divulging the secret to him. The only reason he would look around like that is because he fears that someone will hear that secret. Praise God, Lord of the worlds.

[45] Among the blessings which Exalted God has bestowed upon me is that I barely notice accepting my emir's gift if I bear his burden when he is dismissed, imprisoned, the subject of an inquest, etc., unlike some imposters. The mendicant's duty is to be charitable to the emir and his children if they suffer an ordeal, analogous to what the scholars say about preparing food for the family of a deceased person.

I heard Sayyidī ʿAli al-Khawwāṣ, may God have mercy on him, say: "The most ugly thing is when a mendicant befriends an emir and is covered in his charity, he and his children. Then, when the emir suffers an ordeal, he has no interest in bearing his burden or demands some worldly goods in exchange for bearing his burden." I saw one of them request some worldly goods from the emir with a euphemism, saying, "What would you give to someone who bears your burden?," deceiving the emir into giving him a gift, clothes, or a votive offering. One of them would say to the emir, if by providence his worry and sorrow came to an end, "You owe us a present; we have borne your burden." All of this diminishes the manliness of the mendicant. The intelligent man bears his emir's burden for the sake of Exalted God, fulfilling his duty to him, and is charitable to the emir's children during his imprisonment or house arrest, for example, to the best of his ability, as is the custom of the sincere mendicants. Praise God, Lord of the worlds.

Among the blessings which Exalted God has bestowed upon me is that I command my emir to be patient if his enemy frequently harms him; and I forbid him to answer in kind, even by cursing him to himself, just between him and God, may He be honored and glorified. I strongly discourage him from this and command him to say, "God is my sufficiency and the blessings of the Deputy." If he entrusts his affairs to Exalted God, God will defeat his enemy and may break him entirely. This is something unknown to most people. One supposes that by saying "God is my sufficiency in dealing with so-and-so" there is no request for retaliating for the harm done by his enemy, but this is an incorrect assumption. Had he considered the matter with insight, he would have found that his retaliating for the harm done by his enemy is less damaging than retaliating by saying, "God is my sufficiency and the blessings of the Deputy," such that my brother Afḍal al-Dīn, may God have mercy on him, used to pretend to retaliate against his enemy with a similar harm with the intention of reducing the harm done his enemy were God to repay him with its like. The more a person entrusts his affairs to God, the greater God's retaliation against the enemy.

I heard Sayyidī 'Alī al-Khawwāṣ, may God have mercy on him, say: "Whoever wants to destroy his enemy quickly, let him say, 'God is my sufficiency and the blessings of the Deputy' concerning him and not retaliate by doing him harm. Whoever wants to preserve his enemy and delay his punishment, let him pretend outwardly to retaliate by doing him harm." Exalted God has commanded His most intimate servants to endure the harm done by their enemies and has not permitted them to retaliate against them. Indeed, He commanded them to forgive and reform, that is, to pray that their enemies be reformed. He permitted only the common people to retaliate. Because of their weakness they are incapable of withstanding harm [46] without retaliating. For this reason, He vented their emotions in saying, "and the recompense of evil is evil the like of it,"[80] thereby calming them in His mercy, may He be exalted, which encompasses all things. As for the mystics, He permitted them to retaliate only with the human minimum, as has been mentioned, having gifted them with understanding of his saying "and the recompense of evil is evil the like of it." He, may He be exalted, called the compensatory evil "evil," and confirmed it by saying "the like of it," implying that one should abstain. God's people do not wish to be evildoers, even if this is permitted to them in the human minimum, which in them is very little. They said, "If we recompense the evildoer with the like of his evil deed, we become evildoers like him." No intelligent person should do that.

I heard Sayyidī 'Alī al-Khawwāṣ, may God have mercy on him, say: "Everyone who gazes with the eye of certainty and whose vision penetrates into the Hereafter, its accounts and balances, knows with certainty that the harm his enemy does to him is more beneficial in this world than the kindness of his friend. That is because Exalted God gives the victim of wrongdoing power over the good deeds of the wrongdoers on the Day of Resurrection. They seize their good deeds in the amount of the wrong done to them, and Exalted God forgives the evil deeds of the wronged in the amount of the wrong done to them and places them on the shoulders of

80. Sūrat al-Shūra 42:40.

the wrongdoers, it is said. This is not the case with the kind deeds done by one's friends. Intelligent emirs and other people put up with the harm and deceptions done by their enemies and forgive them and reconcile with them without demanding what is owed to them in the two abodes." Praise God, Lord of the worlds.

Among the blessings which Exalted God has bestowed upon me is that I will not allow my emir to slander any of his enemies, much less his friends, even if he claims that his slander is legitimate, such as if the person slandered openly admits to committing sins, so that I can completely close the door to slander. But the master of this station must be especially careful not to eat the emir's food or accept his gifts, so that he looks annoyed and his face is sullen if he offers him one thousand dinars, for example. He should think that the emir did this sort of thing with him only because of his contempt and disdain for him, and because he assumes that if he returns some worldly object, he is only pretending to return it to maintain his reputation. Otherwise, his heart loves worldly goods, as has already been mentioned in this book. If the mendicant has not reached this station of self-restraint, in most cases he will necessarily ignore his emir's slandering people, and his tongue will be tied, preventing him from criticizing the emir. The intelligent man enters people's homes by their front doors.

I heard Sayyidī 'Alī al-Khawwāṣ, may God have mercy him, say: "If the mendicant does not think that he is capable of criticizing his emir if he slanders people, he certainly should not befriend him, since it is forbidden for a person to be present where sins are committed if he is unable to put a stop to them. Whoever befriends an emir who slanders people, oppresses the peasants and others, and refuses his intercession on their behalf, this ruling applies to him." I heard him say: "Rare is the mendicant these days who is free of persistent sin. Let the mendicant who befriends an emir be extremely cautious for his own sake." Praise God, Lord of the worlds.

[47] Among the blessings which Exalted God has bestowed upon me is that I will not befriend an emir who accepts my intercession on behalf of persons who have been wronged, unless I have confidence in my ability to restrain myself from accepting gifts from the aggrieved person, unlike some people who make a business out of interceding with their emir so that they can pursue gifts of money, food, clothes, etc., to the point that everyone becomes aware of this when they possess so many clothes, riding animals, and food, and there is no explanation for this other than their intercession with their emir. Let the mendicant who intercedes with his emir be careful.

I heard my brother Afḍal al-Dīn, may God have mercy on him, say: "A mendicant must not accept his soul's claim to be sincere in befriending the emir, and that the only reason he has befriended him is for the sake of Exalted God and for the reward in the Hereafter, until he tests it. What if his emir were to cease to have faith in him and to accept his intercession, to meet with one of his enemies and to begin to accept the enemy's intercession, and the gifts that used to come to him were to shift to his enemy? If his soul is happy with that, he has befriended his emir for the sake of Exalted God. If a single hair is annoyed or he frowns once because of that beyond the human minimum, his friendship is not purely for God's sake." This is a scale that can be tipped by a speck of dust, so test your souls with it, my brethren, if they claim to be sincere with regard to emirs. Praise God, Lord of the worlds.

Among the blessings which Exalted God has bestowed upon me is that I do my best to protect my emir's reputation and prevent his being embarrassed in front of people, thereby fulfilling my duty to him. If I intercede with him for an aggrieved person, I do not attribute that wrongdoing to him, lest he be overcome by his ego, defend himself, and then it is proved that he permitted this wrongdoing and he is embarrassed. Instead, I blame the wrongdoing on his followers, without his permission or knowledge, and make it his station to intercede with his followers for the aggrieved persons. This is a tactic that few people who intercede with the emirs for aggrieved persons know. One of them might speak harshly with the emir and treat him as the wrongdoer, although he lacks a spiritual state to protect himself. The emir may attack him and insult him, and will lose the respect that the emir and other people have for him. They will not accept his intercession because the intercessor is required to be outwardly protected against anything that diminishes his respectability and awe in people's hearts, as was customary among the active scholars in former times.

I heard Sayyidī ʿAlī al-Khawwāṣ, may God have mercy on him, say: "The mendicant must learn to be tactful if he befriends an emir and intercedes with him for the victims of wrongdoing. He must not begin by accusing him of wrongdoing on the basis of his first impression, saying to him, 'You are forbidden to do this and thereby you sin, you who have little fear of God,' etc. Instead, he should blame the emir's followers for the wrongdoing and consider it an opportunity for him to do a good deed by interceding with his followers for that victim." I heard him say: "If you enter into the presence of an emir to intercede for an aggrieved person or to rebuke him for the commission of some sin of which he is guilty, prepare the way for him first so that he learns the wealth or benefit in this world or the Hereafter that he will receive for accepting this intercession or abstaining from this sin, so that he takes the initiative in doing what you have suggested without your having commanded or forbidden it. The egos of most emirs cannot be pressured into accepting the commands of one of their subjects." It has already been said in this book that it is [48] tactful for the mendicant when writing to him about people's rights, if they ask him to write to the emir or meet with him to intercede for one of their family members or friends who has been wronged, to say to the emir in his letter, or when meeting with him, "the family of so-and-so or his children asked us to ask you to free their imprisoned relative," for example, "and we know that you must have imprisoned him for a legitimate reason. If you are owed something and you are willing to give it up, put it aside as a voluntary act of charity. If someone else is owed something, or the prisoner is a wrongdoer and his punishment has not been completed, we do not wish to intercede for him. Indeed, we are with you against him." With this tact, the barrier of the emir's anger may be broken down.

My brother Afḍal al-Dīn, may God have mercy on him, when they asked him to go with them to intercede with a powerful emir such as the pasha or daftardār, would send him a letter greeting him saying: "The family of so-and-so have told me some stories and asked me for God's sake to go to you to intercede for so-and-so. If you are willing to receive me, send me a message with this messenger and I will come. If you are not willing to accept my intercession for him for any reason, such as fear that his release will result in strife, let me know so that I abstain from participating in this intercession." I did something similar to this with the pasha and daftars in Egypt. I would not go to any of them until he said to me, "Come and intercede and we will accept your intercession," thereby preventing my being embarrassed in a way that would diminish the station of intercessors. Praise God, Lord of the worlds.

Among the blessings which Exalted God has bestowed upon me is that I will not write to my emir or to anyone else saying, "Exalted God greets so-and-so," for example, unless Exalted God has gifted me with the station of revelation that He, may He be exalted, has granted him safe conduct from punishment in this world and the Hereafter, forgiven him, and absolved him. Greetings from God is a safe conduct and whoever gives his emir or anyone else a safe conduct from Exalted God or tells him that he will not be punished for a sin, without it being revealed to him, risks joining those who lie about God. The duty of whoever has not received a revelation that the Real has given safe conduct to his correspondent is to not say to him, "God greets so-and-so." Instead, he should say, "I greet so-and-so," and give him his own safe conduct that he will not harm him or disobey his advice, for example, on the condition that he is confident that he will never harm him as long as he lives. Otherwise, let him write after "In the name of God" and "Praise God" something like the following: "The mendicant so-and-so asks so-and-so to please do such-and-such and gives him safe conduct from himself," out of caution and fear that he may tell a lie. Praise God, Lord of the worlds.

Among the blessings which Exalted God has bestowed upon me is that I will not agree to befriend an emir unless I know that I am capable of observing his errors and missteps on the straight path in his words and deeds, or I know that he will repent immediately if I point out his missteps, as has already been said in this book. This is a rare station that few attain. Most people who befriend the emir [49] barely notice his false states from the moment he befriends him until they part, but this is not the friendship of sincere mendicants. It has already been said that one sign of the sincere mendicant is that he observes the emir in all his states until he crosses the bridge, and this is rarer than red sulfur. It would be best for people like us to abstain from befriending emirs as long as we live and to treat them like ordinary Muslim brethren without entering into an intimate friendship. Praise God, Lord of the worlds.

Among the blessings which Exalted God has bestowed upon me is that I am very cautious about talking about the visits I receive from important emirs, such as the pasha, daftardār, or chief judge, because this contains a whiff of arrogance and opens the door to having my honor sullied by my peers and other people, and to their sinning by slandering me by saying, "So-and-so flew with joy when the pasha visited him," for example, "and turned into a storyteller telling everyone who came to visit him." If talking about the visits of emirs to the mendicant causes this sort of thing, he must conceal the visits of important people to him in order to protect his faith and that of his brethren.

I heard my brother Afḍal al-Dīn, may God have mercy on him, say: "One sign that the mendicant is rooted in the station of proper conduct is that he practically dissolves in embarrassment and shame if he is visited by an important person, and he says to himself: 'Aren't you embarrassed by the many obscenities that you commit but God conceals for you? Don't you fear that you will be unmasked before these important people who visit you, thereby making a scandal of yourself among them and becoming the most hateful thing to them?' Whoever rebukes himself in this manner experiences no joy from the visits of emirs to him or from telling people about their visits to him since he has such great contempt for himself."

I heard Sayyidī 'Alī al-Khawwāṣ, may God have mercy on him, say: "One sign that the mendicant is a deceitful imposter is that he envies his brother being visited by an emir and does not envy his being in the company of his Lord, may He be honored and glorified, and His Messenger, may God bless and save him, most of the time. Were he sincere in glorifying God and His Messenger, he would be extremely envious of his brother being in the presence of God and His Messenger and wish to be like him, and he would pay no attention to his envy of him for being in the company of a weak man who cannot benefit or harm him in God's eyes." Know this, my brethren, and act upon it. This is correct conduct that is rarely practiced these days. Praise God, Lord of the worlds.

Among the blessings which Exalted God has bestowed upon me is that I mostly follow what is pleasing to God, may He be honored and glorified, if I befriend a pious, good emir, so that I love him more than my own son and family, especially if I am confident that he will accept my intercession, ease the suffering of the miserable, and abstain from every sin that I forbid. If I am confident that he will do that, he is more beloved by me than my family and son, who disobey my instructions. This is unusual conduct that is rarely practiced. Most people prefer to love their son and family instead of the emir, even if he accepts their intercession and relieves the suffering of the miserable, since their natural love overpowers their love for the Holy Law, although this diverges from the path of our people. Know this, my brethren, and act in accordance with it. Love your just, pious emir, and love him more than your son and family in the legitimate manner. [50] Do this publicly and pay no attention to people who say, "So-and-so has great love for the emir because he receives some ill-gotten worldly goods from him." Praise God, Lord of the worlds.

Among the blessings which Exalted God has bestowed upon me is that I am extremely happy when people revere my peers and the emirs venerate them, prefer to visit and respect them instead of me, and that I frequently implore God to preserve them from the defects that might result from being visited by emirs and being greatly respected by them. This is unusual conduct that can be undertaken only by one who has been weaned by his sincere shaykh from all the temptations of this world and all of his soul's frivolities. Few are those who are so weaned.

I heard Sayyidī 'Alī al-Khawwāṣ, may God have mercy on him, say: "One sign of the mendicant's sincerity in befriending the emir for God's sake is that he is extremely happy if the emir leaves him for one of his peers and starts putting him down in gatherings, saying: 'It was a mistake to befriend that man. Had I known of his great defects—deceit, hypocrisy, and love for worldly things—I would not have befriended him.' Know that whenever a single hair on the mendicant more than the human minimum is annoyed when the emir ceases to have faith in him, criticizes him, and meets with one of his peers, he is insincere in claiming to have befriended him for God's sake." This is a scale that can be tipped by a speck of dust, as has already been indicated in this book, so weigh yourselves in it so that you know whether you are sincere or deceitful. I heard him, may God have mercy on him, say, "If your emir leaves you for one of your peers, be happy, but implore God to protect that peer from harm and assist him in fulfilling the duties of friendship to the emir until they part because of death or some other reason." I heard him say, may God have mercy on him: "If an emir enters into friendship with you, and subsequently you perceive a whiff of his losing faith in you, brush him off. Do not command him to return to believing that you are pious; that will only lower you in his eyes. Instead, do your best to show self-respect and that you have no need of him. The benefit derived by each friend from his brother is only due to their strong love for one another. It has already been said in this book that a mendicant who has befriended an emir is not permitted to tolerate his sharing his friendship and love with anyone else since this would be a swindle, unless the mendicant with whom he shares the friendship is more knowledgeable than him in the secrets and performance of the Holy Law. The first mendicant must not be annoyed by this sort of person and must do his best to persuade the emir to put his faith in him. Praise God, Lord of the worlds.

Among the blessings which Exalted God has bestowed upon me is that I always immediately perceive the superiority of my emir over me and almost never consider myself superior to him, thereby fulfilling the duty of friendship. I know that if I considered myself superior to him I would be claiming a higher station in arrogance than that of the emir, and that is considered immoral on the part of mendicants.

[51] I heard Sayyidī ʿAlī al-Khawwāṣ, may God have mercy on him, say: "It is bad for a mendicant to consider himself superior to the emir who visits him, especially if the emir is charitable to him and his children, giving them cash, food, clothes, etc., as is common among the mendicants who befriend emirs today and the opposite of what was done by the mendicants in the old days. One of them would melt from shame if an emir visited him, saying to himself, 'What an embarrassment this emir will cause you on the Day of Resurrection when scandals are made known,' although he would not accept his emir's gifts or eat his food as long as they were friends. In what respect does the mendicant consider himself superior to the emir? On the contrary, if the mendicant thought

about it, he would find himself more arrogant than the emir who visits him, as has been indicated previously." One of the emirs who was a ṣanjaq came to visit me and I said to him, "Do you need anything?" He said, "Yes, there is something important I need." I said, "What is it?" and he said: "This evening, I examined my unclean qualities and found them to be more unclean than a dog's. Implore Exalted God on my behalf to grant me its qualities." Let the mendicant who considers himself superior to the emir take a look at his soul: has it said something like this to an emir who visited it and made a similar request, or does he not know his state? I heard him say: "The mendicant who is visited by an emir or someone else must assume there is a good reason for the visit, such as the only reason he visits him is so that he will be charitable to the emir by imparting knowledge or good conduct or to give him some worldly goods, not the reverse, and that his frequenting and visiting him are pure acts of kindness. If he considers himself deserving of being frequented or visited, he abandons the path of the people and joins the arrogant ones." I heard him say: "The mendicant must see perfection in everyone whom he befriends, whether an emir or someone else. If the emir visits him, he interprets this as an act of kindness on his part, and if he does not visit him, he assumes that the only reason he stopped visiting him was because he sees him so frequently in his heart. His vision of him in his heart beyond the human minimum spares him from seeing this person with his external vision."

I heard my brother Afḍal al-Dīn, may God have mercy on him, say: "If someone visits you a lot or stops entirely, assume the best, like that he visits you frequently because he loves you greatly, and that by visiting you frequently he intends to end your arrogance and treat you when he sees that you are arrogant. Similarly, if he stops visiting you, you must assume that he sees your perfection and that you have no need of a visit from one such as he because of your intellect, knowledge, and elevated soul. He concludes, therefore, that visiting you would be pointless." Know this, my brethren, be courteous to your emir and never consider yourselves superior to him so that you may fulfill your obligation to him, as was customary among your predecessors. Praise God, Lord of the worlds.

Among the blessings which Exalted God has bestowed upon me is that I am silent when my emir consults me on a matter related to the station of one of my peers, whether in perfection or imperfection, such as if he says to me: "So-and-so wrote to me, saying, 'Rely on me to bear your burden and I will get you out of prison or protect you from someone who seeks your office,' for example. Is this person capable of something like this, such that he should be relied upon, or not?" If the mendicant says "yes" or "no" [52] he may make a mistake, so it would be better to be silent. If the mendicant says "so-and-so is not worthy of that," the emir may assume that the mendicant is jealous or wants to be his sole friend, thus lowering his opinion of him.

My brother Afḍal al-Dīn, when he received a similar question from a friend, would send it back to him, saying: "Consider your own faith in him. I won't say yes or no." I acted similarly with an emir who suffered from rickets for about ten years when he said to me: "The mendicant so-and-so said to me, 'If you give me one hundred dinars, I will save you from the rickets at this very moment.' Is he capable of doing this such that I should give him the money?" I said to him, "Follow your own faith in him." Know this, my brethren, and do your best to fulfill your duty to your brethren in their absence. Do not hope to become your emir's only friend, thereby excluding them. You will regret it when he suffers a catastrophe and asks you to remove it but you cannot. Praise God, Lord of the worlds.

Among the blessings which Exalted God has bestowed upon me is that I do not praise myself to my emir or mention things that raise me above the station of my peers in his eyes. The emir may consider me a fool and cease to benefit from me. Instead, I do my best to abstain from talking to him about the self-denial, caution, self-control, and knowledge that Exalted God has given me, so that it is he who raises my rank when he observes that my deeds and states differ from those he finds in other people. This is something that few callow mendicants understand. One may begin praising himself for his knowledge and actions as soon as he meets the emir, paying no attention to the resulting self-praise and trying to extinguish his brethren's lights in the emir's eyes, which is ignorance.

I heard Sayyidī ʿAlī al-Khawwāṣ, may God have mercy on him, say: "Do not praise yourselves to the emir whom you befriend; it may occur to the emir to consider you fools. Instead, conceal your station from him, and act before him in a blameless, acceptable manner with self-denial, caution, fear of and respect for God, until it is the emir who praises you, either because of a light that occurs in his heart or because of many people praising you. Then, if he praises you, do not agree with his praise; instead, swallow your egos as much as possible without any selfish motives, as was the custom of sincere people before you." I heard him say, "If you know that your emir has great faith in you, as you have swallowed your egos, show him some of your qualities that manifest your arrogance to prevent hypocrisy and self-satisfaction by way of committing the lesser of two evils." I heard him say: "If you befriend an emir, do not impugn the integrity of any of your peers in front of him, lest he turn his attention to you exclusively. The Real, may He be exalted, may repay you with someone who impugns your integrity in front of the emir until he comes to see you as just as filthy and polluted as a menstrual rag. Exalted God is a fair arbitrator, and you must do your best to speak to your emir of your brethren's virtues [53] so that you leave his friendship in safety, victorious, and protected from your enemies' criticism of you in his presence, God willing." Know this, my brethren, and act upon it. Praise God, Lord of the worlds.

Among the blessings which Exalted God has bestowed upon me is that I am extremely happy when my emir, who formerly had great faith in me in his heart, turns away from me, as has previously been indicated. This is a rare station that can be reached only by one who renounces this world and its temptations. Few are they! One of my brethren claimed this station with his emir when the emir had such great faith in him that he could visit his family members without asking permission. When the emir's faith in him changed and he began to meet with someone else, he involuntarily appeared sorrowful and annoyed. I said to him: "Where is your claim to have befriended him for God's sake? Were you sincere in renouncing the world, not a single hair on your body beyond the human minimum would have changed because of the emir's faith in you." He did not know what to say. Know this, my brethren, and do not lay claim to the station of being happy when your emir's faith turns away from you before you master the station of renouncing the world and abstaining from its temptations, lest the judgment turn against you and you are disgraced. Praise God, Lord of the worlds.

Among the blessings which Exalted God has bestowed upon me is that I follow the custom of the pious predecessors in not taking the initiative in becoming acquainted with an emir or judge who enters my country, unless someone I trust informs me that that emir or that judge has decided to meet me. In that case, for me to take the initiative in greeting and getting acquainted with him is preferable for a number of reasons that are well-known to a clever man. I adopted this behavior a number of times with Egypt's pashas, daftars, and chief judges. I would not visit any of them until he sent to me asking permission to meet and until I said to him, "Send me your messenger when you want to meet me," lest I go to him at a time when he did not want to meet me and I would be forced to return in shame and embarrassment. If they sent me their messenger, however, at that point I would go to him and say to him: "I am so-and-so whom you were intending to visit. I have brought you what you would have obtained from me, had you visited me." Know this, my brethren, and do not take the initiative in approaching any official, except in a legitimate manner. The pious predecessors used to say, "One sign of a man's intellect is that he does not try to become acquainted with those he does not know, and that he denies knowing those whom he does know." Praise God, Lord of the worlds.

Among the blessings which Exalted God has bestowed upon me is that I am discrete in rebuking my emir in a quiet manner barely noticeable to those present, lest I embarrass him in front of people, since a rebuke implies diminishing and impugning the integrity of the object of the rebuke in the eyes of any clever person. For this reason, they say, "Whoever rebukes his brother in secret, rebukes him and ornaments him; whoever rebukes him publicly rebukes him and his rank." The emir's ego may shun the mendicant if he opens the door to revealing to people his faults, which God has concealed for his whole life. He may say, if only to himself: "I did not need to meet this mendicant. He has exposed me to my enemies." Let the mendicant who rebukes emirs beware letting anyone hear his rebuke, and rebuke him in private instead. Praise God, Lord of the worlds.

[54] Among the blessings which Exalted God has bestowed upon me is that I will not agree to befriend an emir or tax agent unless I know that Exalted God has given me the ability to protect him from those who would increase the land tax on his villages or the sultan's districts in his care. If God has not given me the ability to do that, I will not agree to befriend him since the only point in an emir or tax agent resorting to a mendicant is for him to protect the emir by his prayers and by his entreating God to protect him from those who would harm him unjustly, especially from those who increase the land tax on the villages or the sources of the sultan's revenue under his control. That would be harmful to the emir, to the people responsible for the increase, and to the subjects.

I heard Sayyidī ʿAlī al-Khawwāṣ, may God have mercy on him, say: "A mendicant must follow the custom of former shaykhs by not befriending an emir, tax agent, or other member of the sultan's retinue unless he knows that he has the ability, with God's permission, to protect him from those who would increase the tax burden on his sources of revenue or to seize his office. Someone may wish to harm one of their friends, and he may find that he is behind iron walls with no door, on which is written the name of this emir's shaykh, as happened to Sayyidī Madyan with one of the emirs who befriended him and began to repeat His saying, may He be exalted, "We shall get provision for our family, and we shall be watching over our brother."[81] Know this, my brethren, and do

81. Sūrat Yūsuf 12:65.

not agree to befriend an emir or tax agent unless God has given you the ability to protect him from the evils of this world and the Hereafter. Praise God, Lord of the worlds.

Among the blessings which Exalted God has bestowed upon me is that I devote the equivalent of a single hair on a bull's hide to being considerate of my emir's opinion while devoting the equivalent of the rest of the hair on that hide to being considerate of the interests of his subjects, which is unlike callow mendicants. They consider their emir's subjects with a single hair from a bull's hide while considering their emir with the equivalent of the rest of the hide's hair. The master of this station must renounce the world and follow what pleases God, not what pleases men. Otherwise, he necessarily will put pleasing his emir ahead of pleasing his subjects.

I heard my brother Afḍal al-Dīn, may God have mercy on him, say: "He who seeks to be a scale of justice between the emir whom he befriends and those of his subjects whom he has wronged needs abundant knowledge, perfect tact, and mastery of the station of renouncing the world. Otherwise, he may fall into tyranny and following selfish objectives." Know this, my brethren, and enter this station through its door, which I have mentioned. Praise God, Lord of the worlds.

Among the blessings which Exalted God has bestowed upon me is that I take special care to protect my station in the eyes of the emir I befriend if he has little understanding and knowledge of the states of sincere mendicants. If he sends me something permissible as a gift, and I know that Exalted God has apportioned it to me, I do not hurry to accept it; rather, I return it to him and prevent his heart from redirecting it to someone else, saving him from effort and from wasting his time, if my revelation indicates that it must reach me. This is better than hurrying to receive it, which would demonstrate a low and greedy soul.

[55] I heard Sayyidī ʿAlī al-Khawwāṣ, may God have mercy on him, say: "If your emir gives you some worldly good and you know that you will protect your station in his eyes from being diminished by accepting it, take it, and make use of it, if it is permitted, especially if you have more need for it than other people. If it is tainted or someone else needs it more than you, return it to him and spare yourself the dilemma."

My brother Afḍal al-Dīn, when an emir gave him something, would distribute it to the mendicants without keeping anything for himself. He might mix in some of his own property and distribute it, pretending that it all belonged to the emir. Some people might slander him and claim that he held back some for himself. He would smile at that and happiness would appear on his face because he had concealed his almsgiving. This is something that only someone who cares solely about pleasing God, the Most Generous, and not men, would do.

I saw that Sayyidī ʿAlī al-Khawwāṣ did not accept an emir's gift that he considered licit until he had prayed to God that none of his peers learn of it lest he sin by slandering him for it and lest the common people follow his example without sufficient knowledge, and he be recorded among the false leaders. I heard him say, may God be pleased with him: "If you fear that you will have a high opinion of yourself if people agree to respect you and raise your station because of your considerable caution and renunciation of the gifts of emirs and other people, the intelligent thing to do is to publicly pretend to accept them, then secretly send them to needy people and the like. Similarly, it is intelligent if you see that people have agreed on a lack of caution and on accepting many emirs' gifts, to return their gifts, thereby fulfilling one's legal duty. Caution is one of the pillars of religion. If people favor its destruction, less notice will be taken of the fear of pride in returning gifts, but the master of this station needs considerable knowledge and perfect discretion in order to decide which alternative is preferable." Know this, my brethren. Praise God, Lord of the worlds.

Among the blessings which Exalted God has bestowed upon me is that I do not love my emir more than I do his enemy, except in a legitimate manner. If one of them wrongs the other, I support the aggrieved party. If one of them is more obedient to God, he is more beloved by me than the other. This is an unusual practice that can be adopted only by one who has been weaned of the world and its temptations and abstains from both emirs' property.

I heard Sayyidī 'Alī al-Khawwāṣ, may God have mercy on him, say: "One requirement of the sincere mendicant is that he not enter into a friendship with an emir until he stipulates that the emir will not prevent him from loving the emir's enemy or disliking his friend, thereby allying himself with his allies and making enemies of his enemies in an illegitimate manner, for the station of the mendicant is too lofty for him to allow the emir to control him without a legitimate purpose. On the contrary, the emir must leave the mendicant free to act, even if the mendicant does not request that. The mendicant may think that showing love for the enemy of his emir is more pleasing to God and more likely to bring about a reconciliation between them. If the mendicant is not above acting on the basis of partisanship or selfish motives, the mendicant is not permitted to befriend either emir since under these circumstances he will be unable to reconcile them. Instead, he will need an intermediary to reconcile him with those who accuse him of partisanship."

[56] I heard Sayyidī ʿAlī al-Khawwāṣ, may God have mercy on him, say: "Whoever is not more cautious than a crow is not permitted to intercede to reconcile two rivals. The one who reconciles people to one another must be thought by both rivals to be on his side against his rival, and to love him more, because of his good tact, as He, may He be exalted, says, 'When they meet those who believe, they say, "We believe"; but when they go privily to their Satans, they say, "We are with you."'[82] Exalted God did not throw back at them their saying 'we are with you'; instead, he responded with the quality of mocking, saying, 'God shall mock them.'[83] Were it not for the mocking, their saying 'we are with you' would be flattery, which is praiseworthy in the Holy Law, unlike excessive praise. The religious scholars have distinguished between the two in that flattery is pleasing people by a person sacrificing some of his worldly goods, while excessive praise is pleasing them by sacrificing some of his faith, which is blameworthy in the Holy Law."

I heard my brother Afḍal al-Dīn, may God have mercy on him, say: "A mendicant must not agree to befriend an emir unless the emir believes that he loves him like his own mother, who would never advise her son to do something that she thinks would harm him. If he is not like that, he must not befriend him because in that case he would prefer his own intellect and knowledge of affairs over the intellect and knowledge of the mendicant and accuse the mendicant of being too inexperienced to understand what is required of him." I heard him say, "Every emir who does not believe that the mendicant is more knowledgeable than he about matters of this world and the Hereafter, more knowledgeable of

82. Sūrat al-Baqara 2:14.
83. Sūrat al-Baqara 2:15.

what pleases God, and more distant from selfish gain must not be befriended by the mendicant because his ropes will be cut eventually." I heard him say: "It is ignorant for the mendicant to display partisan support for his emir in an illegitimate manner. The sincere mendicant never intercedes between two people in a partisan manner; he always follows what pleases God. Whoever is more obedient to God he supports with every hair on his body." Know this, my brethren, and weigh every emir you befriend in this scale so that you may know whether you profit or lose by befriending him. Praise God, Lord of the worlds.

Among the blessings which Exalted God has bestowed upon me is that I will not agree to befriend an emir unless I think that he will not seek to prevent me from showing love for his enemy, praising him, and frequently praying on his behalf, as was recently mentioned. The mendicant follows what pleases God, rather than selfish motives. If he thinks that his emir is a wrongdoer, he is against him; if the emir's enemy is a wrongdoer, he is against him. If the emir thinks the opposite, he supports whichever of the two is the aggrieved party. He may laugh in the face of the wrongdoer as he prays to Exalted God with his heart and soul to dismiss him from office and put a stop to his wrongdoing. Know that if I think that the emir wants me not to love his enemy or praise him, I will not befriend him, even if he [57] worships God in accordance with the Qurān and Sunna, for the office of the mendicant is above being under the control of any worldly person with respect to the worldly gains they seek.

I heard Sayyidī 'Alī al-Khawwāṣ, may God have mercy on him, say: "Do not enter into a friendship with an emir who loves gold more than dust for selfish reasons unless he comes under your power. Whenever he asks you to ally yourselves with his allies and oppose his enemies in an illegitimate manner, refuse him and leave his friendship." This is unusual conduct that can be practiced only by one who has mastered the station of renouncing the world and is able to control all of the worldly people he knows because they see how lofty his station is and how cautious and abstemious he is. As for one who loves the world, in most cases this implies that they won't follow him because they see that he is just like them in loving the world, especially if the emir whom he befriends is charitable to him; the mendicant falls under his control just like one of his slaves. An emir befriended me and asked me to show hatred for his enemy. I turned that on its head and began to display love for his enemy, praying that Exalted God would make him one of His greatest saints. Eventually, God reformed them and the former enemy came to the emir, showed love for him, and entered under his authority, as if this enmity had never existed. This is a policy that every mendicant must follow. Praise God, Lord of the worlds.

Among the blessings which Exalted God has bestowed upon me is that I quietly reveal to the emir who befriends me the impurities that are contained in his person, bit by bit, until he comes to see himself as a sinner who is in danger of being swallowed up by the ground or transformed into a beast. The purpose of this is that the emir feel at peace and that all those who befriend him feel at ease, and that he exit the station of the arrogant by imitating the just leaders among the pious predecessors. Each one of them considered it one of God's greatest blessings that they were not swallowed up by the ground or transformed into beasts. If he saw some defect or bad manners in his slave, he would say, "How similar you are to your master's situation with his Master, may He be honored and lofty." They would prevent their slaves from standing in their presence. One of them would pour water on his slave's hands after he had eaten. If the slave prevented him from doing this, he would say to him: "The Messenger of God, may God bless and save him, said, 'The master of a people is he who serves them.'[84] Do not deprive me from that which makes me your master." The slave would accept this.

I heard Sayyidī 'Alī al-Khawwāṣ, may God have mercy on him, say: "If you befriend an emir, do not allow him to love being glorified or having people stand in his presence, lest he take that seat in Hell, as it says in the authentic report in which the Prophet said, may God bless and save him, 'Whoever likes people to present themselves to him standing, let him take his seat in Hell.'[85] He, may God bless and save him, made his entering Hell dependent merely on his liking people to stand in his presence, and connected it to that. Even if they do not stand, let the emir who likes people to stand before him be cautious lest he enter Hell. He won't escape that until he comes to hate them standing for him in the strongest terms." I heard him say: "If you think that someone likes people to stand for him for a reason that [58] is not legitimate, and does not fear the evil done thereby, you are forbidden to stand for him lest you become partners in the sin. If you think that he likes people to stand for him for a legitimate reason, stand for him, there is no harm in it."

I heard Sayyidī 'Alī al-Khawwāṣ, may God have mercy on him, say: "Don't befriend an emir who pays attention when imposters

84. Although this tradition is not attested in the major collections of Sunnī ḥadīth, it was popular in Sufi circles.

85. The ḥadīth usually reads: "Whoever likes men to present themselves to him standing, let him take his seat in Hell." With this wording, it is attested by the authorities Abū Dāwūd, Aḥmad ibn Ḥanbal, and al-Tirmidhī.

say, 'You are a righteous man. We think you are more righteous than most of the shaykhs of this age.' Whoever pays attention to this sort of thing is unable to benefit from the shaykhs of his age, such as you, and his state is totally ruined, as we have seen with some emirs who express their piety by giving alms and performing good deeds, such as building mosques, etc." I have followed this conduct with many ṣanjaqs, subprovincial governors, and tribal chiefs. I continuously spoke quietly to each of them to teach him modesty and to uncover the impurities in his personality that would cause people to stone him, if they but knew of them. This is conduct that few mendicants are capable of following; most of them can barely utter a single word revealing an emir's faults to him because they began the friendship with evil intentions. Praise God, Lord of the worlds.

Among the blessings which Exalted God has bestowed upon me is that I will not agree to befriend an emir until I have informed him that trials and tribulations come to those who love me more quickly than a stream flows to its end. If he accepts that, I befriend him; otherwise, I leave him alone. It says in a tradition: "A man said to the Prophet, may God bless and save him, 'Oh Messenger of God, I love you!' He said: 'If you love me, prepare a trustworthy shield for the poor man. Poverty comes to those who love me faster than a stream flows to its end.'" The mendicants imitate the behavior of the prophets. Whoever truly loves them suffers trials and tribulations, his worldly rank is lowered, and his rank in the Hereafter is perfected, unlike one who does not truly love them, who may be favored by this world to punish him for his lack of love for he who would guide him to those things that would benefit him in this world and the Hereafter. This is something unknown to many emirs. Their love for the mendicant may increase if their worldly fortune increases during their friendship, and their love for him may leave their hearts if their worldly fortune declines during their friendship. This is ignorance and deceit.

I heard Sayyidī 'Alī al-Khawwāṣ, may God have mercy on him, say: "It is the task of the sincere mendicant to protect his friends from the world and its temptations, just as the solicitous shepherd protects his sheep from dangerous pasturage, in imitation of God, may He be honored and glorified." The tradition says, "God, may He be honored and glorified, protects His faithful servant from the world, like a solicitous shepherd protecting his sheep." Just as the Real, may He be glorified and sublime, if he loves a servant, favors him with trials, similarly the mendicant, if he loves an emir, is pleased when he suffers trials, tribulations, and catastrophes, because he loves the emir and hopes that his station will rise in the Hereafter. Let the sincere emir begin his friendship with the mendicant aware that worldly [59] blessings may turn away from him because of the mendicant's private prayer to God. He may laugh in the face of the emir and pretend that he wants for the emir those worldly things he wants for himself, when the truth is that his heart prays to God that he will be deprived of worldly temptations out of kindness to him and in hope of reducing what he owes in the Hereafter. Know this, emirs, and be sincere in your love for the mendicant, if you seek great reward in the Hereafter. Praise God, Lord of the worlds.

Among the blessings which Exalted God has bestowed upon me is that I will not agree to befriend an emir until he swears to tolerate the harm done him by his enemies and not to gloat publicly if his enemy suffers a catastrophe. If he won't swear to this, I won't befriend him. This is because I know that he will ask me to aid him against his enemies, and I know full well that whoever is not patient with his enemies and does not abstain from gloating does not have the Exalted Real on his side. Whoever does not have the Real on his side is forsaken. Exalted God mentioned that He is on the side of the forbearing, that is, on the side of those who do not retaliate in kind against those who harm them, do not anger, and, although long-suffering, do not grow weary of the rituals that Exalted God has imposed on them.

I heard Sayyidī ʿAlī al-Khawwāṣ, may Exalted God have mercy on him, say: "Whoever retaliates for the harm done to him by his enemy, if only by privately praying to God to harm him, is forsaken by divine aid and has the Devil for an ally. No intelligent person would befriend someone whose ally is the Devil, instead of God, may He be honored and glorified." I heard him say, "Any mendicant who befriends an emir and tolerates his retaliating for the harm done by his enemy or his gloating when he suffers a catastrophe renders their friendship useless, and the mendicant will be unable to help him at all against his enemy." Know this, my brethren, and impose a similar condition on every emir you befriend. Praise God, Lord of the worlds.

Among the blessings which Exalted God has bestowed upon me is that I feed the emir who has befriended me whenever he comes to visit me, and I clothe him in my clothes every now and then. I do not eat any of his food or wear any of his clothes so that I may manifest the nobility of the souls of the mendicants and in order to inform people that the mendicants control the emirs, not the other way around, which is rare behavior in this age. Most of those who befriend the emirs do the opposite. They eat the emir's food, wear his clothes, not the other way around. I have clothed innumerable emirs, treasury accountants, merchants, subprovincial governors, and tribal chiefs, now living and dead. Those now dead number more than 150 people, including Emir Muḥammad the daftardār, Emir Iskandar the subprovincial governor of al-Gharbīya, Muḥammad Ibn Baghdād, ʿĀmir Ibn Baghdāḍ, and ʿAbdallāh Ibn Baghdād. Those still alive number more than 100, including Emir ʿUthmān, the pasha of Abyssinia, whom I gave a woolen garment given to me by Sultan Selim; Emir Ḥasan the ṣanjaq, administrator of the Dashīsha of the Khāṣṣikīya; Emir Khiḍr, emir of the Hajj, whose garment when he travels to the sultan's villages is my Sufi cloak; Emir Ḥasan Ibn Baghdād, whose garment is a red outer cloak; Emir Muḥammad, chief scribe of the Bureau of the Army; and Emir Muḥammad ibn Dāwūd. As for the garments of the jurists, mendicants, merchants, treasury accountants, and village headmen who befriended me, I am unable to count them, praise God for that. This is something that rarely happens to a mendicant in this age, [60] and most mendicants follow the opposite behavior. They eat the emirs' food, consume their gifts, and wear their clothes, without clothing a single one of them, except in rare cases. Know this, my brethren, and act on it. Praise God, Lord of the worlds.

Among the blessings which Exalted God has bestowed upon me is that when I abstain from an emir's property I stipulate that he not honor me without my knowledge by giving gifts to my companions or children, for this would amount to my accepting his charity and kindness, regardless of the gift. Were it not for me, the emir would not have given them any of this, so it is as if I were not too scrupulous to accept his wealth. This is a violation committed by many a callow mendicant; whatever he refuses to accept from the emir is accepted by his children and companions. Sometimes, if he is an imposter, he joins them in secretly accepting the emir's gift. Let the mendicant beware of being lenient with his companions with this sort of thing; and let the emir know that whenever he gives some worldly goods to the mendicant's companions without his permission, he breaches the friendship. Know this, my brethren, and act upon it. Praise God, Lord of the worlds.

Among the blessings which Exalted God has bestowed upon me is that I don't limit my intercession with my emir to my friends and exclude my enemies, lest I reduce my emir's reward, even if this goes against my selfish motives. No, thank God, I consider it more imperative to intercede with him for my enemy than for my friend, thereby following the example of my shaykhs, such as Shaykh Muḥammad al-Shinnāwī,[86] may God have mercy on him. He used to say, "Every day my enemy has need of me, I regard as a feast day," especially if the enemy has been wronged. This is conduct that many a mendicant fails to observe. It is easy for him to intercede with his emir for his friend, but not for his enemy. This is a sign of insufficient faith, for in truth all Muslims are equal in the eyes of the believer, and he must not love one more without a legitimate reason, irrespective of his natural inclination.

I heard Sayyidī 'Alī al-Khawwāṣ, may God have mercy on him, say: "It is perfection in intercession that an injustice be reversed in its entirety, such as when the subprovincial governors and tribal chiefs imprison someone from the village until its inhabitants who have fled return and they irrigate it from the Nile, they sow the

86. Muḥammad al-Shinnāwī (d. 1526) was the leader of one of the principal branches of the Aḥmadīya Sufi network and officiated at the birthday celebration of Sayyid Aḥmad al-Badawī, the most important saint of rural Egypt, at his shrine in Ṭanṭā in the Nile Delta province of al-Gharbīya. According to al-Sha'rānī, Muḥammad al-Shinnāwī was enormously popular and influential in the province.

land, or they finish paying the land tax, etc. The mendicant may benefit the prisoner held by the emir, who accepts his intercession and frees him and then seizes someone else in his place and imprisons him as a hostage. This sort of intercession is incomplete; it is as if he never accepted his intercession, unless the first prisoner, on whose behalf intercession was accepted, has dependents or is a pauper, and the second is a bandit or person who doesn't pray, etc., as corrupt people behave." There is no harm in this sort of thing, as we said at length in *The Book of Conduct.*[87] Praise God, Lord of the worlds.

Among the blessings which Exalted God has bestowed upon me is that I will not agree to befriend an emir who seeks to befriend me unless I believe that he thinks that I occupy the station of self-sufficiency, like some kings, and more, because a king may die still seeking more worldly goods, while the mendicant has come to rest [61] at the limit of contentment and seeks no more. For this reason it is said, "Contentment is an inexhaustible treasure"; that is, it never runs out or is extinguished, although it is the nature of the mendicant that he never thinks that he shares ownership of anything with God, as has been indicated previously. For this reason, the mendicant refuses to seek more worldly goods than he needs, and it makes no difference to him whether worldly goods are accumulated in his possession or in other people's possession. Someone like this is more self-sufficient than most kings.

87. Most likely a reference to al-Shaʿrānī's *Laṭāʾif al-minan wa al-akhlāq fī wujūb al-taḥadduth bi-niʿmat Allāh ʿalā al-iṭlāq* (The Subtle Gifts and Conduct on the Absolute Obligation to Publicly Acknowledge God's Blessing), his autohagiography, but he wrote a number of works with the term "conduct" (*akhlāq*) in the title.

I heard Sayyidī 'Alī al-Khawwāṣ, may God have mercy on him, say: "One sign that the emir is aware of the mendicant's station in self-sufficiency is that he does not take up his burden if he sees that he and his dependents are in straitened circumstances. If he takes up the mendicant's burden and sends him some money, food, or clothes, he is not aware of the mendicant's station in self-sufficiency, and he deserves to have the contract of friendship voided. He should blame no one but himself if the mendicant expels him from the friendship because he sent gifts or necessaries to his zāwiya or home, because the mendicant expelled him only after there were indications that he regarded the mendicant as imperfect, and that he abandoned the world and fell into straitened circumstances involuntarily, and not by choice." I heard him say, "Whenever the mendicant thinks that the emir believes that he does desire the worldly goods that people offer him because he is a hypocrite and dissembler or to pursue something of greater value, as imposters and beggars do, the mendicant must expel him, since his station in the emir's eyes is so low." This is conduct that is unknown to many mendicants and emirs. The mendicant thinks that the reason the emir brings him worldly goods is because he holds him in high esteem, while the emir thinks that the mendicant will love him more if he brings him gifts or alms, but both are incorrect in thinking so. The true mendicant thinks that were it not for the emir's low opinion of him, he would not offer him the world that the mendicant has abandoned and whose love he has rejected with the first step he took on the path. Had the emir thought him perfect and recognized his renunciation of the world, he would not have sent him any worldly goods. Similarly, had the emir thought that the mendicant would hate him more if he sent him any worldly goods, he would not have sent any nor have been worried or concerned about it. I heard him say, "One sign of the mendicant's ignorance and love for the world is that his love for the emir grows the more the emir gives him charity; and one sign of his great knowledge, renunciation, and cautiousness is that his hatred for the emir grows the more gifts the emir sends him." I heard him say: "One sign of the emir's sincere love for the mendicant is that he not send him any worldly goods except in cases of legitimate necessity, lest the mendicant be defiled and leave his station of love for him, and God's love for him, as the tradition says: 'Renounce the world so God will love you, and renounce other people's possessions so people will love you.' They say, 'The emir who befriends the mendicant [62] is like the sincere disciple with his shaykh. Just as the sincere disciple protects his shaykh's heart from being defiled by the world and its temptations, which would make him useless, similarly it is the nature of the sincere emir to protect his shaykh's heart from being defiled by sending him worldly goods, the opposite of the false emir's love.'" Know this, my brethren, praise God, Lord of the worlds.

Among the blessings which Exalted God has bestowed upon me is that I will not agree to befriend an emir unless I think that he will not rely upon the intervention of any of my peers between him and Exalted God. When I think that he will rely on someone other than me to weigh money to be paid to officials to remain in office or to obtain office, for example, to spare me and him, I will never agree to befriend him. On the other hand, if he makes me an intermediary in his appointment to office, for example, I fulfill my obligation to him scrupulously, with Exalted God's permission, to the best of my ability. I solve his problem in the presence of heaven before I solve it with the people on earth, so that the officials and subjects all implore Exalted God and implore the officials to appoint him without his having to weigh any money, and so that the only fees he has to pay are the presents for the robe of honor and for the drummers who will accompany his procession to his home. Something like this happened to me with the appointment of Emir Muḥammad ibn Dāwūd ibn 'Umar, who was unlike other tribal chiefs. He swore to me by Exalted God that he would rely on only mendicants, not officials, but he has never ceased to pay fees in exchange for his reappointment to office from that day until now. Thus, it became clear to me that he was not truthful when he pretended to rely on the mendicants as his intermediary to be appointed.

I heard Sayyidī 'Alī al-Khawwāṣ, may God have mercy on him, say: "Any emir who claims to rely on the mendicants as his intermediary to be appointed to office but weighs money to be appointed, or increases the land tax on his villages, is a liar; he relies on worldly people and paying bribes. Do not befriend the likes of him, for he will disgrace you in this world and in the Hereafter." Know this, my brethren.

Among the blessings which Exalted God has bestowed upon me is my lack of natural reliance on the emir whom I befriend; I rely on him only for a legitimate reason. For this reason, I have never been disturbed if the emir was dismissed, jailed, beaten, or fell out of favor. Nor was it ever said to me after his dismissal, for example, "Where are the emir's goods that he left in your custody?," unlike what happens to most people who befriend emirs and rely on them.

I heard Sayyidī 'Ali al-Khawwāṣ, may God have mercy on him, say: "Harm comes to those who befriend the emirs to the extent that they rely on them. Were a person who befriended them and was troubled, concerned, or worried to say, 'I did not rely on them,' they would call him a liar." His being troubled, [63] concerned, and worried betrays his dependence on them, whether rarely or often. Whoever is often reliant on them is often concerned, and whoever is rarely reliant on them is rarely concerned. This is a scale that can be tipped by a speck of dust. We have derived this rule of conduct from His saying, may He be exalted, "Do not rely on those who do wrong, lest you be touched by Hellfire."[88] Although this verse refers to the infidels, it includes those monotheists who wrong themselves by sinning. This is also supported by sense perception and experience. Know this, brethren, and befriend those emirs who wrong men without relying on them with your nature if you wish to be safe from the consequences of befriending them. Praise God, Lord of the worlds.

Among the blessings which Exalted God has bestowed upon me is that I love the emir who gives me a small, licit gift if I need that sort of thing and make an exception in accepting gifts from my emir, more than I love someone who gives me a large gift. For one who gives me a small gift has satisfied my need, and one who gives me more worldly goods opens the door to insolence. It says in the Glorious Qurān, "No indeed; surely man waxes insolent, for he thinks himself self-sufficient."[89] The tradition disparaging the world says, "A little of it is sufficient; a lot of it is insufficient."

I heard Sayyidī 'Alī al-Khawwāṣ, may God have mercy on him, say: "One sign of a sincere mendicant is that he loves those who deny him the world more than he does those who give it to him because they protect him and his brother. On the other hand, one

88. Sūrat Hūd 11:113.
89. Sūrat al-'Alaq 96:6.

who gives him many worldly goods thinks neither of himself nor of his brother." Praise God, Lord of the worlds.

Among the blessings which Exalted God has bestowed upon me is that I do my best to prevent people from taking greater notice of me than of my peers. If I fear that an emir will visit me because of my reputation for learning and righteousness, for example, I implore God, may He be honored and glorified, to conceal my learning and righteousness from him, so that he does not visit me, even by sending me an enemy who puts me down and frequently mentions my defects, out of kindness to us both. I do not consider myself learned or righteous, and I do not have the power to bear the emir's hardships as he asks me to, if he has faith in me and visits me, or even to share his misfortunes. One of my friends used to visit some of the daftars and pashas of Egypt. I asked him, "Why do you visit the pasha and daftars?" He said, "I heard that he loved the learned and the righteous, and I wanted to meet him." I said, "What makes you think that you are a righteous, learned man so that he should love you?" He did not know what to say and became embarrassed. My son 'Abd al-Raḥmān said to him, "Tell my father 'I went to see him only because of his love for the learned and righteous men, regardless of whether I am a learned and righteous man.'" He told me that and I whispered into his ear, "This is not your station." He became embarrassed again, for this station [64] can be attained only by one who renounces the world and learns to follow what pleases God, rather than his selfish motives. He is content that God should know him and does not seek any status in the hearts of men or bestow on his brethren the respect that people have for him in their hearts. I have acted in accordance with this station on a number of occasions when I learned that Emir Musṭafā, the pasha of Zabīd, planned to visit me, accompanied by Muḥammad the daftardār. I implored Exalted God to turn his heart away from visiting me, except with a pious intention, which would have no negative consequences for me or them in this world or the Hereafter. They have yet to visit me. Know this, brethren, and do not publicize your learning or righteousness to the emirs or important people, unless one of you is protected from being seduced, lest one of them visit you and believe you to be learned and righteous, although one such as you is beneath being believed to have attained the station of learning and righteousness. Praise God, Lord of the worlds.

Among the blessings which Exalted God has bestowed upon me is my great fear that my emir will unwittingly diminish his faith because of me. I might ask him for some worldly goods for a mendicant without knowing whether he would be happy or unhappy to do this. His faith would be diminished if I receive something because of his fear of being shamed, and he will be deprived of his reward if he refuses. He may fall out of divine favor because of his refusal, if the mendicant is very needy and Exalted God is protective of that mendicant or because the mendicant invokes God against him. It is obvious that this violates the duty of friendship owed to the emir.

I heard Sayyidī 'Alī al-Khawwāṣ, may God have mercy on him, say: "We have heard that the Real, the August and Most High, sent some needy mendicants to someone to whom He entrusted with His favor and inspired them to beg him persistently for something that he would find it difficult to part with at that moment. His refusal of the mendicant would be the occasion of His favor turning away from him, as happened to Ibn al-Zarzīrī in Upper Egypt." I heard him say, "A mendicant who befriends an emir must not ask him for any worldly goods on behalf of another mendicant unless he thinks that the emir will be happy and joyful about this; otherwise, it is better not to ask." This is something many callow mendicants who befriend emirs are unaware of. One may ask his emir for something for a mendicant and the emir will be too embarrassed to refuse and give him something for fear of being shamed without the mendicant realizing this. He asks the emir a second time, and a third, and it becomes burdensome for the emir, and his soul develops an aversion to it. The emir may repeatedly give gifts to the mendicants whenever they ask him through their shaykh, and he becomes famous for this. People rush to him and he gets sick of it, annoyed, and angry with his shaykh, if only to himself, because of his shortsightedness. Were the mendicant farsighted, he would consider the consequences of this and abstain from asking the emir for anything in the way of extra alms he does not think will please him, unlike obligatory alms, where he pays no attention to whether he will be pleased.

I heard Sayyidī 'Alī al-Khawwāṣ, may God be pleased with him, say: "No mendicant who befriends an emir should ask him for some worldly good a second time unless he saw that he was happy and his face was cheerful the first time. Otherwise, he should not ask again since the Lawgiver,[90] may God bless and save him, described the acceptable alms as that whose giver is willing and eager. Whoever asks his emir for something on behalf of a mendicant, although he does not think he is willing and eager, exposes him to a bad transaction with God." I heard him say, "If a mendicant asks you to ask your emir for some worldly goods for him, and you fear

90. The Prophet Muḥammad.

that the emir will not be happy with this, give him what he wants and avoid asking [65] anyone else, even if you give him your extra clothes, such as a turban, jacket, quilt, etc." Thank God, I have followed this conduct innumerable times. If a mendicant asks me to ask my rich brethren among the emirs and others on his behalf, I give him my clothes. I don't ask anyone who I think will be made unhappy by this.

This is why Mawlānā 'Abd al-Raḥmān, the chief judge, has great faith in me and why he preferred me to many of my peers when a debtor told him that I gave him my new jacket when one of my friends wanted to have him imprisoned for debt. Then, when another jacket was made for me in its place, a group of people wanted to have him imprisoned, so I gave it to him. The chief judge said: "This man is unique in this age in his self-restraint and great manliness. I don't know of anyone equal in this sort of thing. Look how manly he is, how he gives the needy person his own clothes and abstains from asking people, lest they refuse, he be embarrassed, and they fall into sin." I heard him say: "Do not claim that you are one of the people when you are too tightfisted to give a mendicant what he asks you for, although he is needier than you. They say, 'There is nothing uglier than a miserly Sufi.'" Know this, my brethren, and do not ask your emir for something on behalf of a mendicant, unless you know that the emir will be made very happy by this and that he will thank you very much for asking. Praise God, Lord of the worlds.

Among the blessings which Exalted God has bestowed upon me is that I frequently guide the emir who befriends me and teach him to be polite toward the people of the Sufi cloak of mendicancy, even if one of them is ordinarily one of my biggest enemies, to the point that I do not allow him to prefer me to my peers, much less impugn their honor, as has been indicated previously. This is something that turns a believer into a grave sinner.

I heard Sayyidī ʿAlī al-Khawwāṣ, may God have mercy on him, say: "If an emir befriends you, teach him to be polite toward those of your peers who hate you, much less those who love you. Do not allow him to be impolite to any of them; that would be harmful to your faith and that of your emir. Don't fail to teach him good manners unless he reaches the point where he would be ashamed before God to meet a mendicant, kiss his hand, or send him greetings because he considers himself and his tongue too defiled and impure. He would say to himself, 'How can I face one of God's people with a face and tongue that have disobeyed their Lord?'" Among those I have met who are like this among the chief judges are the Qāḍī Darwīsh, the Qāḍī Nūr al-Dīn, qāḍī of the khānqāh of Siryāqūs, and among the emirs, Emir Sulaymān, the current *aghā* of the ʿEzab.[91] He said to me, "Pray to God on my behalf that he will grant me the conduct of a dog, for I have examined my conduct and found it to be filthier than that of a dog." If your emir reaches this level of good manners with the mendicants, let him be, if you wish, or help him progress to a higher station than that. Praise God, Lord of the worlds.

[66] Conclusion in which is mentioned a number of ways in which the emir can be polite to the mendicant. We mention them

91. The term *qāḍī* means judge, although it could also designate a high-ranking civilian official. The khānqāh of Siryāqūs was a Sufi monastery founded in the fourteenth century around which a town grew up. The ʿEzab was one of the regiments of the Egyptian garrison during the Ottoman period. It was made up of volunteers, and its commander had the title of aghā.

for increased benefit. Just as the mendicant is polite to the emir, the emir must be polite to the mendicant. Now that you know this, we say, and success comes from God:

For the emir to be polite to the mendicant, he should consider him a greater authority than a worldly king, as was indicated at the beginning of this section. If he is fated to give considerable money to the mendicant or his group as charity, he should see this as totally insignificant in comparison to his request from the mendicant that he take his hand in times of hardship and that he frequently pray to Exalted God to protect him from the ills that beset his body, faith, and worldly goods. It is the task of the mendicant if he befriends an emir not to leave his side until he crosses the bridge. So let the emir take care not to think himself superior, for example, to the mendicant to whose zāwiya he sends wheat, lentils, honey, or cheese, etc. In comparison to what the mendicant suffers on his behalf in this world and the Hereafter, this is like a speck of dust.

I heard Sayyidī ʿAlī al-Khawwāṣ, may God have mercy on him, say: "Do not ask a mendicant to solve your problems quickly; if you belittle his honor, that is an error and is ignorant. The speed with which your problems are solved depends on how much you venerate the mendicant and how strong your faith is in him, so that every hair on your body testifies that Exalted God will not refuse any request from him. If you manage that, then ask him to solve your problems quickly; otherwise, blame no one but yourselves." I heard him say: "The shaykh's station is too exalted for him to see how great is his station with God. He continually sees himself as a sinner exiled from Exalted God. Whoever wants a mendicant to solve his problems with God, let him have faith in the mendicant's sanctity and power; otherwise, none of his problems can be solved at the mendicant's hand, even if he be an axial saint." Know this, emirs, and venerate your shaykh before you ask him to solve your problems. Praise God, Lord of the worlds.

For the emir to be polite to the mendicant, he must also not insist that the mendicant accept his gifts, eat his food, drink his beverages, wear his clothes, wear his perfume, smell his incense, put on his cream, ride his mount, relax with him in a garden, or allow him to recommend him to the sultan, etc., because this is bad manners. One mendicant smelled some incense provided by his emir and his heart grew hard for a long time and he did not long for sermons or enjoy worship.

I heard my brother Afḍal al-Dīn, may God have mercy on him, say: "It is impermissible for an emir to control a mendicant. It is the emir's duty to allow the mendicant to control him, willingly and happily, so that even if the mendicant wanted to saddle the emir and ride him like a donkey, it would be the emir's duty to accept this, as happened to Sayyidī Yūsuf al-'Ajamī with Emir Shaykhūn, the founder of the great madrasa near al-Rumayla.[92] We have heard a story about Sayyidī Muḥammad al-Ḥanafī,[93] who is buried at his zāwiya in Suwayqat al-Subā'īyīn, that when Emir Ṭaṭar, *qānī martabat* Sultan Sha'bān,[94] went to visit the

92. Emir Shaykhūn (or Shaykhū) (d. 1357) was a powerful political figure in the Mamluk sultanate who founded a mosque and khānqāh.

93. Muḥammad al-Ḥanafī (d. 1443) was a prominent shaykh of the Shādhilī Sufi network who was influential in the courts of a number of fifteenth-century sultans.

94. Emir Ṭaṭar (later sultan, 1412–21) was a leading Mamluk emir. Sultan al-Ashraf Sha'bān reigned from 1363 to 1375. The meaning of the term *qānī martabat* is unclear but may mean that Ṭaṭar had acquired the same rank or status as Sha'bān. Al-Sha'rānī seems to have mixed up at least two different stories about powerful emirs who allowed themselves to be governed by Sufi shaykhs.

shaykh, the shaykh commanded him to remove his clothes and fill the fountain for ablutions and the [67] toilets from the well. This made Emir Shaykhūn happy and he said, 'Every day I am employed by the shaykh I consider a feast day.' Sultan Sha'bān, when he went to visit Sayyidī Muḥammad and found the door closed, would wait by the door without knocking. He would shift from one foot to the other until the shaykh's slave woman or male slave came out, and would say, 'Tell my master that his servant Sha'bān is at the door.' Sometimes the shaykh would permit him to enter, and sometimes he would say to the slave woman, 'Tell him that my master won't meet with anyone at this time.' He would kiss the shaykh's doorstep and return to the citadel." We have already said in this book that the emir's duty if his shaykh asks him for food, drink, or clothes is not to hurry to give it to him lest the shaykh use tainted things of which the food, drink, and clothes of emirs are rarely free. No, he should delay and say, "Your servant and all he possesses belong to your lordship, but I am concerned that you will be defiled by food, drink, and clothes like mine, but it is up to your lordship to decide." If the mendicant withdraws his request, fine; otherwise, he should give him what he asks for. Praise God, Lord of the worlds.

For the emir to be polite to the mendicant, he also should never leave him, day or night, but should tie himself to him and never part from him in any of the divine presences he enters, so that he can protect him from bad consequences. The mystics say: "Whoever claims to be the constant friend of his shaykh and suffers some bad consequences, call him a liar. The shaykh's heart is always in the presence of God, may He be honored and glorified, and those in the presence cannot suffer a trial. That could only happen while he was veiled from witnessing his Lord and had left the presence."

I heard Sayyidī 'Abd al-Qādir al-Dashṭūṭī, may God have mercy on him, say: "No trial can befall a disciple as long as he is connected to his shaykh and has faith in him. If his connection to him is broken, or he has doubts about his sanctity and righteousness, he exposes himself to a trial befalling him. Since the saint cannot suffer a trial as long as he witnesses that he is before his Lord and that He, may He be exalted, gazes upon him perpetually, the servant should blame no one but himself if his connection is broken." Know this, my brethren, and examine your souls concerning the truthfulness of your faith in the mendicant whom you ask to solve your problems. If you find certainty in your hearts about his sanctity and righteousness, ask him to solve your problems; otherwise, leave him be, out of kindness to him and good manners on your part. Praise God, Lord of the worlds.

For the emir to be polite to the mendicant, he also must not place his whole burden on the mendicant if he falls very ill, is dismissed from office, has his property confiscated, etc. Instead, he should implore God with all his might to prevent this and ask the mendicant merely to assist him, as perfect men do. They say, "Whoever places his burden on someone else while seeking to take it easy himself is a woman, even if he has a big beard, since He indicates, may He be exalted, 'Men are the managers of the affairs of women.'"[95] One thing that happened to my brother Afḍal al-Dīn, may God have mercy on him, [68] is that he had a vision of himself in which he was dead. He was carrying half of

95. Sūrat al-Nisā' 4:34.

himself, while Sayyidī 'Alī al-Khawwāṣ was carrying the other half. Afḍal al-Dīn told him this and he said, "Afḍal al-Dīn, be a man and carry your other half."

I heard Mawlānā Shaykh al-Islām Zakarīyā, may God have mercy on him, say: "Do not bear the entire hardship that befalls your emir in order to have mercy on him and be kind to him, thereby insulting him and treating him like a weak, lazy, deficient woman. Instead, command him to implore Exalted God to keep this hardship from him and to do his best to prevent it. Then bear the part you are certain or think he cannot bear, as shaykhs do with their disciples." I heard him say: "It is imprudent for the mendicant to rush to bear his emir's burden without examining the consequences for himself. He may harm his own body and the emir's faith. The emir may not deserve the help in preventing this hardship because he has committed a major sin and persists in committing minor sins, such as fornication, sodomy, drinking wine, or mistreating the peasants and shopkeepers among his subjects by depriving them of their rights or taking from them more than they owe him. Perhaps he was very jealous of his peers, mentioning their deficiencies behind their backs, insulting them to their faces, did not perform his prayers on time, enjoyed himself in gardens, had intercourse with women, and ate sweets and fruits on the days when the mendicant prayed to God that he could bear his burden, as is common among oppressive emirs. Let the emir or mendicant be clever and observe the duty of friendship and its rules of conduct so that neither of them harms himself or his brother."

I heard Sayyidī 'Alī al-Khawwāṣ, may God have mercy on him, say: "No one who suffers from a hardship should rely on his brothers to avoid it since this would overburden anyone with manly qualities. A man asked the Messenger of God, may God bless and save him, to watch over him in Paradise. He said, 'Take care of yourself with frequent prostration.' See how he, may God bless and save him, guided him to great manliness, that he should not reduce himself to laziness and ease and place the burden on someone else." I heard him say: "It is characteristic of manly people that they implore Exalted God to avoid hardships and do not ask other people for help, except with the human minimum that requires one to seek help and assistance from people because one is forgetful of one's Lord, may He be honored and glorified. For this reason, they say, 'The servant must work to obtain the station of witnessing, at first glance, without thinking or contemplation, as do the prophets and their perfect heirs, that whatever help people give him is actually help from God, may He be glorified and exalted.' The Lord Jesus, may God bless and save him, said 'Who are my helpers to God?,' that is, with God, asking to use intermediaries, without considering whether they would be rewarded. [69] He was required to consider their assistance of him as part of God's help, may He be honored and glorified. Exalted God has the power to act through intermediaries or to act without an intermediary, as He indicates, saying, may He be exalted, 'Fight them, and God will chastise them at your hands,'[96] although He, may He be exalted, says, 'You did not slay them, but God slew them.'"[97] I heard him say, "It is ignorant of the emir to place his burden on the shaykh without helping him, especially if his shaykh eats his food and accepts his alms and charity." He will be unable to bear

96. Sūrat al-Tawba 9:14.
97. Sūrat al-Anfāl 8:17.

any of his emir's burden, as has previously been indicated, quoting the statement of our lord Sultan Sulaymān,[98] "Any mendicant who eats any of the food of kings and emirs loses his power to pray to Exalted God and is no longer qualified to intercede with Exalted God for another person." Know this, brother emirs and mendicants, and act upon it. Praise God, Lord of the worlds.

For the emir to be polite to the mendicant, he also must not ask him to support him in vanquishing and defeating his rival, for that would be ignorant, tactless, and an occasion for his rival to prepare snares for him. His duty is to explain his side of the story to the shaykh, so that he can intervene between them in a tactful manner and judge between them so that neither of the two rivals vanquishes the other. If the rival is defeated and vanquished, he will certainly plan stratagems and snares until he vanquishes and defeats his enemy and takes revenge on him, as most emirs do to one another. Had the emir turned the affair over to the mendicant, and not asked him to take his side against his enemy, he might have prayed to Exalted God to judge between him and his rival in a manner in which neither was vanquished. Let the emir consider the story of Iblīs with Adam, may God bless and save him, which will show him the truth of what we have said.[99] When Iblīs was ordered by the Real, may He be glorified and exalted, to prostrate himself to Adam and he refused, the Real, may He be exalted,

98. Sultan Sulaymān I "the Magnificent" ruled from 1520 to 1566, during most of al-Sha'rānī's adult life.

99. The story of Iblīs's expulsion from God's presence and his temptation of Adam and Eve is told in a number of places in the Qurān, but the passage referenced here is most likely Sūrat al-Ā'rāf 7:11–27 or Sūrat Ṭāhā 20:116–23. There is no reference to the serpent in the Qurān, but it appears in a number of exegetical works.

expelled him from Paradise, vanquishing him and expelling him from His presence. Whenever Iblīs remembered the bounty he had formerly enjoyed, he began to hatch plots to return to Paradise and take revenge on Adam. Eventually, he managed to enter into the serpent's mouth and whisper to Adam to eat from the tree, so that he too was expelled from Paradise. Had Iblīs not been vanquished by being expelled from Paradise because of his refusal to prostrate before Adam, he would not have hatched a plot to return there. The intelligent man is he who asks God to judge between him and his rival without vanquishing his rival, indeed by making him happy and pleased. God possesses power over all things.

I heard Sayyidī 'Alī al-Khawwāṣ, may God have mercy on him, say: "The intelligent man isn't happy to vanquish and defeat his enemy because he fears that he will prepare traps for him and the victor will become the vanquished. If the enemy is defeated and vanquished once, he will necessarily hatch plots to take revenge on his rival, as one can witness among enemy emirs, jurists, financial officials, tribal chiefs, peasants, etc. Know this, [70] emirs, and do not go against your shaykh's advice or you will regret it. The scale of justice among men does not tilt in anyone's favor to accommodate selfish motives. Praise God, Lord of the worlds.

For the emir to be polite to the mendicant, he also must not ask him for assistance in obtaining an unavoidable office, just as he must not ask him to pray to God that he remain in his current office, unless it causes him no bad consequences, and that is rarer than red sulfur in this age.

I heard Sayyidī 'Alī al-Khawwāṣ, may God have mercy on him, say: "An emir must not ask his shaykh to accommodate all of his worldly motives. The shaykh's station is too exalted for this. His duty is to accommodate his shaykh's motives, even if he says to him, 'Dismiss yourself from this office,' his duty is to obey him, especially if he can escape from it and there is someone more deserving of this office than he." I heard him say: "A mendicant must not help an emir, a tribal chief, or a tax agent obtain office in this age, unless he knows his intention to be righteous, and that he seeks to reduce the unjust burdens on the subjects, to protect their property, blood, and families from rebellious and corrupt people. If he knows or thinks that the emir is seeking this office to accumulate property and to obtain more food, drink, wives, and ships, he must not help him; indeed, that is prohibited to him. This increase in wealth usually comes about through a lot of wrongdoing, bribery, and criminal behavior.

Imām al-Shāfiʿī, may God be pleased with him, said: "The emir is the same as the judge. When his property, goods, food, and drink increase during his term in office from what they were before he assumed the office, convict him of wrongdoing, tyranny, bribing others, and receiving bribes. Where did he obtain this increased livelihood, if not by accepting gifts from the subjects and propertied people?" The authentic tradition says, "Gifts from tax collectors are fraud," and we know that fraud is forbidden, as is testified in the Qurānic verses and reports from the Prophet.

I heard Mawlānā Shaykh al-Islām Zakarīyā al-Anṣārī, may God have mercy on him, say: "Let the mendicant beware of assisting the emir to obtain office in this age. Most emirs have evil intentions in seeking office and almost none of them seeks office unless he intends to follow in his predecessor's footsteps in wrongdoing. Whoever helps an emir do this sort of thing will share his disgrace in this world and punishment in the Hereafter." I heard him say: "Any emir who asks his shaykh to help him be appointed to an office that is unavoidable deserves to be expelled from the shaykh's friendship. The shaykh's duty is to implore God to deprive the emir of that office or dismiss him from it, if it is in his possession. If he assists the emir in this, he cheats him and cheats himself." I heard him say: "A mendicant must not help an emir to obtain office unless he knows his intention to be righteous, such as if he intends by being appointed to take the victims of injustice by the hand and restrain the wrongdoers, so as to honor the community of Muḥammad, may God bless and save him. If his intention is worldly enrichment, laying snares for his enemies, and enjoying [71] power without regard for the obligations of his office, one must not assist him with one's tongue or one's heart." I heard him say, "Any mendicant who thinks that his emir's intentions in holding office are bad, such as if he intends to use the office to set snares for his enemies, take out his anger on the intimates of the preceding emir, or unjustly expropriate their property, is forbidden to assist him, even by prayer." In the *Testament* of al-Khiḍr,[100] may peace be upon him, to 'Umar ibn 'Abd al-'Azīz, may God have mercy on him, he says: " 'Do not take out your selfish anger on those over whom God has given you power. By a fair verdict, God will bring you one who will take his anger out on you whom you cannot control.' He said, 'Prophet of God, tell me more.' He said, 'Do not reach out your hand to the property of your subjects and seize it unjustly or God will remove their respect for you from their hearts and they will rebel against one another and you will not be able to stop them.' He said, 'Prophet of God, tell me more.' He said, 'Take care not to be God's ally in public and his enemy in secret.'" Know this, emirs, and act upon it. Do not ask your

100. Al-Khiḍr is a mysterious figure often associated with mystical inspiration. The source of the *Testament* quoted here is unknown.

shaykh to help you obtain office or remain in office unless you seek thereby to act for the sake of God or the Hereafter. Praise God, Lord of the worlds.

For the emir to be polite to the mendicant, he also should not send him or the mendicants in his zāwiya any food or clothes unless the mendicant requests them from him, especially on Friday eves and feast days. The food of emirs comes from their fodder and their produce, which are rarely free from taint. Whatever profit he gains from seeking reward with this food or clothes, he will lose from the hidden wrong that results from this food or these clothes. Indeed, more harm may result from the wrong than the good that results from this food or these clothes, even if the only harm done is that the mendicant is unable to enter into God's presence in prayer and at other times because he has eaten this food or put on these clothes and cap, as people have experienced. Emirs should know that the sincere mendicant returns an emir's property purely for the benefit of the emir and the mendicant, just as he never accepts anything except to benefit them both. Praise God, Lord of the worlds.

For the emir to be polite to the mendicant, he must also pay no attention to the other shaykhs of the town or region, no matter how exalted their stations in sainthood. He should think that meeting with his shaykh is more beneficial than meeting with any other shaykh, even if they be axial saints. Whoever's attention is drawn to another shaykh and whoever asks him to solve his problems strays from the path and wastes his shaykh's time, as has been indicated on a number of previous occasions in this book.

I heard my brother Afḍal al-Dīn, may God have mercy on him, say, "God has built human affairs on a foundation of monotheism. Just as the world cannot have two Gods, a man two hearts, or a woman two husbands, similarly, a disciple cannot have two shaykhs because that would slow down his journey [72] and create many obligations." The *Treatise* of Shaykh Abū Madyan al-Tilimsānī,[101] may God have mercy on him, says, "The heart can have but one direction; when it turns toward it, the other directions are concealed." So witness the perfection of your shaykh and ask him for what you need. The shaykhs follow divine conduct. Just as the Real, may He be honored and exalted, does not forgive having partners ascribed to him—that is, inclining toward someone else without His permission—and shaykhs are similar, may God have mercy on them. I heard Afḍal al-Dīn say: "Place love for your Lord in the middle of your hearts, love for your prophet after that, and love for your shaykh after love for your prophet. As for your prophet, he is the greatest intermediary between God and his servants, while your shaykh is the greatest intermediary between you and your prophet. Just as no axial saint can do without the mediation of the Messenger of God, may God bless and save him, between him and his Lord, similarly, the disciple cannot walk a single step on the path to the Real without his shaykh's mediation." Beyond the truth, what can there be but error? I heard him say: "Al-Khiḍr sought to befriend a certain disciple. He refused, saying, 'My shaykh is such that I have no need to befriend anyone

101. Abū Madyan al-Tilimsānī (1126–98) was a leading Sufi in the Maghreb. Originally from near Seville, he was buried in Tlemcen. The *Treatise* (*Risāla*) in question is "The Intimacy of the Recluse and the Pastime of the Seeker" ("Uns al-waḥīd wa nuzhat al-murīd"). See Vincent J. Cornell, *The Way of Abū Madyan: The Works of Abū Madyan Shu'ayb* (Cambridge: Islamic Texts Society, 1996), 118–19, aphorism nine.

else.'" Sayyidī Shaykh Muḥammad al-Shinnāwī asked his shaykh, Abū al-Ḥamā'il al-Sarawī,[102] may God have mercy on him, to give him permission to visit one of the saints of his age. He said, "Muḥammad, if I am not enough for you, why did you make me your shaykh?" He never visited any other shaykh, living or dead, as long as his shaykh lived.

I heard Sayyidī 'Alī al-Marṣafī,[103] may God have mercy on him, say: "If the mendicant learns that his emir's heart leans toward one of his peers, he must expel him or renew the friendship, especially if he swore an oath at the beginning of the friendship not to pay any attention to anyone else. The shaykhs and disciples have learned by experience that dividing one's love between multiple shaykhs prevents them from advancing, the opposite of what happens when they have a single shaykh." I heard him say, "Whoever asks for something he needs from a shaykh while dividing his submission between him and another, wastes his shaykh's time." They say, "Attach yourself to your shaykh and then ask him for what you need." Exalted God, may He be honored and glorified, swore by His honor and glory in one of His divine scriptures that whenever a servant of His asks another servant for what he needs, He, may He be exalted, will be with that servant and fulfill that need so that his servant is not ashamed. This is within the power of divine generosity, as has been explained in the interpretation of His saying, "And as for the unbelievers, their works are as a mirage in a spacious plain,"[104] etc. If the Real, may He be exalted, is present in

102. By Abū al-Ḥamā'il al-Sarawī, al-Sha'rānī presumably means Ibn Abī al-Ḥamā'il al-Sarawī (d. 1525).

103. Nūr al-Dīn 'Alī al-Marṣafī (d. 1523) was an important Sufi teacher and influence on al-Sha'rānī.

104. Sūrat al-Nūr 24:39.

a mirage, whose existence is not real and is purely imaginary, what about the situation of the perfect man who conforms to the Holy Law in his knowledge, action, and faith? Understand! Praise God, Lord of the worlds.

For the emir to be polite to the mendicant, he also must not burden him with offering testimony in any dispute that occurs in his presence that is connected to worldly affairs, especially before secular judges, for the shaykh's position is too exalted for something like this.

I heard Sayyidī 'Alī al-Khawwāṣ, may God have mercy on him, say: "An emir who befriends a shaykh and gets into a dispute over some worldly transaction that took place in his presence must not burden him with testifying about it, even if there are one hundred thousand dinars or more at stake, unless the shaykh is willing to do so. If the emir burdens him with testifying in front of judges when his heart is unwilling, this is impolite, and it shows how little [73] he venerates his shaykh, how highly he regards the world, and that he does not deserve to be a friend to shaykhs." I heard him say on a number of occasions: "The hearts of sincere mendicants pay no heed to the affairs of worldly people, so do not impose upon them to testify about wealth. His forgetfulness, his lack of precision, his great contempt for the world, and his witnessing that it isn't worth a mosquito's wing in God's eyes will cost you this testimony." He said: "Someone called a mendicant in the age of Sayyidī Ibrāhīm al-Matbūlī to testify before a judge about one thousand dinars. Sayyidī Ibrāhīm reprimanded this person and said to him, 'You are calling a mendicant to appear before a judge for some worldly matter?' He said, 'It is one thousand dinars.' The shaykh said to him, 'Those one thousand dinars aren't worth a single step taken by the mendicant that will besmirch his reputation and violate his sanctity in the eyes of his rivals.'" If this is the case with an ordinary mendicant, what about the shaykh who has the responsibility of guiding people? The intelligent man has too much respect for his shaykh to make him testify in a dispute about worldly matters that occurred in his presence. Praise God, Lord of the worlds.

For the emir to be polite to the mendicant, he also should not get annoyed with the mendicant if he fails to honor him by rising or offering him food when he had previously risen for him and offered him tasty food. No, his duty is to be happier about this than if he were honored, since the mendicant may have honored him at first in order to become familiar with him, but when he realized that he was sincere in his love, there was no need to honor him by rising for him or offering him food. I have often done this sort of thing with subprovincial governors and tribal chiefs to the point that I would give one of them a dry crust to eat and he would eat it happily. This is because I know that the emirs have no need for the kind of food eaten by mendicants; they eat it only to seek a blessing from their food. Many times, I have poured honey on the floor of my home for someone who ate it so he could imitate the poor and indigent who have no vessels from which to eat. Know this, brother emirs, and adopt kind answers to the mendicants you befriend. Don't impute to them what you impute to one another. Praise God, Lord of the worlds.

For the emir to be polite to the mendicant, he also should not begin a friendship with him until he witnesses that he is so sincere in loving him and forming a connection to him that no devil, whether man or jinnī, could get between him and his shaykh by changing one of their hearts. If the emir claims to be sincere in this but later there is a change of sentiment between him and the mendicant, his claim is not sincere. The explanation [74] of this is that the emir is connected to the presence of the mendicant and the mendicant is connected to the presence of God. Were a devil, whether man or jinnī, to enter into that presence, he would be burned and reduced to liquid and be unable to accomplish his objective of whispering to turn one against the other. Know this, emirs, and be sincere in your connection to your shaykh so that you may be free from harm. Praise God, Lord of the worlds.

For the emir to be polite to the mendicant, he must also be honest with him in seeking worldly positions for the sake of God, may He be honored and glorified, so that the mendicant can help him to obtain them, if only by prayer, and so that he and the emir can avoid bad consequences. If in the emir's heart he seeks to obtain them for selfish motives but pretends otherwise to the mendicant, he is impolite to the mendicant in using him for lowly purposes. The mendicant may detest the emir, since Exalted God detests him, for having used him in abhorrent matters. Exalted God is too protective of his saints to see them used for things He has not permitted.

I heard Sayyidī ʿAlī al-Khawwāṣ, may God have mercy on him, say: "An emir must not deceive his shaykh and claim that he is sincere in obtaining appointment to worldly offices, such as a subprovincial governorship, tribal chieftaincy, or tax agency. The mendicant may be veiled from witnessing his bad intention and assist him, relying on the apparent meaning of his saying, 'I swear to God, the only reason I want this office is to reduce the wrongs inflicted on the subjects and to prevent them from wronging one another, without increasing my food, drink, clothes, mounts, etc.' It is obvious that this is bad manners and hypocrisy toward the shaykh. Let the emir take care not to manifest to the shaykh something other than what is in his heart." Praise God, Lord of the worlds.

For the emir to be polite to the mendicant, he also must not invite him to attend his feast, unless the mendicant will be pleased with this. Whoever invites his shaykh to attend his feast when the shaykh is unhappy with this is impolite to him, especially if the feast brings together the shaykh's peers who are not so cautious as not to eat from this sort of feast, which may not be free from taint. If he agrees with his peers and eats, he abandons precautionary piety; and if he refuses to eat, he stands out from them and they are embarrassed to eat. Their souls may be moved to impugn his integrity and interpret his refusal to eat as intended to distinguish him from his peers in that company. They may be moved to insult his honor and mention those of his defects that are hidden from people, even though these qualities that he manifests may also be their qualities, and the shaykh is their mirror. It is well-known that a man sees only his own image in a mirror, not the mirror itself.

[75] I heard Sayyidī 'Alī al-Khawwāṣ, may God have mercy on him, say: "An emir must not invite a mendicant to a wedding or circumcision feast, or any other feast that brings together various kinds of people, such as scholars, emirs, financial officials, and merchants, unless he knows that his shaykh's heart will be happy to attend. There are times when the mendicant's heart has no room for anything but God and being devoted to obeying Him. If the emir must invite him to this feast with a good intention, let him present this to him as an offer, not a command. If the shaykh wishes, he can attend; if not, he can refuse." I heard him say, "A shaykh must not eat his emir's food, either privately or in public, because eating his food defiles his heart since the emir's station in precautionary piety is beneath that of a shaykh." This assumes that his food is free from being contaminated by his peers, but what if they contaminate it? It is preferable not to attend emirs' feasts at

all, unless for some legitimate objective. Praise God, Lord of the worlds.

For the emir to be polite to the mendicant, he also should not ask him to begin a friendship unless he has been purified of wickedness and lewdness, manifest and hidden, either by the pure nature granted him by God or by sincere repentance. If the emir seeks to befriend the shaykh while continuing to commit lewd acts, he exposes himself to being detested for having belittled the person of the shaykh by befriending him with lewdness and impurity. The mendicant may think that the emir can be purified only when he has been dismissed from his current office, which implies ruining him or his suffering a physical trial, such as syphilis,[105] which afflicts his body with joint pains so that he is deprived of the pleasure of eating food, drinking, intercourse, and sleep. Then he implores God, may He be honored and glorified, to purify him of this sort of thing, out of love for him and concern for his faith. Let the emir beware of befriending the mendicant as long as he remains impure. Praise God, Lord of the worlds.

For the emir to be polite to the mendicant, he also must not listen to what the mendicant's enemy says about him, and to his accusing the mendicant of defects. If the emir realizes that he is listening to what his shaykh's enemy says, this is impolite to him and he must renew the friendship. When one listens to people putting one's brother down, these defects take shape in one's mind and one is no longer able to remove them from one's mind. If one tries to see some perfection take shape in one's mind, one cannot.

105. The term translated here as "syphilis" (*al-ḥabb al-franjī*) literally means "Frankish boils." The disease first appeared in Europe at the end of the fifteenth century and then spread to the Ottoman Empire.

It is well-known that the emir's befriending this kind of mendicant does more harm than good.

I heard Sayyidī ʿAlī al-Khawwāṣ, may God have mercy on him, say: "If the emir loses faith in his shaykh, it is the emir's duty to inform the shaykh of this so that he can treat this illness or drive him off tactfully and with fine words, such as by encouraging him to befriend one of his peers and proclaiming that the peer, whose student he is not worthy to be, is of a higher station. Perhaps he will turn from his shaykh to the peer and the shaykh will be relieved of his evil. [76] Nonetheless, brethren, if you sense that the emir has faith in someone else, you must ask Exalted God on behalf of that mendicant to whom your emir has turned to protect him from the harmful effects of that friendship lest you be impolite toward your brother and cause him to suffer harm." I heard him say: "Do not encourage one of your emirs to have faith in one of your peers unless there is a higher purpose that outweighs your alienating that emir from him. Follow higher purposes, not selfish motives. Protect your brother as you would yourself, and ask Exalted God to protect him from harmful effects." Praise God, Lord of the worlds.

For the emir to be polite to the mendicant, he should also raise his station above the station of ordinary mendicants—such as imposters and devils—who have no part in the station of certain knowledge of the path of righteousness, which is well-known among our people, even if they are popular among worldly people who put them ahead of the people of certainty. If the emir considers the station of his shaykh to be lacking, he will not benefit from his friendship and the shaykh is obliged to expel him from his friendship.

I heard Sayyidī ʿAlī al-Khawwāṣ, may God have mercy on him, say: "The emir who befriends mendicants must be clever in distinguishing the righteous from the wicked so that he can increase the faith of the righteous and drive away the wicked. Among the best indications that a man is righteous is that he is learned, active, and abstains from the property of most people; that he renounces the world; and that he is austere in his food, marriage, mount, residence, and other forms of wealth in this abode. The wicked man is the opposite of this."

I heard Sayyidī ʿAlī al-Khawwāṣ, may God have mercy on him, say: "One of the strongest indications that a man is a saint and righteous is that he abstains from all of the property of officials and bears all of their burdens. When his emir is dismissed, falls ill, is imprisoned, or is placed under house arrest, you almost never see him eat, drink, or smile, except for some legitimate necessity, thereby fulfilling the duty to the friendship. Anyone who claims to tell an emir that he is righteous and accepts his charity and gifts, but later finds that his heart is free of the burden of his concerns, is an imposter who makes false claims." I heard him say: "An emir must not be satisfied to believe that his shaykh is as righteous as an ordinary man, thereby wronging him, being impolite, and putting an end to his usefulness. When the true mendicant realizes that the emir thinks that he has no greater claim to the path than those beneath him, such as imposters and fakes, his heart shuns the emir and he does not think that he deserves anyone bearing any of his concerns because he lacks full faith in the mendicant." Know this, emirs, and give preference to your shaykh over his peers if you want him to take your hand during hard times, as has already been said in this conclusion. Praise God, Lord of the worlds.

[77] For the emir to be polite to the mendicant, he also should not conceal any of the wealth he has acquired while in his current office if the mendicant asks about this. He should say, "I made

such-and-such from agriculture, such-and-such from crimes and bribes, such-and-such from fees, such-and-such from gifts," and so on. If he conceals any of this from the shaykh, he betrays the friendship and will benefit little from him.

I heard my brother Afḍal al-Dīn, may God have mercy on him, say: "An emir must not conceal from his shaykh any of the wealth that he acquired while in office. This is so that the shaykh can bless his licit wealth and command him to return wealth derived from crimes, bribery, terrorizing people, and unnecessary fines on his subjects. Then if it is fated that that emir cannot return this wealth to its owners, he must ask the mendicant to intercede for him with God and with the victims of his wrongdoing, so that the sin may be lessened, assuming God accepts the mendicant's intercession. This is something that emirs usually conceal from mendicants, which is liable to speed up their destruction, the loss of their wealth, and their ruination, as a punishment for their unjust treatment of people and whole villages. Had they informed the mendicant of the property they acquired through the prestige of their office, he might have done his best to stop them from receiving ill-gotten gains." I heard him say: "The emir must not conceal his affairs related to his office from his shaykh, mistreat people and whole villages while claiming to be a just person, and then, when God treats him as He would a village of evildoers, place himself under his shaykh's protection, saying, 'Bear my burden for me.'[106] This is one of the most impolite things one can do to the

106. The reference here is to Sūrat al-Nisā' 4:75, "How is it with you, that you do not fight in the way of God, and for the men, women, and children who, being abased, say, 'Our Lord, bring us forth from this village whose people are evildoers, and appoint to us a protector from Thee, and appoint to us from Thee a helper'?"

shaykh since the shaykh is the one who will bear the burden of the emir's mistakes forever." Know this, emirs, and be honest with your shaykh. Don't conceal any of your affairs or wealth from him, and he will bless them if they are licit or keep you from them if they are forbidden. Praise God, Lord of the worlds.

For the emir to be polite to the mendicant, he also should not consider himself superior to the mendicant because of the lentils, wheat, clarified butter, sheep, etc., that he sends to his zāwiya from time to time, as has been said previously. If the mendicant swears on his life to bear his hardships for him, whatever the emir sends him as gifts is like a speck of dirt in comparison to bearing these hardships. Let the emir take care lest his generosity to the shaykh cross his mind, much less take hold in his heart. Praise God, Lord of the worlds.

For the emir to be polite to the mendicant, if the mendicant expels him from the friendship, he also should not leave the mendicant's door or meet with other mendicants, even as a ruse. The common saying goes, "Whoever was no good in the past will be no good in the future." The meaning of this is that the emir is to the mendicant as the disciple is to the shaykh; the shaykh may drive him away, but it is the disciple's duty to offer the shaykh whatever will cause the shaykh's heart to incline in his favor. If the shaykh drives the emir away and the emir is unaffected by that, the shaykh is obliged to wash his hands of him since he is of no use to the emir.

[78] I heard Sayyidī 'Alī al-Khawwāṣ, may God have mercy on him, say, "The mendicant should act superior to the emir and the emir should show as much deference and humility to him as his spiritual ambition and ability allow." I heard him say: "For the emir to be polite to the mendicant, he should not leave his door,

even if the mendicant drives him away. Nothing can turn the lover from the beloved; he cannot be stopped by swords or destruction." He said, "Any emir whose faith in his shaykh is strengthened when people rush to him and weakened when they turn away and strongly denounce him should not be befriended by the mendicant because the emir lacks faith in him and love for him." I heard him say, "Any emir whose faith in his shaykh depends on other people's opinions is impolite to his shaykh because his faith in him and love for him are liable to be shaken." This is common among emirs these days; rarely does any of them find in his heart cause to have faith in a shaykh [unless] he sees that people have great faith in him. If he sees them turn away from the shaykh and denounce him, he forsakes him in his heart. If he happens to visit him, this amounts to hypocrisy and corrupt intentions, such as fearing that people will reproach him if he stops visiting his shaykh. Know this, emirs, and have faith in your shaykh, even if everyone on earth denounces him, as long as you witness that he is righteous in following the Holy Law. Praise God, Lord of the worlds.

For the emir to be polite to the mendicant, he should also fulfill all the promises he made to the shaykh before he was appointed to office to take good care of the shaykh's friends who are peasants, street hawkers, shopkeepers, etc. In order to honor the shaykh and avoid hypocrisy, he should not ask them to weigh any of the fines that are placed on corrupt people. One sign of a hypocrite is that he breaks all his promises, lies whenever he speaks, and violates every trust. If this is true of the shaykh's friends, what about the shaykh? He should not force the shaykh to ask him to abolish them or weigh them for him. The position of shaykh is too exalted for this sort of thing.

I heard Sayyidī ʿAlī al-Khawwāṣ, may God have mercy on him, say: "Any emir who claims to have strong faith in his shaykh and then forces him to ask him to help his friends is not sincere in his faith. It is the duty of the faithful man to help anyone related to the shaykh and not to force the shaykh to ask him for this, verbally or in writing." I heard him say: "Let the emir take great care not to ask the shaykh's friends for any of the fines that he is capable of preventing or weighing on their behalf so that he may fulfill his duty to the shaykh. If he forces the shaykh to ask for help for his friends, he goes beyond the boundaries of good manners." I heard him say: "The emir is blameless if he fails to reduce the wrongs done to his shaykh's friends, unless he is capable of it, such as if he is the one to benefit from these fines. As for those that he cannot prevent, such as customary sultanic fines, for these he is blameless." I heard him say: "The lowest level of intercession by the shaykh with the emir on behalf of a victim of wrongdoing is that the emir not reject his intercession except in a matter in which it is right that he reject the intercession of someone like the pasha, in a situation where reason indicates that he cannot accept the shaykh's intercession. If he accepts the pasha's intercession in matters where he would reject the shaykh's intercession, [79] he is impolite to the shaykh." I heard him say: "A mendicant must befriend only those emirs whose station he regards as higher than that of any emir. The station of the shaykh is too exalted for anyone to regard him as equal to any worldly person. This rarely exists anymore; most people venerate anyone who is a client of a powerful, worldly person more than they venerate someone who is a client of God and His Messenger." I attempted to get my deputies in my zāwiya to pay attention to the mendicant who comes to visit, just as they take care of worldly people, but love for the world was too strong in their hearts for them to comply. How often would I see them, when a worldly person came to visit me, competing to bring him to me in the hope that he had brought some worldly goods to distribute to them, but if a *sharīf*[107] or poor, blind man came to visit me—he might sit around all day without anyone informing me or asking to bring him in, they thought so little of him. Know this, emirs, be familiar with the ranks of the mendicants, and raise their station above the station of emirs in respect and honor more than you do with fellow emirs, in order to honor those whose exclusive clients they are—God and His Messenger. Praise God, Lord of the worlds.

For the emir to be polite to the mendicant, he should also have greater love and veneration for him the more he intercedes with him on behalf of victims of wrongdoing. In doing so, the shaykh only wishes to increase the emir's reward in the Hereafter and make him happy in his grave as a recompense for his treatment of his subjects. Blessed is he who obeys his shaykh, and woe unto he who disobeys him.

I heard Sayyidī Afḍal al-Dīn, may God have mercy on him, say: "Exalted God causes the emir in his grave worries and concerns or joy and happiness, depending on what he caused his subjects. Let the emir be careful not to reject the mendicant's intercession for an aggrieved person who, for example, has long been imprisoned, worrying and suffering. The Real, may He be glorified and honored, might cause him similar suffering in his grave as an appropriate punishment." Praise God, Lord of the worlds.

For the emir to be polite to the mendicant, he also should not force him to wear himself out obtaining any of the emir's worldly

107. A sharīf or "noble" is a descendant of the Prophet Muḥammad.

objectives. No, his duty is to say to the mendicant: "I ask you by God not to assist me in obtaining any selfish objectives; indeed, I thank you for your kindness if you oppose me in them. I am ashamed before God to employ a mendicant in base matters that lower my station in the eyes of my Lord." This is to bring ease to the shaykh's heart. Then, if he wishes, he can wear himself out in his devotion to solving the emir's problems, or, if he wishes, he can relax. When Sultan Qāyitbāy befriended Sayyidī Ibrāhīm al-Matbūlī, he said to him: "Shaykh Ibrāhīm, I swear to God, I have not befriended you for worldly reasons. I befriended you only so that you would take my hand in the entry halls at the Resurrection. I am too ashamed to employ any of God's saints in a worldly matter." Know this, emirs, and act on it. Praise God, Lord of the worlds

For the emir to be polite to the mendicant, he should also befriend his friends and be an enemy to his enemies. Let the emir take great care not to allow a mendicant who condemns his shaykh to enter his house, much less sit with him and smile to his face, in imitation of God, may He be honored and glorified. [80] The shaykh is an intermediary between the emir and the presence of God, may He be honored and glorified. Whoever opposes the shaykh, opposes God, and there is nothing to be done with him. As the tradition says: "On the Day of Resurrection, a man will be brought forward with good deeds equivalent to several mountains, but the Exalted Real will command him to go to Hell. The angels will say, 'Our Lord, How could you send him to Hell when he has all of these good deeds?' God, may He be honored and glorified, will say, 'Take him to Hell. He neither befriended my friends nor was an enemy to my enemies.'" Just as the Exalted Real did not accept any of this man's good deeds because he did not befriend

His friends and was not an enemy to His enemies, similarly, the shaykh, in imitation of God, must not sympathize with the emir who befriends his enemies. Know this, emirs, and abandon your shaykh's enemy so that the shaykh will take your hand in hard times. Praise God, Lord of the worlds.

For the emir to be polite to the mendicant, he also should not ask him to bear his burden in the hard times that he suffers in this world and the Hereafter unless he has repented of all of his sins, manifest and hidden, lest he waste the shaykh's time. How can the shaykh bear the burden of someone with whom Exalted God is displeased, even angry? This is one of the hardest things in the world. Let the emir seek Exalted God's forgiveness for all his transgressions, manifest and hidden, and only then ask the shaykh to bear his burden. If he asks him to bear his burden without repenting, he makes inappropriate use of him and it is obvious that this is bad manners toward the shaykh. One who persists in sins such as fornication, sodomy, wine drinking, extortion, theft, profiting from criminal penalties, and so on deserves only greater punishment. Exalted God said, "We tried them with good things and evil that haply they should return."[108] Any shaykh who does not investigate the truth of his emir's repentance is not permitted to take up his burden; indeed, God might hold that against him. Know this, emirs, and ask your Lord's forgiveness for every sin so that your shaykh can take you by the hand during hard times, just as he would with most people. Praise God, Lord of the worlds.

For the emir to be polite to the mendicant, his faith in the shaykh must also not be shaken if he promises him that he will be appointed to office at a certain time but the appointment is

108. Sūrat al-Aʿrāf 7:168.

delayed beyond the time he specified. It may be that the shaykh's gaze is fixed on the 360 Tablets of Erasure and Affirmation, which are of a lower level than the Protected Tablet and the Supreme Pen.[109] The news he gave the emir of his appointment at a certain time was nothing but the truth, but the decision was later changed and his appointment at that time was erased and something else was written. Had the emir asked the shaykh when the change was made, he would have informed him of it, but he did not ask, so he stuck to the first statement, not the second.

I heard Sayyidī ʿAlī al-Khawwāṣ, may God have mercy on him, say: "A shaykh must not reveal any future events to anyone unless his gaze is fixed on the Protected Tablet. If his gaze is fixed on the Tablets of Erasure and Affirmation, he must not reveal this to anyone lest his prediction not come true, people make fun of him, and they cease respecting the people of the Sufi cloak." [81] I heard him say: "Any emir who asks his shaykh to reveal the future to him is impolite and violates the duties of friendship. If someone says, 'How does the mystic view the Protected Tablet?' the answer is that there are two ways. Sometimes his vision rends the veils until he reads what is there, and sometimes he knows what is there because it is inscribed in his heart. For the heart, when it is burnished, becomes like a spherical mirror. When it is facing the supernal and sublunary worlds, they are all inscribed in it. This depends on the power or weakness and breadth or narrowness of one's vision."

I heard Sayyidī ʿAlī al-Khawwāṣ, may God have mercy on him, say: "The Protected Tablet is where Exalted God has written everything that will be until the Day of Resurrection. Nothing He

109. God used the Supreme Pen to write the Protected Tablet.

has written can change or be altered. He whose heart is burnished from human tarnish may see all the events that are inscribed in his heart reflected in the Protected Tablet, few or many, depending on how far his vision reaches." Praise God, Lord of the worlds.

For the emir to be polite to the mendicant, he also should not ask him to dress him in any of his clothes, such as a cloak or cap, unless he has reached the mendicant's station in great caution, in righteous deeds, and in purifying himself of all impurities, manifest and hidden. This is so that he doesn't mistreat the cloak or cap by removing it from its immaculately pure location and placing it on a location defiled by violations of the Holy Law and filthy things. Moreover, the shaykh must not agree to let the emir, with his impurity, do this, lest he be the emir's partner in mistreating the clothing.

I heard Sayyidī 'Alī al-Khawwāṣ, may God have mercy on him, say: "An emir must not ask his shaykh to give him his clothes to wear, except as a blessing that some of his clothes be in his possession without being worn out of respect for his shaykh. Indeed, if the shaykh bestows an item of his clothes on the emir, the emir would be polite to refuse it and say to the shaykh, 'I am too protective of your clothing for it to be on a body like mine, which is defiled by sins.' Then, if the shaykh insists that he accept it and stresses that, it is polite for the emir to accept it out of respect, and wear it at those times when he is obedient to the Holy Law, and take it off when he commits sins or is heedless, unless by wearing it when he sins his intention is to protect himself from the bad consequences by depending on his friend's blessing." Know this, emirs, and act on it. Praise God, Lord of the worlds.

For the emir to be polite to the mendicant, he should also fear the mendicant turning against him more than he fears his father turning against him, since the spiritual father is owed greater deference and has a more certain claim than the physical father. The explanation of this is that the physical father is nothing more than your locus before you appear from nothingness into being, while the spiritual father at the very least takes you by the forearm and, with God's permission, escorts you to the path of guidance and righteousness. Without a doubt, that is superior to your merely physical generation, unless the physical father is one of the people of the path. In that case, he is superior to the merely spiritual father because he combines both types of merit.

I heard Sayyidī ʿAlī al-Khawwāṣ, may God have mercy on him, say: "Let the emir be extremely careful not to socialize with his shaykh's enemy, who puts him down and mentions his faults lest his faith in the shaykh be changed by this enemy's words and he cease to benefit from the shaykh at all. This is especially true if the enemy is an imposter who falsely claims to be on the path and wants the emir to become his disciple. He will be completely torn up, [82] since he will no longer be the friend of the shaykh and have faith in him to take him by the hand in hard times, nor will the enemy be able to take his place. This happens to many emirs who do not differentiate between sincere mendicants and the other kind. Emirs, do not socialize with your shaykh's enemies unless you are protected from hearing what they say against your shaykh's reputation." Praise God, Lord of the worlds.

For the emir to be polite to the mendicant, he also should not conceal from him any of the errors that he makes, even if the mendicant does not ask him about that, as he does with disciples. This is because if the emir mentions them to the shaykh, either he will guide him to repentance and reform or he will intercede for him with God so that he forgives him or delays his punishment and blame or he will protect him from committing similar errors in the future by watching over him. But if he conceals them from the shaykh, he might continue as he is and not find anyone to guide him to repentance, ask God to forgive him, or delay his punishment. Emirs often deceive their shaykhs in this, when one says to himself, "Since God has protected your reputation and not informed any of His creatures of your errors, there is nothing wrong with your concealing this from people who may look down on you because of the sins you commit and reproach you for them." He overlooks that this is the case only with people other than the shaykh because the sinner is like a sick person and the shaykh is like a doctor. If the sick person conceals his illness from the doctor, he will receive no treatment until he dies or the illness grows more severe. Indeed, were the emir to think about it, he would find that the shaykh is kinder than his mother and more protective of him than he is of himself. Whoever conceals anything from his shaykh fails in his duty to him and his duty to himself. I heard him say: "An emir must not be too embarrassed to mention his faults to his shaykh, as ignorant people are. No, he should mention them to the shaykh so that he can treat them either with repentance and forgiveness, or by asking God to bestow repentance on him immediately, whenever he commits a sin. Emirs, who are dominated by natural shame, not legitimate shame, rarely do this." Praise God, Lord of the worlds.

For the emir to be polite to the mendicant, he also should not promise him to reduce the wrongs done to his subjects unless he knows himself to be sincere, lest the shaykh despise him with God's permission if he extorts the subjects, loots their property, imprisons them, and beats them without just cause.

I heard Sayyidī ʿAlī al-Khawwāṣ, may God have mercy on him, say: "One sign of the emir's sincerity in promising his shaykh to reduce people's grievances to the best of his ability is that he possess wealth in cash, clothes, animals, gardens, and houses when he begins his term in office, before becoming impoverished, with a limited livelihood and no wealth." It is just as Imām al-Shāfiʿī said about the judge with the commonality that both are busy with other people's tasks and forget their own tasks for worldly gain; they are no longer concerned with agriculture or trade despite their many children and expenses. Imām al-Shāfiʿī's exact words are, "Whoever serves as a judge and is not impoverished thereby is a thief." The emir should be compared to him. We have heard that ʿUmar ibn ʿAbd al-ʿAzīz, when he was appointed caliph, owned clothes with one thousand fringes. He sold them all and put the money in the treasury. Before a few months had passed [83] he had only one shirt. When he wanted to wash it, he stayed at home naked, with only a cloth to cover his privates until his shirt dried. He acted similarly with his wife, Fāṭima bint ʿAbd al-Malik. He donated the price of her whole trousseau, which he sold with her permission to the treasury, and she owned only one robe, like her husband.

I heard my brother Afḍal al-Dīn, may God have mercy on him, say, "Whenever an emir who promised his shaykh to reduce grievances if he is appointed to office increases his household furnishings, including garments, utensils, animals, etc., this is a sign that he has betrayed his promise." Know this, emirs, and do not increase your household furnishings if you begin a term in office, claiming that is due to your shaykh's blessing. This is an abuse of the truth. Praise God, Lord of the worlds.

For the emir to be polite to the mendicant, he also should not ask him to help him get appointed to an office that people are competing for, but if he must, he should say to the shaykh: "Master, pray to God, may He be honored and exalted, to appoint over the Muslims whoever His prior knowledge indicates will be more kind to them than others. Whomever God chooses in answering the shaykh's prayer is most deserving and preferable." Then, if someone other than the emir who asked the mendicant to pray to his Lord that he be appointed happens to be appointed, it is his duty to be happy, not unhappy, about this. For he is the best of the two or more men who were competing for that office. Know this, emirs, and do not think that your shaykh prefers you to others in appointment to office or prefers others to you on the basis of personal bias or for personal advantages. That would be ignorance on your part of your shaykh's station. Praise God, Lord of the worlds.

For the emir to be polite to the mendicant, he also should not ask the mendicant to solve his problems with God or men, except with the greatest humility and contrition, and by showing his want and need for this sort of thing. For the mendicant is accustomed to following divine conduct; if he does not see humility, contrition, and need from the needy person, he will not hurry to solve his problem. Let the emir beware of asking the mendicant to implore God, may He be honored and glorified, to solve his problem as long as he continues to act as if he can do without that need and is not wanting of anything. He may find it impossible because of his lack of commitment and bad manners.

I heard Sayyidī ʿAlī al-Khawwāṣ, may God have mercy on him, say: "An emir must not ask his shaykh for his needs unless he is extremely humble and submissive and shows his extreme want and need. The only reason shaykhs set themselves up as shaykhs is to take the hand of the sorrowful who don't ask for their help." Know this, emirs, and be humble in the presence of your shaykhs, and manifest your need for them in every hardship so that they take your hand. If a shaykh and his followers stand to pray for you, stand with them like you are one of them, in extreme humility, so that the Real hurries to solve your problems. Praise God, Lord of the worlds.

[84] For the emir to be polite to the mendicant, he also should bear his own fatigue and not ask him to help him with all of his problems. He should ask him only in important matters in which he is powerless to reduce his debt to the shaykh, and be characterized by the station of manliness. Any emir who needs his help to perform his tasks belongs to the category of women and has no share of perfect manliness. They say, "The perfect man is he who lives under the protection of his own righteous deeds, not he who lives under the protection of his shaykh or brethren."

I heard Sayyidī ʿAlī al-Khawwāṣ, may God have mercy on him, say: "Let the emir be extremely careful not to ask his shaykh to share all of the hardships that befall him. What is polite is for him to ask the shaykh for help in anything he is totally incapable of dealing with." He said: "Let the emir also beware not to place his burden on the shaykh, while he goes to indulge his appetites in eating, drinking, sex, and enjoying himself in gardens and by rivers, saying, 'My shaykh has no need of my assistance with the burden I placed on him.' This is a sign of failure and lack of manliness. Indeed, just as the shaykh abstains from indulging his appetites and keeps himself from them until he feels that his body is engulfed in fire, so too should the emir. Indeed, this is truer of him than of the shaykh since the problem is his and the shaykh is merely helping him with it." Know this, emirs, and lift your burden from your shaykh to be polite and kind to him, and so that you may be characterized by the station of men, not the station of women. Praise God, Lord of the worlds.

For the emir to be polite to the mendicant, he should also trust him with his children and female household members. If it so happens that the shaykh meets with the women in private, it should never cross the emir's mind that he gazes upon any of them lustfully or with any other appetite. Should this thought occur to him, he is being impolite to the shaykh since the believer is he who trusts people with his own life, property, and dependents. Whoever does not trust his shaykh in this way excludes him from the station of perfect faith and ceases to benefit from him; he must repent and renew the friendship. Know this, emirs, fulfill your duty to your shaykh, and trust him with your lives and your dependents in a legitimate manner. Praise God, Lord of the worlds.

For the emir to be polite to the mendicant, he also should not ask him to speak to his superiors among the emirs and viziers in order to keep him in his current office or transfer him to a higher office or abstain from carrying out an inquest on him, if the subjects complain about him, since the shaykh's station is too exalted for this kind of thing, which is not his business. The emirs and viziers may be taking measures that benefit the Umma[110] that are the opposite of what the emir requested of the shaykh and he may be impolite with them. The emir's duty is to leave his fate to God, then to his shaykh. If he thinks something is appropriate, fine; otherwise, he will be silent for fear the emirs and viziers will tarnish the shaykh's reputation and say: "Why has this shaykh

110. The universal Muslim community.

involved himself in the affairs of the sultanate and officialdom? His duty was to stay in his zāwiya and stick to his task of training mendicants, guiding them, and taking care of their livelihoods."

[85] I heard Sayyidī ʿAlī al-Khawwāṣ, may God have mercy on him, say: "An emir must not ask his shaykh to speak to the pasha or sultan to get one of his friends appointed subprovincial governor, tax farmer, or tribal chief over some villages, to protect his shaykh's reputation from being tarnished and his being blamed for the corruption caused by whomever he gets appointed. Indeed, the emir's duty is to say to his naïve, gullible shaykh if he intervenes with officials in the appointment of a subprovincial governor or tribal chief: 'Master, don't intervene in things like this; leave it to those in charge. I fear that those who seek to be appointed will commit corrupt deeds and you will be blamed and they will no longer accept your intercession.'" Know this, emirs, and act on it. Praise God, Lord of the worlds.

For the emir to be polite to the mendicant, he also should not press him to intercede to get him appointed to an office that the mendicant promised him; rather, he should be patient and continue to be polite with the shaykh until the shaykh is moved to intercede for him of his own accord, God willing. Matters are contingent on the moments when the Exalted Real wishes to manifest them. This is what the learned call providence and they utter after fate, saying, "All matters depend on fate and providence." Providence is pre-eternal, while fate is the moment at which the providential event occurs. Just as some providential events are uttered later than others, they are manifested later.

I heard Sayyidī ʿAlī al-Khawwāṣ, may God have mercy on him, say: "The mendicant may promise the emir a certain appointment but later come to the opinion that it would be better if he were deprived of it because of the bad consequences involved, for example. He may ask God, may He be honored and glorified, to make it unattainable for him out of mercy and kindness to him. Let the emir submit to the mendicant in this sort of situation." I heard him say: "The emir may press the mendicant to ask the Exalted Real that he be appointed to a certain office immediately, and so that the emir is relieved of his need for the mendicant. The mendicant says, 'You will certainly turn away,' that is, 'Turn your back to me, as soon as you leave my company.' The emir thinks that he is saying, 'You will certainly be appointed to this office,'[111] and starts pestering the shaykh for no reason." Know this, emirs, and beware of asking your shaykh to help you obtain appointment to office in this age, even if he promises it to you. His opinion may change and he may start imploring God to deprive you of it out of mercy and kindness to you and your faith. Praise God, Lord of the worlds.

For the emir to be polite to the mendicant, he also should obey the mendicant's command if he orders him to be kind to his enemies, not to mention enduring their slights against him. He will command the emir only to do what is best for the emir's faith and worldly interests. This is especially true if the enemies are the emir's relatives and have intimate knowledge of his machinations while in office. Perhaps he levied taxes on the subjects without the knowledge of the sultan or his deputies. It is most imperative that the emir put up with their slights against him after he has been kind to them lest he be exposed, unless something like that would cause people's rights to be returned to them, in which case he should pay no heed [86] to his being exposed. Some emirs

111. Al-Sha'rānī is making a pun on the word *tawlīya*, which can mean "turning away" or "appointment to office."

have overlooked this sort of thing and have not been kind to their relatives. Inform those in power that everything one receives from the subjects unfairly and as arbitrary fines is cause for his dismissal and ruination. Had he restrained his anger and been kind to his enemies, even without pleasure, lesser evils would have befallen him. Know this, emirs, and rush to obey your shaykh's command to be kind to your enemies so that you may prosper. Praise God, Lord of the worlds.

For the emir to be polite to the mendicant, he also should not hold back any of the cash, food, clothes, and so forth that he asks him for if the mendicant's doctrine allows him to accept gifts from emirs and to eat their food. The only reason the mendicant asks him for things in the first place is in some higher interest of the emir, and nobody else.

I heard Sayyidī ʿAlī al-Khawwāṣ, may God have mercy on him, say: "An emir must not begin a friendship with a mendicant until he gives the mendicant firm control over his life and his wealth and puts his fate totally in his hands, to the degree that the mendicant can emancipate any of the emir's slaves he wishes and donate any of his lands to a charitable endowment. As long as this is not the case, the mendicant must not agree to befriend him."

I saw our Shaykh Muḥammad al-Sarawī, may God have mercy on him, when he was visited by the retinue of Judge Shams al-Dīn ibn ʿAwaḍ, who asked him to take up the judge's burden when he was dismissed by Sultan al-Ghūrī,[112] who turned him over to

112. Sultan Qānṣūh al-Ghūrī governed the Mamluk Empire from 1501 until 1516, when he fell at the Battle of Marj Dābiq against the Ottoman sultan Selim. Although many chroniclers present al-Ghūrī as a tyrannical ruler who imposed numerous illegitimate taxes, al-Shaʿrānī praises him for his respect for the Sufis.

be punished. The shaykh said to them, "Bring him to me." When they brought him to the shaykh, he was in chains. He said to him: "Take off your robe and turban and put a towel around your waist. Go out and return home like this and I will take up your burden." The judge hesitated to do this and rubbed his ear. The shaykh took a huge pot and threw it from the window of his home into the Ḥākimī Canal,[113] saying, "Ibn 'Awaḍ's burden, go to someone besides me." They punished him that evening by shaving his head, making him wear a cap full of beetles, which they tied under his chin, and binding his hands behind his back. The beetles began to dig into his skull, and blood flowed over his face until he almost died. They explained his situation to the aforementioned Sayyidī Muḥammad, and he said: "That is what he deserves. How could he begrudge me a robe that he acquired by illicit and tainted means and that will become rags, and begrudge the person who would bear these punishments in his stead?" The aforementioned judge Shams al-Dīn heard this and sent him this robe and another like it, but the shaykh would not accept it from him. He said: "That correct thought is gone. There is nothing left to do but neglect his burden, and that won't spare him anything." Know this, emirs, and give your shaykh whatever he requests if you believe that he is a saint and a righteous man. Do not send him anything without being asked; he may not need that sort of thing. The mendicant should not indulge any of the soul's temptations except in extreme necessity and should consider anything he doesn't need as tantamount to useless, not to mention that rejecting it will single him out among his peers. Praise God, Lord of the worlds.

113. The Ḥākimī Canal (Khalīj al-Ḥākimī) connected the Nile to the Red Sea.

[87] For the emir to be polite to the mendicant, he also, as a matter of course, should not refuse his intercession for a victim of wrongdoing, unless there are valid, indisputable reasons to refuse the sultan's intercession, or that of one of the subordinate emirs. The authority of the mendicant is like the authority of a king, or even greater, for those who understand and have the insight provided by the light of the heart and nearness to the Presence of the Lord.

I heard Sayyidī ʿAlī al-Khawwāṣ, may God have mercy on him, say: "The emir must not rush to accept the mendicant's intercession until he interrogates him cleverly and shrewdly. If he does not do that, he is like those mendicants who have little knowledge of what people are like. The emir has the right not to accept his intercession, but only if he makes it clear to the mendicant why this person whom he considers a victim is actually a wrongdoer, so that the mendicant's heart is not burdened." I heard him say: "It is polite of the emir, if the mendicant intercedes with him for a peasant whose property has been stolen, who has been forced to pay the land tax on fallow land, and who has fled his village, to rush to accept his intercession, ask God's forgiveness, and to turn to Him in repentance. It is not permissible for him to refuse his intercession for fear of being despised or losing prosperity, as is the practice of tribal chiefs and subprovincial governors." I heard him say: "Any emir who befriends a mendicant or claims to have great faith in him, then refuses his intercession, violates the covenant of friendship, and the mendicant is obliged to drive him away unless he immediately repents of his mistreatment of people. This has become rarer than red sulfur among emirs; virtually none of them ever accepts a mendicant's intercession for people whose property he has seized and upon whom he has imposed impossible burdens in land tax and fines." Praise God, Lord of the worlds.

For the emir to be polite to the mendicant, he should also believe that the mendicant's intellect is more perfect than his own intellect and the mendicant's instructions are more perfect than his own instructions. This is so that he does not deviate from the mendicant's instructions to act or not act. Indeed, he should surrender control over his affairs to him just as the disciple turns control over his affairs to his shaykh. This is something that has become rarer than red sulfur among emirs, which is why they suffer and relapse in their frequent disobedience to the mendicant they have befriended. The mendicant is like the captain of a ship and the emir is like one of the sailors. As long as the sailors follow the instructions of the captain, the ship remains safe from harm; but if they disobey, they are in danger of being destroyed. Let the emir who befriends the mendicant be careful; more emirs are destroyed than saved[114] by befriending mendicants whose instructions they ignore. The pleasure of commanding and prohibiting and the honor of being an emir may dominate the emir who accuses the mendicant of having no experience of what people are like and ignores his instructions. Had the emir not befriended the mendicant and instead acted on the basis of his own ignorance, he would have been in less trouble. The mendicant can only offer the emir unselfish advice so that he no longer has any valid excuse. Then, he will be destroyed by disobeying. Know this, emirs, and act on it. Praise God, Lord of the worlds.

For the emir to be polite to the mendicant, he must not break his promise not to take out his anger on those of his enemies over

114. The available manuscripts read "fewer emirs are destroyed than saved," but this is the opposite of what the context implies. It is likely that an error was made in an early copy and reproduced in subsequent copies.

whom he has power, especially the retinue of the emir who held the office before him. Anyone who unjustly takes out his anger on one of his enemies will be sent an enemy by God whom he is powerless to keep at bay, who will take out his anger on him as an appropriate punishment.

[88] I heard Sayyidī 'Alī al-Khawwāṣ, may God have mercy on him, say: "It is foolish of the emir to take out his anger on the retinue of the emir who held his current office before him, to expel them from their homes, seize their property, and then ask his shaykh to repel his enemies who want to take out their anger on him. No, his duty is to never ask his shaykh to avert any punishment for his evil deeds. Indeed, he should consider everything the Exalted Real does to repay him in kind to be merely part of what he deserves. It was said earlier in the *Testament* of al-Khiḍr, may peace be upon him, to 'Umar ibn 'Abd al-'Azīz, that the emir's taking out his anger on his subjects without just cause cuts his rope to the presence of his Lord, may He be honored and glorified. No human being will ever help him, especially if he seizes their property, imprisons many people, and beats them without cause. The intelligent emir puts up with the harm done to him by his subjects, is lenient toward them, and forgives them; he does not repay them in kind. Praise God, Lord of the worlds.

For the emir to be polite to the mendicant, he also should be sick when he is sick, grieve when he grieves, be happy when he is happy, oppose his enemies, befriend his friends, and abstain from sending him a gift that he secretly knows the mendicant abhors. The mendicant does not need to inform him of this since there is a powerful hidden connection between them, as has already been said with regard to the conduct of the mendicant with the emir. If the mendicant falls ill, grieves, is happy, becomes someone's enemy or friend, without the emir knowing, falling ill, grieving, befriending that friend or becoming an enemy of that enemy, this is a sign that there is no connection between him and the shaykh. This is rarer than red sulfur these days; only a few mystics achieve it. One friend who became sick when I was sick, grieved when I grieved, was happy when I was happy, befriended my friends and was an enemy to my enemies without anyone informing him of this was Emir Yūsuf ibn Abī Iṣba', may God have mercy on him. If one of his personal slaves informed him that I had recovered from an illness, he would emancipate him out of happiness, may God have mercy on him. Know this, emirs, and act on it. Praise God, Lord of the worlds.

For the emir to be polite to the mendicant, he also should not attribute unavoidable appointments to office as being through the intervention of his shaykh; this is bad manners toward the shaykh. The sincere man cannot assist him in any unavoidable appointments to offices. Indeed, his task is to protect him from contingent acts of fate and keep them from his friend. The opposite is true of avoidable appointments; the emir can attribute these to his shaykh's assistance.

I heard Sayyidī 'Alī al-Khawwāṣ, may God have mercy on him, say: "Let the emir be extremely careful not to attribute to him assistance in unavoidable offices, since this sort of thing can be attributed to only the appetitive soul, the Devil, or those who hold office at the time. The shaykh can involve himself in an emir's appointment only if there are no negative consequences. God permitting, he can loosen the knot from the heavenly presences and both the subjects and those who hold office at the time will ask him for this appointment and kiss his foot to persuade him to accept it. He will not have to pay any worldly fees to obtain the appointment except the customary bonus for officials' retinues in exchange for the robe of office and drums.[115] If he pays additional fees in dinars or is not asked by the subjects or officials to accept the appointment, he cannot attribute it to the shaykh. Let the emir know that one sign of someone being the cause of his being appointed is that [the same person] is the cause of his being dismissed. Just as Exalted God foreordained that he would be appointed, He foreordained his [89] dismissal. This is something unknown to many emirs. One may be appointed and dismissed at the hands of the shaykh, but he ignorantly attributes this to another official. He is unaware that the manifest officials are merely deputies of the mendicants in adjudicating between people, not the reverse. A certain subprovincial governor of al-Qalyūbīya[116] relied on a mendicant for his appointment until he was appointed to the post, and he attributed this to another person. He was immediately dismissed at the hands of the pasha to whom he was dear, and who took him back with him to Rūm,[117] as a punishment for attributing powers to the wrong people. Then he went to the mendicant and apologized, but the mendicant refused to accept it in order to teach him a lesson." I heard him say: "The emir who relies on a shaykh must consider all of the good fortune and prosperity that come his way from the sultan on down as the blessings of the shaykh. If it so happens that officials turn against him and turn their hearts away from him, this results from the shaykh's heart turning against him because of some sin he has committed. Let

115. High-ranking officials received ceremonial robes of office and were entitled to have drums beaten outside their residences and during processions.

116. A subprovince north of Cairo.

117. Rūm may refer to Anatolia or the Balkan provinces of the Ottoman Empire.

him be more wary of his shaykh's heart turning against him than he is of officials' hearts turning against him; they are dependent on the shaykh." Know this, emirs, and do not attribute to your shaykh assistance in obtaining an appointment unless it is free of negative consequences and you were appointed without spending any money. Praise God, Lord of the worlds.

For the emir to be polite to the mendicant, he also should not think that he can do without his advice and guidance at any time, day or night. Indeed, he must always think that he is crooked and debauched in the lexical sense and the legal sense, for it is rare for an emir to be free of committing acts that make him debauched legally and lexically. Let the emir take care not to listen to those who praise him and describe him as reformed, the opposite of his shaykh's description of him; this is fatal to his faith. I had heard much fine praise about an emir, but when I met him to intercede with him, I found him to be extremely crooked and evil inside. I investigated him and found this was a rumor spread by the beggars who begged wheat, rice, lentils, and other things from him that he extorted from peasants in customary fees invented by tyrannical emirs before him. I explained his shortcomings to him, but not a single word entered his ear. I asked God to reform him and distance him from his evil peers. Know this, emirs, and accept your shaykh's advice, accept his characterizations of you, and hurry to repent from this and to seek forgiveness. Praise God, Lord of the worlds.

For the emir to be polite to the mendicant, he also should not try to hurry him to give him the office that he promised he would be appointed to and that is someone else's possession. The sincere mendicant does not lie. If it is foreordained that the Exalted

Real will not give it to him while he is awake, he will give it to him while he is asleep so that His saint is not trapped in a lie. This is what happened to Shaykh al-Dabbās[118] with Sayyidī 'Abd al-Qādir al-Jīlī. A merchant consulted him about a journey. He said to him, "If you travel, thieves will murder you and take your wealth." The merchant traveled and returned safely, with his wealth intact. Some people thought that the shaykh was not truthful. The shaykh said to them, "Ask him whether he had a dream in which he was murdered and his wealth taken or not." He told them, "Yes, I had a dream in which they murdered me and took my wealth." The shaykh said, "I asked Exalted God to change that to a dream, and He did."

[90] I heard Sayyidī 'Alī al-Khawwāṣ, may God have mercy on him, say: "The emir must not doubt anything the mendicant promises; it must happen, even if it takes fifty years. They have likened an appointment in someone else's possession to a fetus in its mother's womb. It is impossible for it to leave that other man's possession until the end of the term in which God's prior knowledge indicates the appointment will stay in his possession." Let the emir trust his shaykh's promise that he will obtain the appointment, for example, but with patience, with good manners, and without being in a hurry. God guides whom He will to a straight path. Praise God, Lord of the worlds.

For the emir to be polite to the mendicant, he also should not mention to any emir the miracles and wonders he witnesses since this would amount to revealing his shaykh's privates to people so

118. Abū al-Khayr Ḥammād ibn Muslim al-Dabbās (d. 1131) was the teacher of 'Abd al-Qādir al-Jīlī.

that they can see them, which is reprehensible[119] among sincere persons.

I heard Sayyidī ʿAlī al-Khawwāṣ, may God have mercy on him, say: "Every emir must conceal his shaykh's privates and not mention to any of his peers the miracles and wonders he witnesses. Just as the common people are affected by having their manifest privates uncovered, the sincere mendicants are affected by those who show people their hidden perfections, which for them are like private parts because of negative consequences that the mendicants suffer if they let the emirs see their shame." Sayyidī Ibrāhīm al-Matbūlī, may God have mercy on him, said: "A mendicant in this abode whose perfections are revealed is like someone sitting in a water closet. If he closes the door, he relieves himself and exits with his privates concealed; if someone opens the door on him, his privates are revealed, his honor is violated, and everyone who passes by curses him." Most people are the opposite; they believe that manifesting perfections conceals their shame completely, but that is shortsightedness. The perfect man looks with both eyes and sees manifesting his perfections with one eye and their imperfection with the other eye. Know this, emirs, and conceal your shaykh's shame in this abode by concealing the perfections you see from all your peers, unless there is a necessary reason. Praise God, Lord of the worlds.

For the emir to be polite to the mendicant, he also should not get annoyed if the mendicant puts him down in gatherings, ac-

119. "Reprehensible" is a translation of the word *makrūh,* which seems to be the word intended, although all the manuscripts have the word *maqrūn* (connected) or *maqrū.* There seems to be a copyist error here.

cuses him of injustice and wrongdoing, and disassociates himself from his friendship, even without a manifest cause, for the rank of the sincere mendicant is too exalted for him to lie. Let the emir examine himself; he will find that the shaykh is telling the truth in characterizing him as unjust and a wrongdoer, Exalted God willing.

I heard Mawlānā Shaykh al-Islām Zakarīyā, may God have mercy on him, say: "It is polite of the emir to love the mendicant more when he puts him down, disassociates himself from him, severely rebukes him, and doesn't flatter him. Any emir who is annoyed by that sort of thing must be driven away by the mendicant from his friendship since it is clear that he befriended him for some reason other than God, may He be honored and glorified, unless the mendicant wants to continue the friendship to enable him to straighten the emir's crookedness. Then there is no harm in continuing the friendship." Praise God, Lord of the worlds.

[91] For the emir to be polite to the mendicant, he also should not allow him to eat a single morsel of his food, even if the mendicant forgets and absentmindedly eats, in order to protect his shaykh's person from being defiled inside by his food and to prevent his prayers to Exalted God to solve his problems from being weakened. If the emir allows him to eat a single morsel of his food, he betrays their friendship, as has been set forth in this book. Praise God, Lord of the worlds.

For the emir to be polite to the mendicant, he also should accept that he prays for his dismissal or that he be beaten, if he does wrong, is unjust, kills people, and violates the boundaries set by God, and that this is tantamount to his fate as decreed by the Exalted Real for no ascertainable reason. If he does not accept this, at least by being patient, once patience runs out, there is nothing left but anger and impatience at what God has fated, and everyone agrees that that is forbidden.

I heard Sayyidī ʿAlī al-Khawwāṣ, may God have mercy on him, say, "The emir must believe that the mendicant is kinder to him than he is to himself and that he prays to God only for what he knows will benefit the emir in his faith and worldly affairs." I heard him say, "For the emir to be polite to the mendicant, he should love him more whenever he sees a poison arrow coming toward him in the darkness of the night, if he does wrong and is unjust, and [think] that the mendicant intends to purify him and lessen his sin by his death." [The Prophet Muḥammad], may God bless and save him, said, "If You intend to cause Your servants affliction, take me to You now, without affliction." The mendicant prays for the emir's death only out of love for him, so let the emir be joyful and happy with his shaykh's cursing him, if he cannot repent. Praise God, Lord of the worlds.

For the emir to be polite to the mendicant, he also should not ask him to obtain an office or allow him to continue in it unless he is totally just and never, ever commits injustice, or unless he is more righteous than others would be. This is rarer than red sulfur; in this age most offices are nothing but wrongdoing, injustice, and great sin. Any emir who asks his shaykh to help him obtain something sinful betrays the friendship, since it is required of the mendicant that he wish for the emir only what he wishes for himself. It is well-known that were officials to offer the mendicant the post of tribal chief, tax agent, subprovincial governor, vizier, or market inspector and they offered him a lot of money in exchange, he would not agree. Even if the mendicant knew that he would behave justly, he would take precautions to protect himself. The divine grace might abandon the mendicant, leaving him to commit wrongs and injustices and to seize people's property illegally. If this might happen to the mendicant, what about the emir?

I heard Sayyidī 'Alī al-Khawwāṣ, may God have mercy on him, say: "Just as mendicants violate their duties in their friendship with emirs, emirs violate their duties in their friendship with mendicants. In most cases, there is nothing left but deceit, fraud, and pretending on both sides. If it happens that one claims to be sincere, this is rare." Praise God, Lord of the worlds.

[92] For the emir to be polite to the mendicant, he should also accept his judgment just as he would accept the judgment of his master. If the emir does not accept the mendicant's judgment, the mendicant cannot be his friend, since he has gone beyond the limits of good manners. We are talking about the sincere mendicant who renounces the world and will not accept his emir's alms, gifts, or presents. As for the insincere mendicant, the emir is not obliged to accept his judgment because he does not deserve it. Indeed, his insincerity and fraud may become apparent to the emir, who beats and imprisons him to teach him a lesson, as happened to our friend Emir Yūsuf ibn Abī Iṣba' with a certain imposter. The emir had full faith in him, thinking the best of others, and would hold feasts in his honor, invite mendicants, devotees, and reciters of praise poetry, seek his blessing, and wipe his face on his robe. Then it became apparent that he was an imposter without a whiff of righteousness. The emir had him stretched out and severely beaten; his head was shaved and his wool turban torn off. The intelligent man will learn a lesson from this and examine his friend before entering into a friendship with an emir or a mendicant. Praise God, Lord of the worlds.

For the emir to be polite to the mendicant, he should also accept his refusal to let the emir visit him, his public aversion to that, and his severe rebuke if he disobeys and visits him. He must not ask the mendicant about the reason for his refusal to let him visit him since informing him of this might lead to harm or lower the station of one of his peers. Similarly, if the mendicant knows that his peers are being incited to jealousy by the visits of this emir, refusing to let him visit protects his brother's faith from being reduced. If the mendicant says to the emir, "I refused you only for fear that my brother so-and-so's heart would turn against me," he opens the door to putting down his aforementioned brother and accusing him of jealousy and selfish envy. It is polite of the emir not to ask about the reason why the mendicant refuses to allow him to visit, and it is polite of the mendicant too not to mention the reason, thereby fulfilling his duty to his friend.

I heard my brother Afḍal al-Dīn, may God have mercy on him, say, "The emir is to the mendicant like a bad slave with his generous, good master; he rebukes the emir only when he does something harmful, just as the master rebukes his bad slave only when he goes beyond the limits of good manners." Know this, emirs, and act on it. Praise God, Lord of the worlds.

For the emir to be polite to the mendicant, he also should not feel scorn for him if the mendicant complains of his and his dependents' straitened circumstances. It may be that the mendicant complained to him of his and his dependents' straitened circumstances to open the door for him to pleasing God and being satisfied with a modest livelihood, if Exalted God causes him to have straitened circumstances. The shaykh would say to the emir, "Look at my straitened circumstances and be patient as I have been patient." The emir is not permitted to scorn someone with this perspective; indeed, his duty is to venerate him and imitate him. The mendicant ceased to love the world more than the human minimum the day he began to love the people's path. Every day he finds lunch and dinner is like a feast day for him, and every day he has more worldly goods is like a black day for him. Indeed, my brother Afḍal al-Dīn said to me, "I would prefer to lose my beloved son and my virtuous wife and see my wealth vanish than to have them return after I had lost them." Let the emir be extremely cautious of the danger of belittling the station of the mendicant, if he complains to him about straitened circumstances. Praise God, Lord of the worlds.

[93] For the emir to be polite to the mendicant, he also should, every now and then, offer him his best money, clothes, food, and drink to manifest his great love for him and to demonstrate that he is not withholding from him any of his precious wealth. It is for the emir to offer, and for the mendicant to refuse.

I heard Sayyidī ʿAlī al-Khawwāṣ, may God have mercy on him, say: "The emir must explain the shaykh's station in renunciation and caution to his brethren, asking God, may He be honored and glorified, to protect his shaykh from the negative consequences that result from publicizing his high station. How pleasant it is when the emir offers and the shaykh refuses, unlike if the emir does the opposite, which is extremely unpleasant because it contains a whiff of miserliness on the part of the emir and lack of caution and a diminished soul on the part of the mendicant." Know this, emirs, and offer your shaykh your most precious wealth, even if you know for certain that he will refuse, to show your peers how close he is to you. Praise God, Lord of the worlds.

For the emir to be polite to the mendicant, he should have sincere intentions whenever he goes out to visit him. There should be no worldly or otherworldly motive to visit him such as his helping him to be appointed to office or taking his hand during the tribulations and terrors of the Resurrection. If he goes out for a worldly or otherworldly intention, he is impolite to the mendicant and ceases to be perfectly manly or to follow the etiquette of friendship.

I heard my brother Afḍal al-Dīn, may God have mercy on him, say: "Any emir who seeks to befriend a mendicant should not do so for a worldly or otherworldly motive. No, he should do so purely for the sake of the Generous God; then the emir's problems in both abodes will be solved quickly because of the absence of motives that slow down the solving of one's problems and stand between a man and their solution, as people have experienced." This is something rarer than red sulfur; one rarely finds it in an emir. Most emirs befriend the mendicant only for worldly or otherworldly motives, and that is obviously deficient. Praise God, Lord of the worlds.

For the emir to be polite to the mendicant, he should not demand that his shaykh fulfill the conditions of friendship unless the emir knows that he is truly righteous in his words, deeds, and beliefs—and how could he do that? Similarly, he should not demand his help in obtaining appointment to office unless he knows this office was apportioned to him in pre-eternity,[120] lest he waste his shaykh's time. Even then, his request should be expressed by manifesting want and need, just as when the servant asks his Lord to solve his problems.

120. Pre-eternity is the period before God's creation of the world.

I heard Sayyidī ʿAlī al-Khawwāṣ, may God have mercy on him, say: "The aṣḥāb al-nawba may oppose the shaykh in appointing his emir to a certain office, which they have already singled out for an emir who believes in them and in other saints. The emir must not demand it from his shaykh since it is up to the aṣḥāb al-nawba, especially if it is not free from negative consequences, as has been stated repeatedly." I heard him say: "Few mendicants these days know that they are subject to the authority of the aṣḥāb al-nawba in this. One may try to get an emir appointed without their permission but be unable [94] to achieve it by any means. Had he known that he was subject to their authority, he would have asked them for this and waited to see whether they appointed him or not, as we have explained in the book *Advice for Callow Jurists and Gullible Mendicants on Befriending Emirs,* which is a rare book that those who befriend emirs cannot do without. Praise God, Lord of the worlds.

This is the end of what Exalted God has inspired me to say concerning the etiquette of mendicants in befriending emirs and vice versa, by way of brevity and summary. Praise God who guided us to this. Had God not guided us, we would have had no guidance. May God make it purely for His noble sake, and benefit by it the author, he who copies it, he who hears it, and he who views it. I advise all the brethren, should Exalted God grant that any of them acts on the contents of the book, to be grateful for his Lord's favor and not consider himself superior to those not fated to act on it or on part of it, as do those disciples who have not been weaned from human follies at the hands of sincere shaykhs well familiar with the intrigues of the soul, thus acting on the words of the Lord Jesus, may God bless and save him: "People fall into two categories, those who suffer tribulations and those who are cured. Have mercy on those who suffer tribulations and thank God for good health, praise God alone." The author, ʿAbd al-Wahhāb ibn Aḥmad ibn ʿAlī al-Shaʿrānī, the Cairene, said, "The first draft of this treatise was completed on the 27th of Ramaḍān, may it be held in high esteem, in the year 951.[121] Praise God, Lord of the worlds.

121. December 12, 1544.

Excerpts from the *Abbreviation*

[page 100]

Thanks to Exalted God, I befriended Emir Ḥusām al-Dīn ibn Baghdād and his children. To date, I have not accepted any of their gifts, tasted their food or drink, nor worn their clothes, nor used their bedding. If it so happens that one of them sends me some honey or lentils to the zāwiya, for example, I won't taste any, thanks to God's protection, may He be honored and glorified, not due to my own power or might. Muḥammad ibn Baghdād brought me into the private quarters where his children were and ordered them to kiss my sandals. He opened a bottle of apple drink and said, "Humor the children and taste some of our drink, if only a counterfeit dirham's worth." I did not agree to this, and he bent over my sandals and kissed them. He said, "Humor me, then." I said, "Listen, Muḥammad, I did not befriend you to do things like this. I befriended you to help people."

[page 101]

I heard [Shaykh al-Islām Zakarīyā] say: "Do not accept any cows or sheep sent to you by officials on feast days or at other times. They are all tainted or forbidden, taken from peasants by force. Do not go easy on this sort of thing if they say to you, 'This sacrificial victim was purchased by the emir in our presence with his money at a certain market.' Anything purchased with forbidden or tainted money is no different from its source. They said to Aḥmad ibn Ḥanbal, 'What do you say about grape juice, is it permitted?' He said, 'Ask first about the money used to buy the grapes, what was its source?'" An official sent us a cow at the zāwiya. The man who brought it swore that the emir bought it in the market. Then a trustworthy person came to me and informed me that he extorted it from a tax collector who received it as a duty on cows. I returned it to the emir and said to him: "Send it to someone else; we don't need it. And don't send us anything again unless we ask first." I ordered the mendicants in the zāwiya to stop accepting any gifts whatsoever from subprovincial governors and tribal chiefs, and they did.

[page 106]

It is also part of the [mendicant's] conduct with the emir not to consent to the sins he commits, like beating peasants to force them to weigh [pay] the land tax that they cannot pay, or dragooning them into sowing, harvesting, and threshing, or similar things like extortion, and the customary criminal penalties they impose on the subjects. He must censure the emir for this and command him to return the ill-gotten gains to their rightful owners, if he knows who they are as individuals. If he does not know their individual identities, he remains at the mercy of the divine will until the accounting on the Day of Resurrection. Then, if the emir knows the individual identities of the people he has wronged and does not return to them what he has wrongfully taken from them, the religious scholar must expel him from his friendship, and publicly disavow him in this world and the Hereafter. This conduct is rarely found among mendicants these days. Indeed, I have seen one of them accept a bribe from subjects and then give it to the emir. If the emir is then asked to testify to his virtue and faithfulness, he perjures himself, without fearing that any harm will befall his body or faith. This purely is due to his love for worldly goods and ill-gotten gains.

[page 108]

I heard Sayyidī 'Alī al-Khawwāṣ, may Exalted God have mercy on him, say, "The mystic must protect himself and his friends with spiritual states, even if it hurts his body or his friends, since that, although it is of an imperfect station, is perfect knowledge." He said: "We have been preceded in this by Sayyidī Ibrāhīm al-Ja'barī, Sayyidī Muḥammad al-Ḥanafī, and Sayyidī Aḥmad al-Zāhid,[1] among others. They caused the sultan and lower-ranking officials

1. Aḥmad al-Zāhid (d. 1416) was an influential Sufi preacher associated with the Suhrawardī network.

to be unable to urinate, their bodies to swell, their eyes to be sore, and caused them to become bloated until they died or repented of their wrongdoing. Mendicants continued to do this until the beginning of the second half of the tenth century when they were deprived of power over officials as one of the signs these days that the hour is coming. Were a mendicant to implore Exalted God to teach a lesson to officials now, it would be unlikely to be answered, 'but that God might determine a matter that was done.'"[2]

Along these lines, Sayyidī Ibrāhīm al-Matbūlī used to say: "When the year 951 begins, a mendicant must not implore Exalted God to remove wrongs and sins unless he knows through a true vision of the future, in which there can be no deception, that this matter which he wants removed is not one of the signs of the hour mentioned by the Lawgiver, lest he oppose the Lawgiver in something he has informed us will happen. If he must command right and forbid wrong, let him do so solely with his tongue so as to preserve the presence of the Holy Law, without praying to Exalted God that it will not occur, lest he attempt to falsify the report of the Lawgiver."

When I was befriended by Muḥammad ibn Baghdād, may Exalted God have mercy on him, and he was responsible for much injustice and wrongdoing, I implored Exalted God, out of love for him, not hatred, to purify him of the negative influences of people, if only by his being hanged, and I informed him of this. He said, "Not out of hatred?" I said, "Not out of hatred." He said, "God is my sufficiency and the blessings of the Deputy," and was not annoyed with me because he interpreted it as being due to sincerity and a real faith in the Day of Accounting. He was hanged on Bāb

2. Sūrat al-Anfāl 8:42.

Zuwayla[3] after the last evening prayer. When they brought him to the gate, he spread a cloth on the vestibule to the gate and prayed two prayer cycles. He said to the executioner, "Do as you have been commanded." I ask God by His prophets and saints to bestow His ample mercy upon him and make his friends forgive his bad deeds. No one has been as steadfast with me as he.

[page 113]

It is also part of the [mendicant's] conduct with the emir not to eat the emir's food even if the emir swears by God that it is licit, since what is licit in the eyes of the emir may not be licit in the eyes of the shaykh because of his high station. One of the secretaries in the sultan's Dīwān[4] in Egypt whom I trust informed me that they use all of the money that is tainted exclusively for the salaries of the army and the stipends paid to mendicants on the carpet,[5] and send to the sultan's treasury only those parts of Egypt's revenues that are licit, such as the land tax and poll tax on non-Muslims. Therefore, let the brethren take care not to eat the food of emirs and soldiers. They believe that the wage which the sultan has assigned them is licit, even if it comes from tolls, wine sales, and prostitution. Stay away from that. Furthermore, do not befriend an emir who consumes this kind of wage. His first problem is that the Exalted Real will not answer your prayers on his behalf. A trustworthy witness told me that Sultan Selim the Ottoman said

3. One of the major gates of Cairo. Executions were often carried out there.

4. The governing body of the province of Egypt. The Dīwān was headed by the Ottoman governor and included military, administrative, judicial, and religious leaders.

5. A Sufi shaykh would commonly sit on a carpet while instructing his disciples.

one day to a mendicant who asked him for a stipend: "It is better for me to refuse you. Whoever consumes the wealth of kings loses the power to implore Exalted God to solve anyone's problem."

[pages 116–17]

It is also part of the [mendicant's] conduct with the emir not to neglect to protect him with the relevant verses and traditions whenever he thinks of it, so that Exalted God protects him from the evils that befall his faith and worldly goods due to his ruling contrary to the Holy Law, or one of his enemies seeking an office or an increase in the money owed to the sultan, etc., thereby fulfilling his obligation to the emir. If the emir's villages contain dikes and he fears that criminals will pierce them prematurely, causing the villages to be flooded, he should also protect them whenever it crosses his mind. Similarly, he should protect the merchants who travel to village markets from criminal highway robbers lest the merchants' property be lost and the emir be forced to reimburse the value of what the highwaymen stole on his watch.[6] Similarly, he should protect [117] the collectors of the land tax and duties from exceeding Exalted God's boundaries; if the mendicant fears that he will forget to protect the emir, the dikes, and the land tax collectors, for example, he should guide the emir to protect himself and his villages. Indeed, he is more appropriate for the task since it is his burden. Let the shaykh examine in his own mind the duties he owes before befriending him. If he finds that he can fulfill his duties as a matter of course, he can befriend him and not leave him.

6. "On his watch" is a translation of the term *darak,* which refers to the responsibility emirs had for security in rural areas under their control.

[page 120]

When enemies spread a rumor that I promised Emir Ḥusayn ibn Hammād the subprovincial governate of the region of al-Munūfiya because he asked whether he could wear my red robe that year, and then it didn't happen, my enemies said what they said against me, but not a single hair on my body changed, thank Exalted God.

[page 125]

It is also part of their [the mendicants'] conduct to have the foreknowledge to predict who will be appointed, who will be dismissed, and which of the sultan's retinue will die. If the emir asks about that, those without foreknowledge will get nothing out of the emir. If he asks him about something that takes place in another country, for example, like the death of the sultan, the dismissal of a vizier, or something similar, and he says, "I don't know," he will lose the emir's patronage, and the emir will say, if only to himself, "There is no difference between us and him." One who has true foreknowledge, on the other hand, makes the emir his slave and governs him, as happened to Sayyidī Abū al-Su'ūd al-Jāriḥī, may Exalted God have mercy on him. I saw the leading emirs, one of whom was standing before him, but he did not tell any of them "sit," since he had such true foreknowledge that he could tell any one of them what he ate at night and what he did with his children.

[page 127]

I heard Sayyidī 'Alī al-Khawwāṣ, may God have mercy on him, say, "An emir should not enter a mendicant's zāwiya until he has doffed his arrogance and pomp below the threshold to his zāwiya, so that he enters a mere mendicant like him." He said: "This is a secret unknown to most people. Indeed one of them accepts the emir's gifts and charity in wheat, lentils, honey, etc., and comes to be counted as a member of his family. Despite this, he thinks himself superior to the emir." He said: "This sort of thing is not worthy of an emir who renounces the world and does not give in to any of its temptations, except when necessary. As for one who accepts the emir's charity, this is not worthy of him unless he kisses the emir's hand or foot because of his charitable treatment of him." I once saw him, may God be pleased with him, kiss the foot of the market inspector, and a jurist rebuked him for this. He said: "This is forbidden only to those who kiss a foot for worldly objectives. I kiss his foot only because of his robe of honor, which the Exalted Real bestowed on him, in which he commands and forbids. If the goods people need are scarce in the market, he sends his crier, who calls on people to bring out their goods, and the market is filled with goods. Can you, jurist, do likewise?"

[page 129]

My brother Afḍal al-Dīn, may Exalted God have mercy on him, heard an emir insulting a group of toll collectors and financial officials. He said, "Emir, given that you are incapable of bearing the burdens of religious scholars or righteous men, how could you bear the burdens of wrongdoers and toll collectors and copy your good deeds into their records, as it is said?"

[pages 130–31]

It is also part of the [mendicant's] conduct with the emir to befriend him for the sake of Exalted God or the Hereafter, not for any worldly motive, as has been said already in the beginning of the conclusion. Let him beware of making intercessions with the emir on behalf of victims of wrongdoing into a shop where he is paid in dirhams, food, and gifts. 'Āʾisha,[7] may God have mercy on her, is supposed to have said, "Whoever intercedes with an emir and accepts a gift in exchange commits a type of major sin."

I heard one of the Banī Baghdād say about a mendicant who interceded with him: "Don't think that this guy ever intercedes for God's sake. He has made interceding with me into a shop with which to make his living by accepting the gifts of people whenever I accept his intercession." He said, "I often sense this from him and refuse his intercession to save him from consuming something forbidden." I heard him say once to a mendicant: "He is a shaykh only because I accept his intercession. If I refused, no one would have faith in him or make him a shaykh." Someone who had a country estate came to see him with his disciples who were mendicants from Cairo so that they could beg for something on the pretext of interceding for a peasant. The emir accepted his intercession and treated him with honor. He understood the emir correctly and interceded for another. The emir told his financial officer, "Write Sayyidī the Shaykh a voucher for honey, butter, and chicken." He wrote it and gave it to him. The mendicant never mentioned the intercession on his behalf again. Indeed, he forgot all about it because he was so busy with the voucher that had been written for him. The emir and his retinue made fun of that shaykh, and he said, "You have learned that what I said about him is true; he uses intercession as an expedient to beg from me." Another time, a shaykh with an estate came to him during the festival of Sayyidī

7. 'Āʾisha bint Abī Bakr was the Prophet Muḥammad's wife and a revered figure among Sunnī Muslims.

Aḥmad al-Badawī. He said to him, "It is we who should come to you, Sayyidī the Shaykh." Then the emir said to his friends: "This guy is not an Aḥmadī.[8] He just uses his attendance at the festival each year as a pretext to receive his customary payment from me." When he had written him his usual voucher, he said: "May God put an end to you and your being a shaykh. You always do us harm since we are not learned that you might learn from us, nor are we righteous that you might receive our blessing and prayers. We have no licit property for you to receive." This is what I heard from him.

There came into the presence of Emir Muḥammad the daftar a mendicant who had been living in Mecca before coming to Cairo. He said, "What brings you to our country?" He said, "To seek reward for you and our lord the sultan." He said, "How?" He said, "By your building a hospital in Mecca for foreigners and the weak who can find no one to serve and help them." The emir said, "I understood from this that his objective was to be known as one of those mendicants who intervene to help people so that the sultan hears of him and he can then pursue worldly objectives." Then [131] he said: "I will show you what he is really like by giving him some worldly object. If he is sincere, he will refuse it and continue to ask for help. If he is a hypocrite, he will forget all about his request, take what we give him, and leave." The treasurer brought him one hundred dinars and said to him, "The emir has sent you this small gift so that you can wash your clothes after traveling." He laughed and went away. He never again mentioned the hospital, and he traveled without asking the daftar for his answer. The

8. An Aḥmadī is a member of the Sufi network founded by Sayyid Aḥmad al-Badawī.

daftar's intuition that he was interested only in worldly things was shown to be true. Do not do this, brethren, if you are set up as fake shaykhs before the advent of the Anti-Christ! Officials have come to evaluate the mendicants who appear in their age just as they evaluate gold, removing those who are adulterated. There is no one like an expert to inform you. Praise God, Lord of the worlds.

[page 131]

Officials may confide in the emir about his enemy's affairs, and the emir may confide in the shaykh. The shaykh reveals this to people, and this causes great harm to the emir and to the shaykh. Such as if the emir whom the officials want to dismiss has in his possession a large sum of the sultan's money that he has gathered from the land tax. Perhaps he hears that they have decided to dismiss him, seize his property, jail him, beat him, and appoint the emir who visits the shaykh. He becomes afraid and flees with the sultan's money and hides, as has already been mentioned in this conclusion . . .

A number of trustworthy men have informed me that the sheep which subprovincial governors and tribal chiefs send to the religious scholars and the righteous every year for sacrifice are all taken from the peasants illegally and as plunder. It has become an established custom that if they don't find any sheep, they seize the price of the sheep from the peasants.

[page 138]

It is also part of the [mendicant's] conduct with the emir not to ask the emir to intercede for him in paying the toll on people's alms that come to the zāwiya, or honey, rice, wheat, butter, etc., since it is the shaykh's station to intercede for the emir, not the emir's to intercede for the shaykh. Whoever does this loses standing in the emir's heart.

Sayyidī Ibrāhīm al-Matbūlī, may God have mercy on him, said: "The mendicant should keep harm from himself and his friends only with his heart, not with his hand or tongue. If Exalted God enables him to avoid the toll, fine; otherwise, he should be silent, give the sultan's retinue their customary dues, and fulfill his responsibility in this world and the Hereafter, thereby showing chivalry and magnanimity, and fleeing from a humiliating scene before the toll collector were he to ask him for leniency in his customary dues, especially if the toll collector is a Jew and the property owner is a righteous religious scholar, in which case the situation is even more repugnant."

[pages 142–43]

It is also part of the [mendicant's] conduct with the emir who enters his town or the judge appointed by the sultan's gate to go to greet him or to approach if he sees him looking around to greet him, much less if he decides to visit him, and say to him, "May you be a friend to our country and may Exalted God bring good things to his subjects at your hands." If the emir does not look around to greet him, for example, or intend to visit him, it would be better not to greet him, acting on the saying of the Pious Predecessors,[9] may God be pleased with them, "Do not seek to be known by those who do not know you, and deny knowing those who do know you." I followed this conduct on several occasions. I would greet the pasha or judge as soon as he entered Cairo. If he

9. The Pious Predecessors (*al-salaf al-ṣāliḥ*) are the companions of the Prophet Muḥammad who are held up as model Muslims.

had heard my name or looked around to see me, I would go to him at sundown, ask to be admitted, and say to the doorkeeper, "Tell our lord, 'So-and-so whom you decided to visit has come to visit you.'" I would go in, kiss his hand, and leave. If he set aside some money for me, I would not accept it [143] even if it was licit. The learned condemn going into the presence of emirs only by those who love them and use them to obtain worldly goods.

[page 145]

In this book we have already seen the statement of Ibrāhīm al-Matbūlī, may Exalted God be pleased with him: "It is correct conduct by a saint to pretend to err in predicting the future once the second half of the tenth century begins, since that is the age of the concealment of the saints due to the hardships, terrors, injustice, and wrongdoing that will occur then. If people believe a mendicant to be a saint or venerate him, they will crowd his door and charge him with saving them from the trials, tribulations, wrongdoing, and injustice that befall them because of their evil deeds. The saint will be at a loss; the subjects cannot repent of all their sins so that God does not grant officials power over them, nor can the officials refrain from their manifest wrongdoing and injustice, which are a punishment for [their sins]."

I heard Sayyidī 'Alī al-Marṣafī, may Exalted God have mercy on him, say: "A saint should go public only for two reasons: either to guide people to the people's path, or so officials accept his intercession for victims of wrongdoing. These two tasks have become rare, so there is no longer any value in a saint going public. Indeed, the aṣḥāb al-nawba may kill him immediately, as happened to one of our brethren." When Emir Ḥasan ibn Baghdād visited me and had faith in me, and 'Abdallāh deserted me and denounced me, some enemies whispered that I said, "'Abdallāh will be hanged on a certain day and Ḥasan will take over his villages." Egypt and its villages were full of this talk. Don't ask, brother, how people insulted me. Had it been true, every emir in Egypt might have submitted to me, and the aṣḥāb al-nawba might have tried to kill me immediately.

[page 151]

If someone says, "One of the greatest saints used to eat so heartily from the food of emirs that he would eat the emir's entire banquet, what is the story?" [Sayyidī Muḥammad ibn 'Inān][10] said: "Perhaps he was one of those who possesses a spiritual state and gave all of the food to prisoners in the lands of the Franks, but people think that he ate it all. This is like what happened to Sayyidī Muḥammad al-Ḥanafī al-Shādhilī and Shaykh Muḥammad Damurdāsh."[11]

[page 153]

I once said to Muḥammad ibn Baghdād, "What are you worth now?" He said, "I am a poor man with no worldly goods." I said to him, "The mendicants have a true saying that whatever property the tax agent acquires due to the respect in which his office is held must be taken by the sultan's retinue, whether voluntarily or involuntarily." This was true, and after his death they took from him twenty-five jars filled with gold. Still, his concealing it benefited me since he left his property in the care of his friends but did not leave anything in my care for fear of revealing that he lied to me

10. Muḥammad ibn 'Inān (d. 1516) was the disciple of and later successor to Ibrāhīm al-Matbūlī.

11. Muḥammad Damurdāsh (d. ca. 1524), a prominent shaykh of the Khalwatī network, fled Tabriz when it was occupied by the Safavids and went to Cairo.

when he said, "I am a poor man." Everyone whom he entrusted with some of his property suffered grievous harm until he confessed to the property he was holding, except me. I did not suffer a whiff of harm.

[page 157]

It is also part of the [emir's] conduct with the mendicant not to leave his door and service if the mendicant drives him away, and not to meet with any of his peers, for that would confirm his shaykh's hatred for him. Whoever was no good in the past will be no good in the future. Since the mendicant has left behind the soul's follies, the emir can annoy him only by a sin that obliges the mendicant to drive him away, such as the emir's forcing the mendicants and the indigent among his subjects to dig wells, draw water, plow, harvest, or thresh. He prevents the mendicant from plowing his own land or harvesting his crop, for example, until the land dries out or the crop goes bad, and then imprisons him for paying insufficient land tax, or he forgets that the inability of the peasant to pay part of his land tax is purely because the emir forced him to labor, as we have mentioned. This is something that has become customary among the subprovincial governors and tax agents, and they no longer consider them sins for which they should ask their Lord's forgiveness, although these are the acts of tyrants. I once abandoned one of the Banī Baghdād because he forced people to labor and mistreated them. He began to visit the shrine of Imām al-Shāfiʿī, saying, "Imām al-Shāfiʿī is sufficient support to protect me from officials." I said to him, "If Imām al-Shāfiʿī were alive and they brought your case before him, he would rule that you must be dismissed from office and your lands ruined, or that it is permissible to kill you." He paid no attention to what I said. I wrote a question and sent it to the tomb of Imām al-Shāfiʿī, may God be pleased with him. I said: "What is our lord's opinion, may God be pleased with him, about a tribal chief who imposes forced labor on the poor and the indigent, forces their children and their beasts to plow his land, dig his wells, harvest his crops, thresh his wheat, etc., and prevents any of them from taking his own crop or going to preserve it until it is ruined, and makes them responsible for the tax on all his crops? He doesn't reduce the land tax by a single dirham; he takes the tax from lands that the Nile water has not reached; he seizes one neighbor from another, one in-law from another, individual peasants from the inhabitants of the villages who have fled and escaped with their children from frequent wrongdoing; and he loots those who remain behind, leaving them neither beasts, nor wheat, nor anything else. Is it permissible for the ruler to appoint such a person over the Muslims? If he is dismissed by officials who seize his property, put him in prison, beat him as punishment, and kill him for the people he had killed by some criminals, do they sin thereby or not?" That night I dreamed that Imām al-Shāfiʿī ruled that he should be killed. A few days later, they hanged him on Bāb Zuwayla.

[pages 163–64]

I heard Sayyidī ʿAlī al-Khawwāṣ, may God have mercy on him, say: "A tribal chief, subprovincial governor, or agent who collects what is owed to the sultan is entitled only to that part of the money he collects from the peasants and others that constitutes his customary wage, as was established in the beginning [of his term in office]. Any increase over the aforementioned wage is totally forbidden. This assumes that the sultan or his deputy has not assigned him some part of this money. If they have assigned him some part of it, then that is clear." He said: "The emir who collects the land tax and other licit funds due to the sultan is not permitted to give some of it to a beggar or poet, nor to spend it liberally on his household for his children or guests so that they call him generous. The soul of the sultan or his deputy cannot permit something like this, if he hears of it." Know this, emirs, and let each of you perform an inquest on himself about the wrongs he committed and money he seized illegally from the subjects and spent on undeserving people while he was in office. Let him beware of the vanity of poets praising him in front of his guests and others if he is known for his generosity. Generosity is not praiseworthy unless it is licit. The common saying goes: "If you feed orphans by renting out your vagina, it would be better not to fornicate and not to give alms."

When they arrested Emir ʿĀmir ibn Baghdād to be executed, and he was known for his generosity, this was one of the things the Pasha Mehmed rebuked him for: "Remember, ʿĀmir, how liberal you were with the sultan's funds? How you stood leaning on your cane from sunset until the first part of the night had passed [164] saying, 'Feed such-and-such tribe, feed the peasants, feed the ʿArab al-Aṭāyā, feed Muḥārib'?[12] Don't you know that this was the sultan's property?" This is what he told me before his death, may God have mercy on him.

[pages 167–68]

It is also part of the [emir's] conduct with the mendicant not to oblige him to speak on his behalf to the officials of the town so that his office is returned to him if they have dismissed him since

12. The groups named appear to be tribes that received the emir's patronage.

this may not work. The shaykh knows that every office comes from the presence of the sultan and must therefore be obtained through the mediation of the aṣḥāb al-nawba in the sultan's town. Let the emir have patience with the shaykh until the problem is solved at the sultan's gate. If it is solved there, it will be solved here. The intelligent man does things the right way . . .

I heard a chief judge say: "The viziers pay no attention to the prosperity of the material that is the source of the sultan's revenue. If a person increases the tax on the land so much that it is not reasonable to think that it can be collected from the subjects, they permit him that, and when he fails to collect it, they punish him." I once said to the judge of al-Khānqāh, "The villages have been ruined by injustice." He said: "The sultan's retinue pays attention only to the prosperity of the households of Cairo and their inhabitants. As for the peasants, they pay no attention to their suffering and ruin." Then he said to me, "Who, walking from Bāb Zuwayla to Bāb al-Sha'rīya and seeing these huge crowds and streets full of people,[13] would say that Egypt has been ruined?" Know [168] this, emirs, and know the time in which you live and what its people deserve. If you would ask that there be no unjust rulers, first ask Exalted God to create for you a new heaven and a new earth, or that the world return to its beginning. Then ask Him to remove injustice from the world.

. . . I have already said that I have continually been tested by those who belittled me to the emirs, tribal chiefs, daftars, and chief judges who have faith in me, but the army of the Real defeats the

13. Bāb Zuwayla and Bāb al-Sha'rīya, two of the major gates of Cairo, were located in some of the most densely populated and commercially active neighborhoods in the city.

army of the Devil, and they, especially the Banī Baghdād, pay no attention to what the enemy says. Exalted God has continually sent me enemies to put me down; whenever one passes away, to this day, he has been succeeded by another. May God give me the best preparation with each emir who befriends me and forgive every enemy He sends me.

[page 173]

I heard my brother Afḍal al-Dīn, may God have mercy on him, say, "One sign of the emir's evil intention is that thieves and bandits proliferate during his time in office, and that Exalted God so diminishes respect for him in the hearts of the subjects that thieves may steal his beasts from his house, not to mention the beasts of the subjects, as happened to some tribal chiefs."

Index

al-Aḥkām al-sulṭāniya (Rules for Governance), 111
Aḥmad al-Badawī, 216
Aḥmad al-Sha'rāni, 6
Aḥmad al-Zāhid, 209–10
Aḥmad ibn Ḥanbal, 136n85, 208
Aḥmadī Sufi network, 8, 141n86
Aḥmad Pasha, 9
'Ā'isha bint Abī Bakr, 215
Akbar the Great, 15
Aleppo, 4
'Alī al-Khawwāṣ, 5, 7, 8, 29, 32, 34, 36–37, 54–55, 66, 71, 96, 102, 104, 105, 109, 115, 129, 132, 145–46, 148–49, 156, 170–71, 176, 180, 181, 183, 184–85, 187, 193, 194–95, 200, 201, 205, 209, 213–14, 222–23; on acceptance of emir's gifts, 63–64, 65, 79–80, 131; on appointments, 60, 187–88; on bearing hardship, 156–57; on befriending wrongdoer, 85–86; on conditions for mendicant befriending emir, 47–48, 51–52, 72, 76, 78, 201; on dispute testimony, 165–66; on distribution to the poor, 108; on emir's faith in mendicant, 40–41; on emir's faith in shaykh, 175; on emir's glorification, 136–37; on emir's honesty, 167; on emir's love of gold, 134–35; on emir's misfortunes, 69, 112–13; on emir's sins, 82, 83; on enemy, 113–14; on intercession, 92, 93, 132–33, 141–42, 145, 191; on mendicant's control over emir, 189–90; on mendicant's deceit, 121; on mendicant's gift for revelation, 74; on mendicant's modesty, 126–27; on mendicant's promises, 81; on mendicant's refusal of emir's food, 79–80, 100; on mendicant's self-sufficiency, 143; on mendicant's sincere motives, 88–89, 122, 132, 146–47; on mendicant's solving of emir's problems, 152–54, 159–60; on mendicant's superiority, 64, 123; on mendicant's tact, 117; on politeness, 151; on Protected Tablet, 179–80; on retaliation against enemy, 139; on reversal of injustice, 141; on vanquishing enemy, 159
'Alī al-Marṣafī. *See* Nūr al-Dīn 'Alī al-Marṣafī
'Alī ibn Abī Ṭālib (fourth caliph), 5
'Alī Pasha, 11
alms, 51n16, 66, 131, 149–50, 217
alms tax, 51n36
amīr. *See* emir
'Āmir Ibn Baghdād, 140, 223
amulets, 24
Anatolia, 2, 3, 4
anger, 161, 192–93
Ankara, Battle of (1402), 2
al-Anṣārī, Zakarīyā, 7
Anushiravan (Khosrau I), 111
appetites, indulging of, 185–86
appointments, 48–49, 60, 183–84, 187–88, 194–95, 196, 197, 205
'aqīqa (naming ceremony), 102

Arabic language, 4
arbāb al-aḥwāl (type of saint), 83
Ardabil, 3
ʿārif (mystic), 21
arrogance, 135
aṣḥāb al-nawba (type of saint), 83, 205, 224
Ashʿarism (theological school), 12
Ashraf al-Qānṣūh al-Ghūrī, Sultan, 3, 4, 189–90
al-Ashraf Shaʿbān, Sultan, 153–54
ʿaskarī class, 22
ʿAṭāʾ ibn Abī Rabbāḥ, 104
awqāf. See endowments
awrād. See invocations
axial saint, 13, 14, 162, 163

al-Badawī, Sayyid Aḥmad, 8, 141n86
bad manners. *See* manners
Bakrī lineage of scholars, 8
bandits, 225
Banī Baghdād, 9, 10, 18, 46, 98, 215, 221–22, 225
Banī ʿUmar, 9, 10, 46
Bayezid II, Sultan, 2, 4
beverages, 153, 154
blessings, 33–34
Book, the. *See* Qurān
Book of Conduct, The (al-Shaʿranī), 142
bribes, 47, 145, 160, 209
burden shifting, 155–56, 178, 185
bureaucracy, 2, 5
Byzantine Empire, 2

Cairo, 2, 3, 4–5, 17, 216, 218, 224; principal gates of, 84; *zāwiya*s in, 6, 10, 20
Çaldiran, Battle of (1514), 4
caliphate, 13, 14, 15, 58, 85n67, 104n76, 111n78, 183
charity, 94, 112–13, 123, 135, 144, 152, 214; distribution of, 20, 108; mendicant's refusal of, 48, 106
children, 20, 44, 140, 186
Circle of Justice, 16–17
clothing, 62, 79, 139–40, 150, 153, 154, 162, 180, 183, 207
code of conduct, 20–21, 28, 36, 44, 56, 73, 75, 76, 99, 156, 219; of emir, 151–52, 221–24; of mendicant, 120, 121, 122, 124, 127, 135, 141, 146, 190, 208–9, 211–12, 217–18; religious, 24; al-Shaʿrānī's book on, 142. *See also* manners
conscience, 75, 76
Constantinople, 2, 5
contentment, 64, 142
corruption, 187
cosmos, 80n58
cursing standards, 38, 61

daftardār, 34–35, 34n18, 35n31, 59–60, 65, 118, 120, 128, 140, 147, 148
Damascus, 4, 25
Darwīsh, Qāḍī, 151
Dashīsha of the Khāṣṣikīya, 150, 155
David, 14, 70, 107
Day of Accounting, 210

Day of Judgment, 19
Day of Reckoning, 97
Day of Resurrection, 76, 92, 114, 123, 177–78, 179–80, 209
death. *See* Hereafter
debtor, 150
dependency, 20, 54
deviancy, 70
Devil (Iblīs), 24, 139, 225; deception by, 80, 81; expulsion from Paradise of, 158–59
disciple, 163–64
divine. *See* God
Dīwān, 211
dream interpretation, 24

Egypt, 2, 9–12, 25, 104n76, 118–19, 224; *daftardārs* of, 60; economic assets of, 5; Islamic Empire and, 104n76; licit revenues of, 211; Ottoman conquest of, 1, 4, 5, 9–10, 22, 24–25; two major Sufi movements, 8. *See also* Cairo
emir, 17–25; acceptance of fate, 199–200; alms and, 66; anger of, 193; appointments and dismissals and, 60, 183, 184, 194–95; bribes to, 47; burdens of, 67–68; characterizations of, 196; competition for friendship of, 108–9, 125–26; connotation of term, 18–19; consolidation in office of, 57; deception and, 75–76, 182; dependency and, 54; distribution of worldly goods by, 53, 55, 183; enemies of, 45–46, 61, 98–99, 132, 135, 138–39, 158, 177, 188–89, 192–93; enemy's reconciliation with, 135; faults of, 58–59, 119–20, 137, 181–82; feasts and food of (*see* food); fraud in office by, 160, 183, 188; gifts from (*see* gifts from emir); glorification of, 136–37; good manners of, 151; humility and, 56–57; imprisonment and, 92, 97–98; income sources of, 107; indulgence of appetites of, 185–86; integrity and, 49, 167; intercessions and (*see* intercession); mendicant's befriending of (*see* mendicant-emir friendship); misfortunes of, 67–69; mistreatment of subjects by, 84, 90, 93, 156; office seeking by, 48, 80, 159–61; piety and goodness of, 121, 137; punishment of, 85; purification of sins of, 63, 95–96, 97, 169; reliance on, 145–46; religious disobedience by, 82; repentance of, 178; reputation protection and, 116–17; rival's defeat and, 158; self-recognition of impurities of, 135–36; shaykhs and (*see* shaykh); signs of evil intentions of, 225; sins of, 75–76, 82–83, 84, 85, 115, 208–9; standing in presence of, 136; subjects ("flock") of, 50, 50n33, 130; tax collection and (*see* land tax); training of, 50–51; treatment of rival of, 70–72;

God, 34, 70, 85, 127, 161, 164–65, 176, 185, 186, 199, 206, 210, 214, 224–25; blessings of, 51, 58; caliphate and, 13; divine conduct and, 184; divine election and, 75; divine inspiration and, 7; divine processions and, 81–82; etiquette of mendicant-emir friendship and, 205; as Exalted Real, 63, 69, 139, 177–78, 187, 188, 193, 211; expulsion of Iblīs and, 158–59; forbearing and, 139; forgiveness and, 178; as Glorious, 62–63; help from, 157; Holy Law and, 16; human reciprocity and, 23; humility valuation by, 56; injustice and, 224; intercession with, 84, 158, 172; intermediaries and, 157, 177; as the Lofty, 62–63; Messenger of (*see* Muḥammad, Prophet); monotheism and, 162–63; obligated obedience to commands of, 28n1; power of saints and, 75; Protected Tablet and, 50, 80–81, 179–80; retaliation against enemy and, 113–14, 139; revelation from, 75, 119; shyness before, 62; three pious phrases and, 65; the wronged and, 114–15
gold, love of, 134–35
good deeds, 53
good manners. *See* manners
government officials, categories of, 22

ḥadīth, 136nn84, 85
Hajj, 2
Hapsburg dynasty, 15
hardship, bearing of, 155–57
Hārūn al-Rashīd, Caliph, 58n42
Ḥasan Ibn Baghdād, 140, 219–20
Ḥasan the *daftardār,* 34, 60, 65
Ḥasan the *ṣanjaq,* Emir, 140
hatred, 135, 143–44
Ḥaydar, Shaykh, 3
Hejaz, 1, 2
Hell, 67, 136, 146, 177; bridge over, 78–79
Hereafter, 48, 49, 53, 56, 59, 96, 116, 138, 214; accounts and balances and, 97, 114, 210; Day of Reckoning and, 97; emir's hardships in, 78; emir's reward in, 176; emir's sins and, 82; entrance into, 78–79; Iblīs's expulsion from Paradise and, 158–59; mendicant's knowledge about, 133–34; penetration of vision into, 96; punishment in, 161; purification of sins and, 97; rank in, 137; weighing of good and evil deeds and, 53n39. *See also* Paradise, Iblīs's expulsion from
hidden saint, 83, 219
hierarchy, manifest and hidden, 13
holy fools, 7, 50–51, 83, 83n63
Holy Law (*sharī'a*), 13, 14, 28, 50n15, 92, 102, 121, 123, 133, 165, 180, 210, 211, 212; emir's learning in, 43, 44; exemption from, 83, 83n63; interpreter of, 21; justice and, 23; schools of, 6, 30n11; secular law and, 16; two sources of, 30n10

Holy War, 84–85
honesty, 88–89, 167
humility, 55, 56–57, 99, 173–74
Ḥusām al-Dīn ibn Baghdād, Emir, 207
Ḥusayn ibn Hammād, 213
hypocrite, sign of, 174

Iblīs. *See* Devil
Ibn Abī al-Ḥama'il al-Sarawī, 164
Ibn al-'Arabī, *al-Futūḥāt al-Makkīya*, 12
Ibn al-Zarzīrī, 148–49
Ibn 'Awad, Shams al-Dīn, Judge, 189–90
Ibrāhīm (Egyptian *daftardār*), 60
Ibrāhīm al-Ja'barī, 84–85, 209–10
Ibrāhīm al-Matbūlī, 7, 101, 165, 177, 198, 210, 218, 219, 220n10
Ibrāhīm ibn Adham, 103–4
Ibrāhīm Pasha, 9, 15
illegality, 19
illiteracy, 7
Imāmī Shī'ism, 3
immorality, 19, 96
imposters, 136–37, 201
imprisonment, 92, 97–98
incense, 153
India, 1
Indian Ocean, 3, 5
infidels, 146
injustice, 161–62, 200, 224–25; hanging as punishment for, 210–11; reversal of, 23–24, 141–42
integrity, 49, 108, 109, 127, 167
intercession, 115–19, 163, 177, 181, 187, 195; emir's acceptance of, 191; emir's rejection of, 175; with God, 84, 158, 172; by mendicant, 19, 57, 58, 59, 76, 82, 90–93, 94, 109–11, 117–18, 121, 141, 144–45, 172, 176, 187, 191, 215–16; for mendicant, 217–18; power of, 19; to reverse injustice, 23–24, 141–42; between rivals, 132–33; by saint, 219
invocations, 51, 65–66
Iran, 1, 3, 4, 111n79
Iraq, 1, 3, 111n79
Iskandar, Emir (subprovincial governor of al-Gharbīya), 140
Islam: death and, 78; equality of all Muslims and, 147; first two caliphs of, 14; holy cities of, 2; holy law of (*see* Holy Law); holy shrines of, 2, 5; Mamluk defenders of, 2; millennium and, 14–15; political theory and, 12–17; "protected people" and, 92–93; Shī'a and, 3, 4; universal community of, 186. *See also* Muḥammad, Prophet; Sufism; Sunnī Islam
Islamic Empire, 104n76
Islamic law. *See* Holy Law
Ismail, Shah of Iran, 3, 4, 15
Istanbul. *See* Constantinople

Jānim al-Ḥamzāwī, Emir, 9, 34
Jesus, 157, 205
Judgment Day, 19
judiciary, 20, 22, 120, 128, 151, 183

al-Junayd, 72–73, 87, 94
jurist, 21, 28, 30, 30n11
justice, 16–17, 23–24, 130

Kaaba, 103n74
kanun (body of laws), 15–16
Kanuni Sulaymān, 15
Kanunname (administrative code), 9–10
karāma (saintly miracle), 75n54
Khā'irbak, 4
al-Khawwāṣ, Sayyidī 'Alī. *See* 'Alī al-Khawwāṣ
al-Khiḍr, 163–64; *Testament* of, 161, 193
Khiḍr, emir of the Hājj, 140
khilāfa. *See* caliphate
khirqa. *See* Sufi cloak
Khosrau I (Arushiravan), 111
khuluq. *See* code of conduct
king. *See* ruler
knowledge, 133–34

land tax, 47, 103, 129, 142, 191, 211, 212, 217, 221, 222–23, 224
law, 6, 15–16; Shāfi'ī school of, 7, 30n11. *See also* Holy Law
lies, 196–97
living saints, 19, 24
Lofty, the, 62–63
Lotus Tree, 80, 80n58
love, 44, 89, 121, 134, 135, 137–38, 144

madrasa, 6, 153
Madyan, Sayyidī, 129
magic, 71–72
Mahdī, 15–16
maḥyā prayer, 7
Māmāy, Emir, 91–92
Mamluk Empire, 2–5, 7, 9, 10, 59n41, 189n112
manifest hierarchy, 13
manifest sovereignty, 13
manliness, 20, 46, 100, 150, 155–57, 185, 186, 202
manners, 20–21, 151, 155
Marj Dābiq, Battle of (1516), 189n112
masters of states, 83–84
al-Matbūlī, Ibrāhīm. *See* Ibrāhīm al-Matbūlī
Mawlānā (honorific), 21
Mecca, 2, 5, 216; Sacred Mosque, 103–4
mediation. *See* intercession
Medina, 2, 5
Mehmed, Pasha, 223
Mehmed II, Sultan, 2, 9
mendicant, 17, 21, 28, 36, 66; abstention and, 99–101; authentic revelation and, 74; authority of, 191; balance sheet of, 62; caution of, 120; charity and, 48, 106; complaints of straitened circumstances of, 202–3; contentment of, 64, 142; deprivation of power of, 210; emir relationship with (*see* mendicant-emir friendship); enemies of, 108–9, 177; feast attendance and, 168–69; fraud and, 201; freedom from emir, 132; garments given away by, 140; God's

Qurān, 87, 134, 146; expulsion of Iblīs and, 158n99; forbidding of fraud and, 160; justice injunction and, 23; sin of prophets and, 76; interpreter of spiritual meaning and, 13; Sufi miracles and wonders and, 30
Qurān schools, 6
quṭb. *See* axial saint

ra'īya (emir's subjects), 50n33
Ramaṭān, breaking the fast of, 94–95
Real, the. *See* God
Red Sea, 5
religious exemplar, 24
religious practices, 13, 24, 81
religious scholars, 6
renunciation of world, 54, 77–78, 105, 107, 135, 143–44, 171
repentance, 19, 82, 119, 178
reputation, 50, 64, 65, 70, 86, 107–8, 115, 116–17, 147, 165, 181, 182, 186–87
Resurrection Day. *See* Day of Resurrection
retaliation, 113–14, 139
revelation, 74, 75, 88, 119, 179
Revival of the Religious Sciences (Ghazālī), 23, 80n57
righteousness, 24, 39, 43, 70, 74, 137, 147, 185, 200; bridge over Hell and, 78n55; eating of food and, 44; indications of, 171; prayers of, 56; preconditions for, 77–78; requirement of, 62; of shaykh, 204
ruler, 14–17, 142; power of, 111–12, 191; role of, 16; sacralization of, 14, 15; service to, 73–74

Sacred Mosque (Mecca), 103–4
sacrifice, 133, 217
Safavid dynasty, 1, 3, 4, 15, 220n11
saint, 30n12, 31n13, 46n10, 50n15, 53, 55, 61, 62, 80, 81, 141n86, 205, 219–20, 224; axial, 13, 14, 162, 163; hidden, 83, 219; indications of, 171; interpretive function of, 13, 15; living, 19, 24; masters of states and, 83–84; miracles performed by, 75
salvation, 19
ṣanjaq, 33–34, 34n18, 46, 137
Sasanid Empire, 111n79
Sayyidī (honorific), 21
Sayyidī the Shaykh, 216
secrets, 51–52, 111–12
secularism, 14, 15–16
self-sufficiency, 142–43, 146
Selim I, Sultan, 2, 4–5, 140, 189n112, 211–12
serpent, 158n99
Seventh Heaven, 80n58
Shādhilī Sufi network, 8, 153n91
al-Shāfi'ī, Imām, 30, 160, 183, 221, 222
Shāfi'ī school of law, 7, 30n11
al-Sha'rānī, 'Abd al-Wahhāb: authoritative teachers and, 7; concept of justice of, 23–24; life of, 5–11; political influence of, 22; principal

distinction between *Advice* and *Abbreviation* of, 18; Sufi political theology and, 12–17; Sufi school of law and, 30n11; Sufism and, 8–9; works of: *The Abbreviation of Advice for Callow Jurists and Gullible Mendicants on Befriending Emirs,* 12, 13, 18–25, 207–25; *Advice for Callow Jurists and Gullible Mendicants on Befriending Emirs,* 12, 13, 17–25, 27–206; *The Book of Conduct,* 142; *al-Fulk al-mashḥūn,* 103; *al-Minan al-wusṭā,* 14; *al-Yawāqit wal-jawāhir fi bayān ʿulūm al-akābir,* 12
al-Shaʿrānī, Aḥmad, 6
sharīʿa. See Holy Law
shaykh, 9, 17–25, 54, 180–87, 193; befriending of, 212; clothes of, 180; emir's deception of, 182; emir's faith in, 174, 175, 178–79, 186, 204; emir's fulfillment of promises to, 174; emir's gifts and, 41, 55, 162; emir's trust in, 186; enemy of, 181; functions of, 24, 163–64; help from, 184–85; honoring of, 174; as intermediary, 177, 178, 187, 194; mendicant and, 43–44, 46, 52, 77, 197–98, 215–16; more than one, 164; privacy of, 197–98; protection by, 155; refusal of emir's offers by, 203; reputation of, 186–87; revelation of future by, 179; station of, 175, 203
Shaykhūn, Emir, 153–54
sheep, sacrificial, 217
Shīʿa Islam, 3, 4
Shūnī, Nūr al-Dīn, 7
sincerity, 33, 88–90, 93–94, 196–97, 198, 199, 201; of emir, 166–67, 204; signs of, 98, 99, 105, 106–7, 120, 122, 132, 146
sins, 116, 119, 146, 180, 216, 219, 221; axial saint's protection from, 13; of emir, 82–83, 84, 85, 115, 117, 135, 182, 208–9; entrance into Hereafter and, 78; enumeration of, 82, 84, 156, 178; intercession with God for, 84, 172; mendicant's conscience and, 76; men of mercy and, 84; minor, 82, 156; prophets and, 76; purification of, 62, 63, 95–96, 97; repentance for, 19, 82; types of, 82, 84, 156, 178
ṣirāṭ (bridge over Hell), 78n55
Siryāqūs, *khānqāh* of, 151n91
slander, 115
slaves, 135–36
slave soldiers, 2
sodomy, 82, 156, 178
sovereignty, two types of, 13–14
spice trade, 3, 5
spiritual authority, 14, 15
spiritual development, stations of, 31n14
Sufi cloak, 106, 150–51
Sufism, 6–10, 59, 136; authorities of, 7; Baghdad school of, 72n53; divine processions and, 81–82; Ibn

Sufism (*continued*)
al-Arabī's synthesis of disciplines, 12; interpretation of Islam, 7; jurists, 30; lineage, 3; mendicants, 21; miracles and wonders, 30; mysticism, 21; networks/movements, 8, 81n59, 141n86, 153n91; people of the path and, 81; political theology, 11–17, 22; sainthood model, 13, 15; school of law, 30n11; shaykh-emir relations, 17–25; state stipends to, 20; stations and, 31n14; true meaning of, 30; *zāwiya*'s functions, 6–7
Sufyān al-Thawrī, 29, 104
ṣuḥba. *See* friendship
Sulaymān, Emir (*aghā* of the 'Ezab), 151
Sulaymān Pasha, 92–93
Sulaymān the Lawgiver, 15
Sulaymān the Magnificent, Sultan, 9, 15, 158
sultan: concept of, 15–17; intermediary with, 187; money owed to, 59, 223; officeholders and, 224; protected authority of, 99; revenue source of, 224
Sunna, 13, 30, 102–3, 134
Sunnī Islam, 3, 4, 85n67, 111, 215n7; Ash'arī theological school, 12; ḥadīth and, 136nn84–85
Supreme Pen, 179
Sūrat al-Nisā', 172n106
syphilis, 169
Syria, 1, 2, 25, 104n76

Tablets of Affirmation and Erasure, 24, 81, 179. *See also* Protected Tablet
Tabriz, 4
tact, 117, 118
Ta'iz (Yemen), 25
Tamerlane. *See* Timur
Tantā shrine, 8
Ṭaṭar, Emir, 153–54
Tāwūs al-Yamānī, 103–4
tax agent, 59, 92, 129, 130, 212, 220; gifts from, 160
taxation, 3, 4, 51n16, 217; intercession and, 141–42; of non-Muslims, 92, 211. *See also* land tax
tax farmer, 102–3
temptations, 77–78; abstention from, 101, 138
Testament (al-Khiḍr), 161, 193
theft, 178, 225
Throne, 80
Timur (Tamerlane), 2, 15
al-Tirmidhī, 136n85
Tlemcen, 6, 163n101
toll collector, 218
tribulations, 205–6
tribute, 5
Ṭūmān Bāy, 4
Tunisia, 25
Turkey, 25
Turkoman nomads, 3
Twelve Shī'i Imāms, 3

'Umar ibn 'Abd al-'Azīz (caliph), 85, 161, 183, 193

'Umar ibn al-Khaṭṭāb (second caliph), 14, 104
Umayyad caliphs, 85n67
Umma, 186
'Uthman, Emir, 140

veneration, 175–76

Wafā lineage of scholars, 8
wara' (precautionary piety), 19, 41
wealth, 160, 171–72, 183, 203
wine drinking, 82, 84, 156, 178
women, 100; dependency of, 20, 155–56, 185, 186
wonders, 30, 197–98
worldly gains, 53–56, 68, 71, 87, 106, 134, 138, 149–50, 176, 183; dispute testimony and, 165–66; emir's honesty about, 167–68; as friendship motive, 204; renunciation of, 54, 58, 63–65, 66, 77–78, 105, 107, 135, 138, 142–44, 171
wrongdoer: blame of, 117; emir as, 76, 84–87, 160, 200, 208–9; intercession for victims of, 90–92, 110, 172, 175, 176, 191; mendicant's view of, 134, 199; prayers of victims of, 86, 114–15. *See also* sins

Yāqūt al-'Arshī, 88
Yūsuf al-'Ajamī, 66, 153
Yūsuf ibn Abī Iṣba', 194, 201

Zabīd (Yemen), 34n18
Zakarīyā, Mawlānā Shaykh al-Islām, 30, 36, 59, 75, 90, 156, 160, 199, 208
zāwiyas, 6–7, 9, 10–11, 20
Zodiac, 80n58